# Using Technology in K–8 Literacy Classrooms

**Rebecca S. Anderson**
*University of Memphis*

**Bruce W. Speck**
*University of North Carolina—Pembroke*

Merrill
Prentice Hall

Upper Saddle River, New Jersey
Columbus, Ohio

**Library of Congress Cataloging-in-Publication Data**

Anderson, Rebecca S.
    Using technology in K-8 literacy classrooms / Rebecca S. Anderson and Bruce W. Speck.
       p. cm.
    Includes bibliographical references (p. ) and index.
    ISBN 0-13-936337-8
      1. Language arts (Elementary)—Computer-assisted instruction.   2. Computers and
literacy.   3. Critical thinking—Computer-assisted instruction.   I. Speck, Bruce W.   II.
Title.

LB1576.7 .A43 2001
372.133'4—dc21
                                                      00-030531

**Vice President and Publisher:** Jeffery W. Johnston
**Editor:** Linda Ashe Montgomery and Bradley J. Potthoff
**Editorial Assistant:** Jennifer Day
**Production Editor:** Mary M. Irvin
**Production Coordinator:** Kathleen M. Lafferty/Roaring Mountain Editorial Services
**Design Coordinator:** Diane C. Lorenzo
**Text Designer:** Rose Marie Votta
**Cover Art:** Artville
**Cover Designer:** Rod Harris
**Production Manager:** Pamela D. Bennett
**Director of Marketing:** Kevin Flanagan
**Marketing Manager:** Amy June
**Marketing Services Manager:** Krista Groshong

This book was set in Garamond by The Clarinda Company. It was printed and bound by
R. R. Donnelley & Sons Company. The cover was printed by Lehigh Press.

10 9 8 7 6 5 4 3 2
ISBN: 0-13-936337-8

# PREFACE

## INTENT

*Using Technology in K-8 Literacy Classrooms* is designed to provide K–8 teachers with an array of computer tools to promote reading, writing, and critical thinking in their classrooms. Thus, this text can be used not only in a preservice course but also by seasoned teachers who recognize the need to continue their education by becoming adept at using computers in their classrooms. Each chapter provides rationales for using computer technology to teach literacy and gives many examples of how teachers can use technology effectively. The chapters deal with issues such as how the teacher can facilitate students' use of technology, how the Internet can enhance students' literacy education, how the teacher can develop integrated lesson plans, how technology can be used to help students write and publish their work, and how teachers can use technology to work with ESL and special education students. Each chapter provides information the teacher needs to use technology in the literacy classroom and sample lessons that can be imported into his or her classroom. This two-fold intent, providing continuing teacher education and pedagogical materials for classroom use, structures the chapters. Each chapter consists of a scenario that dramatizes the topic; includes a Classroom Snapshot of a actual teaching situation whereby a teacher handles the topic in his or her classroom; and provides discussion of the topic, Electronic Classroom Examples, Techno-Teacher Tips, and Frequently Asked Questions. In short, *Using Technology in K-8 Literacy Classrooms* covers the major concerns K–8 teachers face as they integrate computer technology into their classrooms and provides numerous suggestions for applying the ideas described in the text in real classrooms.

# FEATURES

The following features make *Using Technology in K–8 Literacy Classrooms* particularly valuable:

- The book provides teachers with theoretical information so that they have the assurance that the information conveyed is based on solid research.
- The book focuses on major issues and gets to the point; it allows teachers to save time by looking at the significant issues without getting bogged down in the details.
- The Computer Classroom Snapshots provide real-life examples of how teachers are integrating technology into the K–8 literacy curriculum.
- Lists of electronic sources provide teachers with easy access to URLs that can give them more materials for their classes.
- The Techno-Teacher Tips provide important pointers on using technology in the classroom.
- Print sources cited throughout the book provide numerous resources, including References at the end of each chapter that identify sources to promote the integration of technology and literacy in the classroom.
- As an ancillary text, *Using Technology in K–8 Literacy Classrooms* does not belabor points but treats each subject in enough detail to get the message across.
- The book is practical, so that teachers can either use the materials straight from the book or easily adapt them for their classes.

# ACKNOWLEDGMENTS

This book would not have been possible without the support and help of many people. That the book was published was due to the faith that our editor, Brad Potthoff, had in us, and we know that we tried that faith during our prolonged period of writing the text. We thank Brad for bearing with us and giving us the opportunity to provide a book that will help K–8 teachers integrate literacy via computer technology into their classrooms. We are also grateful to the reviewers who provided helpful comments on drafts of the book: Donna Camp, University of Central Florida; Kara Dawson, University of Virginia; Laurie Elish-Piper, Northern Illinois University; Patricia P. Fritchie, Troy State University–Dothan; Joan Hanor, California State University–San Marcos; Kim MacGregor, Louisiana State University; Michael Moore, Georgia Southern University; Richard Robinson, University of Missouri–Columbia; and Mary Tipton, Kent State University. We appreciate the many useful responses they provided to enable us to revise our drafts effectively.

Because the Classroom Snapshots are a significant part of the chapters, we are indebted to the classroom teachers who wrote those snapshots–Karen Anderson,

John Bauer, Carol Ann Brown, Kim Buie, Fran Clark, JoAnne Lancaster, and Whitney Miller. Our goal was to produce a book that would be useful to classroom teachers, and the Snapshots help readers see that their peers, other classroom teachers, are successfully dealing with issues of integrating computer technology into the K–8 literacy classroom. Two professorial colleagues also helped us by writing sections of Chapter 7 related to their disciplines. Anita Pandey's expertise in ESL enriches the chapter immensely. Janna Siegel Robertson's expertise in special needs and insights into the use of technology to promote literacy among special needs students adds greatly to the chapter.

We enlisted the help of Kelly Wise and Jennifer Jackson, former students in a graduate class we taught on integrating technology into the literacy curriculum and classroom teachers themselves, who helped us prepare the Computer Classroom Examples. We thank them publicly for their assistance and are grateful that they were willing to work on this project with us.

Others at the University of Memphis—including Renee Weiss, the interim director of the Center for Academic Excellence; Heather Knowlton, a graduate student in English; John Bauer, a graduate student in Education; and Raj Poutturi, a graduate student in Engineering Technology—were instrumental in helping us prepare the book for our editor's approval. We are particularly grateful that Renee provided so much advice about graphics for the text and allowed us to work with her staff as we prepared the final draft.

We are also grateful to our employers for supporting us as we prepared this textbook. Rebecca thanks her department chair, Dennie Smith, for his support; and Bruce, now working at the University of North Carolina at Pembroke, appreciates the support of the provost, Charles Jenkins. Without institutional support, neither of us would have had the resources to produce a textbook that requires significant technological resources to write about the useful ways in which technology can be used in the K–8 classroom.

To all our collaborators, we offer our gratitude for the many ways you have worked to make this book a reality.

## DEDICATION

We dedicate this book to our student-colleagues in Computer Applications in Reading Instruction who have helped us understand ways to use technology effectively in the literacy classroom.

*Rebecca S. Anderson*
*Bruce W. Speck*

# DISCOVER THE COMPANION WEBSITE ACCOMPANYING THIS BOOK

## THE PRENTICE HALL COMPANION WEBSITE: A VIRTUAL LEARNING ENVIRONMENT

Technology is a constantly growing and changing aspect of our field that is creating a need for content and resources. To address this emerging need, Prentice Hall has developed an online learning environment for students and professors alike—Companion Websites—to support our textbooks.

In creating a Companion Website, our goal is to build on and enhance what the textbook already offers. For this reason, the content for each user-friendly website is organized by topic and provides the professor and student with a variety of meaningful resources. Common features of a Companion Website include: the following.

## FOR THE PROFESSOR

Every Companion Website integrates **Syllabus Manager**™, an online syllabus creation and management utility.

- **Syllabus Manager**™ provides you, the instructor, with an easy, step-by-step process to create and revise syllabi, with direct links into Companion Website and other online content without having to learn HTML.

- Students may logon to your syllabus during any study session. All they need to know is the web address for the Companion Website and the password you've assigned to your syllabus.

- After you have created a syllabus using **Syllabus Manager**™, students may enter the syllabus for their course section from any point in the Companion Website.

- Clicking on a date, the student is shown the list of activities for the assignment. The activities for each assignment are linked directly to actual content, saving time for students.
- Adding assignments consists of clicking on the desired due date, then filling in the details of the assignment—name of the assignment, instructions, and whether or not it is a one-time or repeating assignment.
- In addition, links to other activities can be created easily. If the activity is online, a URL can be entered in the space provided, and it will be linked automatically in the final syllabus.
- Your completed syllabus is hosted on our servers, allowing convenient updates from any computer on the Internet. Changes you make to your syllabus are immediately available to your students at their next logon.

# FOR THE STUDENT

- **Topic Overviews:** outline key concepts in topic areas
- **Electronic Blue Book:** send homework or essays directly to your instructor's email with this paperless form
- **Message Board:** services as a virtual bulletin board to post—or respond to—questions or comments to/from a national audience
- **Chat:** real-time chat with anyone who is using the text anywhere in the country—ideal for discussion and study groups, class projects, and so forth.
- **Web Destinations:** links to www sites that relate to each topic area
- **Professional Organizations:** links to organizations that relate to topic areas
- **Additional Resources:** access to topic-specific content that enhances material found in the text

To take advantage of these and other resources, please visit the *Using Technology in K–8 Literacy Classrooms* Companion Website at

www.prenhall.com/anderson

# CONTENTS

## CHAPTER 3

### Using the Internet to Teach Literacy                                            43

## CHAPTER 4

### Using Additional Electronic Tools to Teach Literacy                          81

## CHAPTER 5

### *The Writing Process, Computers, and Your Classroom*     *119*

## CHAPTER 6

### *Using Electronic Technology to Publish Students' Writing*     *139*

## CHAPTER 7

### *Working With Special Education and ESL Students*                    *159*

### *Index*                                                                                                        *192*

## CHAPTER 1

# TEACHING LITERACY USING COMPUTERS

"I'm uneasy about all this talk about computers in the classroom," Milton says to Wynette as they are having lunch in the faculty lounge. "For one thing, I don't even own a computer!"

"I can identify with you," Wynette responds, while unwrapping her dessert. "I was petrified of computers until I took that summer institute at the University. I began the course not knowing anything about computers and ended up creating an electronic portfolio—all in five weeks. It was grueling. I think the professors who taught the course were masochists in very little disguise, but the course was a lifesaver."

"Look, Wynette," Milton retorts, with a bit of frustration in his voice, "I don't have five weeks in my summer to devote to a summer institute. I've got to work to put the kids through college."

"Milt," Wynette says sympathetically, "it's tough keeping up with everything we're expected to do as teachers. The summer institute may not work for you. But you and I know that computers are here to stay. We have ten more years to teach, and we can't just cruise out of our teaching career hoping that we don't have to become computer literate."

"I was afraid of that," Milton says.

"So we've got to make strategic plans. How can we fit computer training into our schedules? How can we begin to use computer projects in our classes? If you can't attend a summer institute, suck it in and take a night class at the University or register for the technology workshop offered at the local district office. Talk with the woman we just hired—what's her name?"

"Miss Devers. The brand spanking new college graduate who knows everything about computers."

"Yes, talk with Miss Devers and find out when you can use the computer lab here. She'll probably be willing to help you get started."

"It's embarrassing. It's humbling," Milton admits reluctantly.

"You bet," Wynette says, "but just because we're the senior faculty doesn't mean we're trained in all this new technology. When I took that summer institute, I was the oldest participant, and at first I felt funny being in a class with so many younger teachers. But I said to myself, 'Wynette, you either stick this out and get up to speed or you keep slinking past the computer lab at school, hoping it will go away.' It's not going away, and I'm not slinking. Besides, Milton, the younger faculty who know the ins and outs of computers are willing to help us learn about technology. I haven't found that they look down on us because we don't know how to turn on a computer. They're fairly new at this game, too."

"Of course, you're right," says Milton. "I've just got to suck it in and learn about computers. From what I've seen of you, seems like sucking it in has rewards."

"Yep. I've joined those in teaching who are doing interesting things with technology in their classrooms. I can talk with lots of other people—like students' parents—about computers, something I avoided altogether until the summer institute. I even bought my own computer."

"But my kids' college—" Milton begins.

"No excuses, Milt. Start having the credit union take out $25 a month so that you can make payments on a computer. Did you know that the school district has a plan so that teachers can get a good deal on computers?"

"Do now."

"That's right, and you've got to be strategic about this whole thing. Work out your schedule to allow for training, and save your lunch money so that you can buy a computer."

"Hey," Milton says laughing, "that's sucking it in a little bit too much."

## ATTACKING LITERACY WITH COMPUTERS

Milton could be sensing that his own teaching situation is much like the computer that was not—as the industry called it during the anxious period before January 1, 2000—"Y2K compliant." He would not, of course, "shut down" in seconds because of a technical glitch, but in broader terms he knows that unless he upgrades his own technical skills he will suffer the anguish of falling behind in his career, standing by as computer-literate teachers guide their students to the launch pads of cyberspace. Veteran teachers like him are coming to the conclusion that they should be choosing the exciting dawn of a new era in educational instruction over the comfortable dusk of the old. They know that computers are in the classroom to stay and that their students are armed with untold skills, itching to use them.

That's where this book comes in. There is a transition period in which teachers are testing the waters with computers, and it is our intention as authors of this book to keep them afloat, turning latent panic into the controlled thrill that only the deep waters of a new adventure can bring. And we're doing it in the field of literacy—reading, writing, comprehension—the wellspring from which all else flows.

In this chapter, we discuss what it means to integrate computers into the literacy curriculum and why we advocate this. We believe that before teachers can communicate with students, parents, and administrators about how they are going to use computers in their classrooms, they must first have a clear vision about what they are trying to do and why they are doing it. To set the stage for discussing the integration of computers into the literacy curriculum, the following electronic classroom snapshot describes why Kim Buie, a first-grade teacher, decided to use technology in her classroom and relates her first adventure in integrating computers in her literacy curriculum.

## COMPUTER CLASSROOM SNAPSHOT

### Context

My name is Kim Buie, and for the past several years I have watched teachers, administrators, and students become engrossed in computers and what they had to offer. I began to feel as if I was missing out on something that could enhance my teaching, so I enrolled in a class at the University of Memphis in hopes of finding out what all of the excitement was about. I soon realized that computers could be a valuable teaching tool in my literacy program.

My first attempt at putting all that I was learning into practical use began in March 1998. In my university class I was required to complete a problem-based project involving my first graders and the computer. Because my computer experience had been so limited, I started with a simple project with the following goals:

1. Introduce the computer keyboard.
2. Encourage and motivate students to write.

To accomplish these goals I decided that I would need help to oversee and facilitate my first graders on the computer. I realized that I couldn't give my students the one-on-one attention they needed, so I enlisted the help of a colleague who taught a third-grade class. I suggested to my colleague that her students pair up with my students as one-on-one tutors. The students consisted of 16 first graders and 16 third graders. The ethnic makeup was 29 African Americans and five Hispanic students. My colleague liked the idea of pairing our students, so I had some confirmation that I was on the right track in integrating technology into my literacy program. To collect data for this project, I took notes during each class based on my observations of the conversations and interactions of each pair of students.

### What I Did and Why

To meet my goals of introducing my students to the computer keyboard and to encourage and motivate students to write, I decided to have each first-grade student write a story and then have the students compile the stories in a book. To prepare students to write their stories, I reviewed the steps in the writing process and discussed potential topics.

Then we went to the computer lab to begin writing. The lab contains 25 Macintosh computers, but computer time was difficult to obtain because other classes were scheduled throughout the day. We were allowed 30 minutes from 1:00 to 1:30 P.M. twice a week. Each first grader, with the help of a third-grade tutor, wrote his or her story at the computer without the use of pencil or paper. First, each student created a file for his or her story. Second, student typed their stories with the help of their tutors, who assisted them in learning the keyboard. In addition, the tutors acted as peer reviewers for the students' stories. Third, the students learned to print their stories so that they could combine them into a book. (Alternatively, the students could have learned how to compile their stories into one file and use publishing software to produce a book, but, as I noted, we had limited time in the computer laboratory.) My first goal of introducing the function of the computer keyboard was achieved with the help of the third-grade tutors.

### *What I Learned*

After the project was complete, I read over the notes I had taken and found that my second goal of encouraging and motivating students to write also was achieved. In fact, my first graders' motivation for writing increased. For instance, many times I overheard my students engage in lively discussions about their stories. Not only were they concerned with their own writing, but they also were curious about each other's writing. My students were full of excitement and pride about what each one in the class was accomplishing. According to my notes, while at the computers the students' interactions were more spontaneous and extensive than I had ever seen. In addition, I was amazed at some of the story lines my first graders were generating. This was the first time during the year—and it was late in the school year—that I had seen so much interest in and excitement about writing. In fact, every day my students would ask excitedly if today was a computer day. Overall I was extremely pleased with the change in my students' attitudes and motivation to write.

My project was also a success in that I learned ways to improve my writing program for next year. The first part that I would change is to start going over the keyboard at the beginning of the year and spend time letting the students become familiar with the keyboard. I would also spend more time with the tutors and find out exactly how much computer experience each student has. I will continue to use the computer as a tool to enhance my students' desire to write, because I realize how much of a positive impact technology can have on my teaching and in the lives of my students.

## WHY TEACH LITERACY WITH COMPUTER TECHNOLOGY?

Evidence abounds that technology is revolutionizing the way people function in society (Anderson & Lee, 1995; Means, 1994). Computers are common in the workplace, and their use in homes is growing. A strong argument for increasing computer technology in schools is that computers are essential for preparing students for the digital future (Reinking, 1997). If teachers accept that "To prepare our students for the challenges of their tomorrows, the Internet and future technologies will be central to our mission" (Leu, 1997, p. 63), they need to provide the tools for that to happen. Add to this the likelihood that the school will be the only place the urban poor will ever use a computer before going into the job market, and it becomes even more imperative that schools make the most of the time dedicated to computer use. Just as schools have always stressed the lifelong importance of good reading skills, the word *computer* must be mentioned in the same breath. As Costanzo (1994) argues: "computers are altering the way many of us read, write, and even think. It is not simply that the tools of literacy have changed; the nature of texts, of language, of literacy itself is undergoing crucial transformations. Along with these transformations come shifts in the sites of literacy. From the home and the classroom to the market and the workplace, computers are reshaping the environments in which language is learned, produced, and practiced" (p. 11).

Many state and national educational initiatives are supporting technology reform efforts in the schools. Educators realize that electronic communication is becoming less an option and more a requirement for students' success in the 21st century. Little wonder, then, that government officials at the national level are advocating that every student in the United States have access to the Internet.

Many teachers have come to appreciate the limitless possibilities that creative software and Websites offer to enhance traditional teaching methods. In fact, it is much easier to access the Internet than it is to pore over dated texts for fresh ideas. Today the text is still the classroom standard, with the computer as an optional resource. As the current gale force of technology becomes a hurricane, the roles will be reversed.

In spite of reform efforts, however, computers have not revolutionized schools to the extent that many people once predicted (Bork, 1987). Nor is there a significant body of research literature supporting technology-based instruction over other forms of instruction, although a growing number of studies support the use of computers to teach literacy (Atkinson & Hanser, 1996; Labbo, 1996; Labbo, Reinking, & McKenna, 1995; Leu & Reinking, 1996; Reinking, 1996). Nonetheless, Morrison, Lowther, and DeMeulle (1999) suggest that the time is ripe for a computer revolution in schools. These authors base their claim on the new knowledge gained during the past few years about how to use computers in the classroom. For instance, instead of being used as a delivery mechanism, computers are now used as problem-solving tools. Concerning literacy teaching, the new knowledge is helping redefine literacy and is shifting educational paradigms from a behavioral to a constructivist learning approach.

## *Redefining Literacy*

Our vision of using computers to teach literacy is connected to our understanding of what it means to be literate. As literacy teachers, we must first ask ourselves, "What are we trying to teach our students?" Historically we have based our understanding of literacy—and our understanding of what we are trying to teach students—on paper texts. For instance, we have read newspapers, novels, term papers, letters, and a host of other documents printed on paper. We have written directly on paper (even when we used a typewriter), not on a computer screen. Discussions inside and outside of classes have been referenced to print documents, whether basal readers or trade books. As educators, we have read paper texts—such as picture books or poems—to students, so they were listening to spoken words read from a paper text. In fact, we have asked students to point to a specific place in a text to provide evidence of the validity of a particular interpretation of the text.

However, many scholars are challenging us to expand our definition of literacy to regard it as a social process that is dependent on cultural and electronic contexts (Flood and Lapp, 1995; Gallego and Hollingsworth, 1992; Leu, 1997; Reinking, 1995). Their arguments are grounded in the assumption that students are expanding their reading and writing activities beyond traditional print texts to include electronic contexts that incorporate print and nonprint forms of communications. As El-Hindi (1998) notes, we are revising traditional notions of reading and writing because "Literacy now involves being able to make sense of and navigate through several forms of information including images, sounds, animation, and ongoing discussion groups" (p. 694). For example, students now spend time responding to e-mail messages, engaging in online conversations, and navigating through vast amounts of information in a combination of print and nonprint forms (Ryder and Graves, 1996–1997). Although students are interacting with electronic contexts through reading and writing, this electronic communication is described as a new literacy (Reinking, 1992, 1994, 1995) that forces us to rethink what and how we teach literacy. Adhering to the current standards for the English language arts, we must ensure that "students use a variety of technological and informational resources (e.g., libraries, databases, computer networks, video) to gather and synthesize information and to create and communicate knowledge" (NCTE and IRA, 1996, p. 3). What principles, therefore, should guide our teaching? The shift from a traditional, behaviorist paradigm to a constructivist learning perspective provides insights to this question.

## *Shifting Paradigms*

For many years, literacy was taught from a behavioral paradigm. Essentially this paradigm assumes that all students should learn a finite list of language arts skills, that it is the teacher's responsibility to teach students facts, and that students demonstrate their learning by "regurgitating" facts on a test. When the behavioral paradigm was the ruling paradigm in literacy education, students worked independently in straight rows of desks and teachers provided lecture or direct instruction followed by worksheet assignments. Computers were generally used for drill-and-practice exercises (Becker, 1994) or were used by students who finished their required class work early. Most classrooms did not have even one computer. Instead, computers were located in a computer lab where once a week students generally received computer instruction in the form of keyboarding skills. Fortunately this scenario is changing in many schools. Many literacy educators are moving away from a behaviorist perspective and instead are embracing a social constructivist learning paradigm that advocates using the computer as a problem-solving tool (i.e., Bruffee, 1986; Dixon-Krauss, 1996; Gavelek and Raphael, 1996; Gould, 1996; Willis, Stephens, and Matthew, 1996).

The social constructivist learning paradigm is based on a theory of learning that regards learning as a problem-solving activity. Thus, Brooks and Brooks (1993) note that the word *learning* from a social constructivist paradigm "is understood as a self-regulated process of resolving inner cognitive conflicts that often become apparent through concrete experience, collaborative discourse, and reflection" (p. vii). Note that "cognitive conflicts" is another way to talk about unresolved problems and that the means of resolving conflicts focus on a student's personal engagement in the learning process through reference to actual experiences, collaborative or interpersonal communication, and reflection that can take the form of journal, essay, and other writing exercises; simulations; case studies; and so forth. In other words, students are actively engaged in their learning, not passively absorbing information via a lecture method so that they can parrot the same information on an exam.

The social constructivist paradigm, by focusing on exploring and solving cognitive conflicts, calls into question a major premise of the behaviorist paradigm, namely, that for every question there is one correct answer. For some questions, this may indeed be the case. If, for instance, three students measure the height of a $2 \times 4$ piece of wood that is 4' 11/16" tall, then 4' 11/16" is the correct answer to the question "How tall is this $2 \times 4$?" However, the rudiments of measuring physical objects should be seen as a tool that will be used in more complex situations such as building a model or, ultimately, a house or school building. The goal of teaching measurement skills, therefore, is to provide students with one small tool that they can combine with other tools to make complex decisions. In fact, students can learn how to measure as part of a complex task—such as determining whether object X will fit in space Y given a variety of other constraints.

If the goal of education is to provide students with the necessary conceptual tools to respond to complex life situations and to apply those tools in the classroom, then the social constructivist perspective has a great deal to offer teachers. Many life problems do not yield to the easily measured answers that a true-false or multiple choice test provide, two of the premier ways behaviorists promote the assessment of student learning. For instance, what is the cause of cancer and how can it be prevented or cured? Why do people of different nationalities and skin colors fear each other, and how might people create harmonious multiracial communities? How does a person determine when to stop life support for a loved one? How should an employee—the hoped-for future status of our students—evaluate ethical dilemmas in the workplace? These and many other tough issues can be addressed in practical and informative ways by using a constructivist learning paradigm. Indeed, a constructivist perspective takes into account the cultures and contexts in which learning occurs (Moll & Greenberg, 1990; Tittle, 1991).

What exactly are the principles associated with a constructivist pedagogy? Brooks and Brooks (1993), building on the work of Piaget (1970), Bruner (1986), and Vygotsky (1978), outline five overarching principles of a constructivist pedagogy:

1. Pose problems that are relevant and meaningful to students.
2. Structure learning around "big ideas" or primary concepts.
3. Seek and value students' points of view.
4. Modify curriculum to address students' suppositions.
5. Assess student learning in the context of teaching.

In constructivist classrooms, students learn through active participation and have opportunities to explore their own ideas through discourse, debate, and inquiry (Anderson & Piazza, 1996; Bufkin & Bryde, 1996; Davydov, 1995; Duckworth, 1987; Gruender, 1996; Kroll & LaBoskey, 1996). Teachers assume a facilitator's role, and students assume more responsibility for their own learning (Fosnot, 1996). Skills, although necessary components of instruction, are not the goal. Rather the goal is to promote concept development, deep understanding, and active learning (Brooks & Brooks, 1993). The focus is not on concrete thinking but on abstract synthesis or higher level mental development that occurs through verbal interaction and use. For instance, as Dixon-Krauss (1996) points out, "This Vygotskian idea is in direct opposition to the traditional basic skills view that a child must learn a word before she can use it. From the Vygotskian perpective, the child would learn the word by using it" (p. 14).

## LINKING CONSTRUCTIVISM, LITERACY, AND COMPUTERS

Even though constructivism is not a theory about using technology, constructivist assumptions are guideposts for developing a vision for integrating technology into the literacy curriculum (Brown, 1997; Wolffe, 1997). These assumptions are outlined in Figure 1.1.

**Figure 1.1** Assumptions of Constructivism

- Knowledge has multiple interpretations.
- Learning is an active process.
- Process and product are emphasized.
- Problem solving is the focus.
- Power and control are shared among students and teacher.
- Learning is a collaborative process.
- Reflection is promoted.

### Knowledge Has Multiple Interpretations

One assumption of a constructivist approach is that knowledge is complex and can be interpreted in various ways. It is extremely difficult if not impossible for everyone to reach a consensus about meaning, because each individual brings his or her background and interpretation to situations that change over time. With this assumption in mind, teachers create classroom environments where students talk, collaborate with, and question others. In addition to conversations within the classroom, this involves conversations via the Internet. For instance, it is not uncommon for students to be engaged in online projects with students in a different state or country and for them to gain new insights about different cultures and develop different perspectives on current literature they are reading in class.

### Learning Is an Active Process

"Learning is a natural, integral, and ubiquitous part of living" (Bintz, 1991, p. 309), not something that is handed as a package to someone else. Students actively search for meanings to transform their present understanding, instead of parroting standard interpretations (Greene, 1988). Students do not sit passively while teachers pour knowledge into their heads. Teachers assume a new role in a constructivist classroom. Instead of being dispensers of knowledge, teachers are facilitators. For instance, they develop tasks that require students to tap into the Internet to find answers to their questions and explore ideas.

### Process and Product Are Emphasized

Generally, what has been valued and assessed in traditional classrooms is students' final products; the assessment is usually based on some sort of objective test (Bertrand, 1993). The final outcomes of students' efforts are assumed to be representative of their learning, with less consideration given to the "how and why" of their learning. In constructivist classrooms, however, the process is valued as much as the product. What, how, and why students learn are given significant consideration (Hutchings, 1993; Johnston, 1992). For example, when students have access to a word processor, they can use technology to engage in process writing by getting feedback from others electronically and making revisions to their drafts.

### Problem Solving Is the Focus

In constructivist classroom environments, students develop real-world problem-solving skills that lead them to observe, think, question, and test their ideas. These problem-based learning environments encourage students to make decisions about how to approach a problem; they call into question the traditional approach that focuses on the teacher as the sole authority in the classroom and the only source of knowledge. In the traditional approach, the teacher dispenses information and the students absorb it in order to demonstrate via a test that they have understood what the teacher said. Under a constructivist paradigm, teachers are facilitators who scaffold instruction to facilitate students' growth while the students assume more ownership and responsibility for their learning. In this environment, the Internet can be a powerful tool that enables students to explore and gather information on a variety of topics.

## Power and Control Are Shared Among Students and Teacher

One assumption of social constructivism is that teachers share the power with students in making decisions about what is to be learned and how it is to be assessed. In this context, students negotiate the curriculum by having a voice in selecting and defining activities that are relevant and meaningful to them, as well as in evaluating the outcomes. For instance, it is well documented that students are more intrinsically motivated and show greater growth in their writing when they are allowed to write on topics of their choice (Calkins, 1994; Graves, 1983). In today's classroom the Internet provides numerous sources of information for students to gather information on topics they find interesting, not topics the teacher assigns. This does not mean, however, that the teacher has no part in developing assignments. On the contrary, in a constructivist classroom the teacher is very much in charge as a manager. For example, a sixth-grade teacher might determine that the students will read and study Shakespeare's plays and at the same time might give students a great deal of freedom in selecting topics for such a study (e.g., Elizabethan costumes, the use of theatrical props at the Globe Theatre, Shakespeare's use of humor in his plays, the relationship between a historical event and Shakespeare's use of that event in a play or series of plays, the politics of Elizabethan England as reflected in the plays). A work of literature exists in a social context, and students can approach that work from a variety of viewpoints, choosing a perspective that is appealing to them.

## Learning Is a Collaborative Process

In contexts that embrace a social constructivist perspective, students and teachers are co-learners, freely expressing and testing their ideas together. In these social milieus, collaborative talk helps students achieve their goals and also builds community. For instance, peer writing conferences help "children connect with another human being in order to learn from him or her, to empathize, to hear peers' stories and to understand their own stories more fully, to care about another person's interpretation of the world, and to be able to identify and respond to another person's perspective" (Gould, 1996, p. 98). Thus, students are not always working independently on reading and writing tasks; they are often working in collaborative computer groups. As Leu (1996) states, "Students often learn about complex multimedia environments by showing each other 'cool' things" (pp. 162–163). Leu point outs that learning "is frequently constructed through social interactions in these contexts, perhaps even more naturally and frequently than in traditional print environments" (p. 163). In addition, these collaborative groups have expanded beyond the traditional classroom to groups throughout the world via the

Internet. For instance, students are able to read, write, and collaborate with others through e-mail, chat rooms, newsgroups, and listservs.

**Reflection Is Promoted**

In constructivist classrooms, students are given opportunities to reflect on their learning. Reflection encourages students to respond to what they are reading and to think about their own learning. Reflection enables them to make informed decisions about what they should learn next. One example of how teachers are promoting reflective behavior is electronic journals. In addition to composing journal entries on the computer, students easily give and receive peer feedback by exchanging their journals via e-mail.

In summary, constructivist classrooms that make use of computer technology to teach literacy are busy, interactive environments. Students freely interact with others to enhance their own learning, both online and in the classroom. Teachers do not teach literacy skills in isolation but, rather, create meaningful and purposeful tasks that are open-ended and problem-based. Students become researchers, exploring numerous sources to collect and analyze data to make informed decisions about their learning. Serving as mentor and coach, teachers use computers not as a delivery mechanism for drill and practice of skills but as a tool to enhance students' learning in numerous ways.

# WAYS TO TEACH LITERACY USING COMPUTERS

Let's return briefly to the opening conversation on page 1, where the teacher named Milton says he has good reason not to take a computer clinic but realizes he should. Do all teachers have to spend money on a high-powered clinic to be able to introduce computer work into their classroom methodology? No way.

With decent keyboarding skills and an enthusiasm for forging ahead into a new frontier, teachers can use the following opportunities to ease into the high-tech field with painless adandon. Veteran computer users will find fresh ideas as well.

**Word Processing**

Students use word processing programs to type, format, and print their writing. If students are expected to engage in process writing—prewriting, drafting, revising, editing, and publishing—then word processing programs are a must. For instance, students will not rewrite an entire draft just to change one word. However, making small changes is easy if they have access to a word processor because they can compose, revise, edit, save, and print their writing on different days without ever having to retype the portions of their drafts that do not need to be revised. Many word processing programs have advanced text and graphics capabilities that enable students to design and publish colorful and visually detailed documents such as newspapers, pamphlets, and yearbooks.

### Technology Texts

The computer will never replace books (Leu & Leu, 1997). There will always be a need for the rich and well-appreciated art form of books. Stories on the Internet, however, have great literacy potential, especially as multimedia forms become quicker and richer. For instance, connecting with students and authors around the world helps create authentic literacy experiences for students. The Internet also provides opportunities to connect reading and writing in the classroom, and it is a resource tool for supporting project-based instruction in an open-ended learning environment.

### Publishing Students' Work

A primary goal in teaching literacy is for students to engage in meaningful and purposeful tasks, because students are motivated and invest themselves in their work when they are engaged in authentic tasks. Publishing students' work is an excellent way to meet this goal, and computers make it easy to publish in multiple ways. For instance, their work is shared with a variety of audiences through reports, books, multimedia presentations, Web pages, or CD-ROMs. Not only do students produce hardcopy documents such as newspapers, but they can also publish their work online in a variety of ways, such as through e-mail and Websites.

### Integrating the Internet Into the Curriculum

As computers have become more widespread, access to the Internet has become increasingly common, providing a place to collaborate with people around the world and an outlet for publication. The amount of information that is accessible in just a matter of seconds on this Information Superhighway is truly amazing. A variety of Internet components are discussed in Chapter 3—including the World Wide Web, FTPs, gophers, e-mail, listservs, newsgroups and chat forums—that enable students to send electronic messages and join in discussion groups about books they have read or issues they have studied.

### Searching for On-Line Information

Students now have access to current information on the Internet and on CD-ROM. For instance, they can read the works of their favorite authors, view the national weather, or read the daily news in reports from around the world. However, because of the vast amount of information available on the Net, students need to develop time-efficient navigation strategies that can help them avoid endless "surf-ing." Students need to know how to access the most appropriate information in the least amount of time. Chapter 3 discusses strategies students can use to make decisions about the value of the information they access on the Net.

## Databases and Spreadsheets

Students can use databases and spreadsheets to collect, organize, retrieve, and analyze information. These learning tools are especially useful when students are manipulating large amounts of data to answer questions about specific topics. For instance, students in the second grade may want to help maintain a class database related to each book they read during that year. Then, by sorting the database, students could find out how many students selected certain authors. In addition, students could use a spreadsheet to create a bar graph showing how many students selected the top ten authors. Students' use of databases and spreadsheets can motivate them to read and analyze data; therefore, databases and spreadsheets expand the ways they learn about the world.

## Instructional Materials

In addition to enhancing students' learning, computers are invaluable in helping teachers facilitate students' learning and manage the classroom. For instance, the Internet is a powerful resource for planning and locating instructional activities for thematic units. The computer also enables teachers to replace overhead transparencies with multimedia presentations, provide individual instruction through personalized worksheets, and use specialized education software. Teachers can also use computers for administrative purposes, such as creating electronic gradebooks to save hours of time in computing grades, employing word processing and databases to expedite communicating with parents through personalized letters (using Mail Merge) or newsletters, and using drawing tools to develop certificates and coupons that recognize student achievement.

## COMPUTER CLASSROOM EXAMPLES

Look for this heading in the other chapters; you will find examples of activities based on the chapter topics to use in the classroom.

## TECHNO-TEACHER TIPS

As noted previously in this chapter, computers can enhance the teaching and learning of literacy in numerous ways. Personally, as authors of this book we are impressed with the great number of teachers who value the computer as a tool for teaching literacy and who are willing to spend time and effort learning how to use the computer effectively to teach literacy. Just as it is important to understand how to use the computer as a teaching tool in the classroom, it also is important to understand the challenges associated with this technology. Although challenges are a part of any type of school reform, computers raise unique issues in a variety of areas.

### Technological Access

Numerous teachers are excited about using computers in their classrooms but don't have access to computers. Other teachers have access to computers but not to the Internet. Unfortunately, many schools are not designed or equipped for the 21st century (Morra, 1995). It is very disappointing to envision your students having keypals in say, Alaska and to realize it may be another year before you can go online. Amazingly, teachers develop resourceful ways to overcome many of these limitations by using the one computer in the library that is online or by using their home computer at night to send their students' keypal messages.

### Financial Issues

Money is always an issue in dealing with computers. A considerable amount is needed not only to set up computers but also to maintain them. Computers break down. New literacy software and the hardware to run it are constantly being marketed. For instance, perhaps you decide that you would like your students to create electronic portfolios this year. To complete this task, you need a scanner and specialized software. But there is no money in the budget. What can you do? Either you postpone using portfolios with your students, or you pay for the materials out of your own pocket.

### Training Needs

Regardless of how knowledgeable and skilled teachers are in using computers to teach literacy, the need for professional development is constant. Advancements are occurring so rapidly that even the "technology gurus" are challenged to stay abreast of the knowledge and skills they need to maintain their status. For literacy teachers, extra time to develop computer skills is virtually nonexistent; generally, the economic incentives are insufficient to invest the time and energy to learn more about the latest technological developments. This is especially true in schools where the administration and faculty are resistant to integrating computers into the curriculum. You may ask yourself why you should learn how to create homepages on the World Wide Web with your students when no one in the work environment appreciates your efforts. Fortunately, this scenario has become less widespread in recent years as the need to use computers has received nationwide emphasis and as computers have become part and parcel of more people's lives.

**Classroom Instruction**

Very few teachers have as many computers as they would like, and even those who do are challenged to determine how to structure classroom time so that students can use the computers. In addition, integrating the computer into existing curriculum may be quite challenging. For instance, perhaps you are accustomed to teaching your students process writing, and you now have three new computers in the classroom. When you are developing lesson plans you will need to consider how and when to introduce your students to word processing. You may wonder what to eliminate from the curriculum to make time for computer instruction. And although these types of curriculum and instructional decisions may not be too difficult for you to think through, they will require additional time on your part.

## FREQUENTLY ASKED QUESTIONS

1. **I would like to e-mail other teachers who are interested in discussing ways to use computers to teach literacy. How do I go about finding these teachers?**

   You could join several listservs. Essentially a listserv provides individuals who are interested in the same topic with a forum for online discussions. See Chapter 3 for a list of listservs of interest to literacy teachers.

2. **I have just acquired a computer in my classroom. How do I begin using it with my students when I'm not yet comfortable with my own abilities?**

   Computers, like most things, seem scary when you first begin using them. Turn the computer on and spend some time each day in class problem solving and learning about it with your students. Tell your class that the computer will be a learning experience for all of you. Try opening yourself up to your students. Ask them about their computer knowledge, and solicit help from those who use a computer at home. Trying to learn all about the computer after the students have left for the day will only add an unnecessary burden to your busy schedule. Remember, teaching and learning constitute a reciprocal process. You teach the students, and they invariably teach you.

3. **Each classroom in my school was equipped with a new computer and printer this year. Soon we will decide on buying grade-specific software or installing Internet connections in each classroom. What should we do?**

Strongly encourage your fellow teachers and administration to install an Internet connection in each classroom in the school. CD-ROM technology has many benefits but cannot compare to the endless possibilities of the Internet. Using the Internet, students and teachers can research topics, communicate with others, read books, and publish writing. CD-ROMs are designed to serve specific purposes and may not transfer among grade levels. The Internet can be used in any classroom and with any teacher or grade.

## REFERENCES

Anderson, J., & Lee, A. (1995). Literacy teachers learning a new literacy: A study of the use of electronic mail in a reading education class. *Reading Research and Instruction, 34,* 222–238.

Anderson, D. S., & Piazza, J. A. (1996). Changing beliefs: Teaching and learning mathematics in constructivist preservice classrooms. *Action in Teacher Education, 18* (2), 51–62.

Atkinson, R. C., & Hansen, D. N. (1996). Computer-assisted instruction in initial reading: The Stanford project. *Reading Research Quarterly, 21,* 5–25.

Becker, H. J. (1994). How computers are used in United States schools: Basic data from the 1989 I.E.A. computers in education survey. *Journal of Educational Computing Research, 7* (4), 385–406.

Bertrand, J. E. (1993). Student assessment and evaluation. In B. Harp (Ed.), *Assessment and evaluation in whole language programs* (pp. 19–35). Norwood, MA: Christopher-Gordon.

Bintz, W. P. (1991). "Staying connected": Exploring new functions for assessment. *Contemporary Education, 62* (4), 307–312.

Bork, A. (1987). *Learning with personal computers.* New York: Harper & Row.

Brooks, J. G., & Brooks, M. G. (1993). *In search of understanding: The case for constructivist classrooms.* Alexandria, VA: Association for Supervision and Curriculum Development.

Brown, D. (1997). Kids, computers, and constructivism. *Journal of Instructional Psychology, 23* (3), 189–195.

Bruffee, K. A. (1986). Social construction, language, and the authority of knowledge: A bibliographical essay. *College English, 48,* 773–790.

Bruner, J. (1986). *Actual minds, possible worlds.* Cambridge, MA: Harvard University Press.

Bufkin, L. J., & Bryde, S. (1996). Implementing a constructivist approach in higher education with early childhood educators. *Journal of Early Childhood Instructor Education, 17* (2), 58–65.

Calkins, L. (1994). *The art of teaching writing.* Portsmouth, NH: Heinemann.

Costanzo, W. (1994). Reading, writing, and thinking in an age of electronic literacy. In C. L. Selfe & S. Hilligoss (Eds.), *Literacy and computers: The complications of teaching and learning with technology* (pp. 11–21). Urbana, IL: National Council of Teachers of English.

Davydov, V. V. (1995). The influence of L. S. Vygotsky on education theory, research, and practice. *Educational Researcher, 24* (3), 12–21.

Dixon-Krauss, L. (1996). *Vygotsky in the classroom: Mediated literacy instruction and assessment.* White Plains, NY: Longman.

Duckworth, E. (1987). *The having of wonderful ideas.* New York: Instructors College Press.

El-Hindi, A. (1998). Beyond classroom boundaries: Constructivist teaching with the Internet. In D. J. Leu Jr. (Ed.), Exploring literacy on the Internet. *The Reading Teacher, 51* (8), 694–700.

Flood, J., & Lapp, D. (1995). Broadening the lens: Toward an expanded conceptualization of literacy. In K. A. Hinchman, D. J. Leu, & C. K. Kinzer (Eds.), *Perspectives on literacy research and practice* (pp. 1–16). Chicago: National Reading Conference.

Fosnot, C. W. (1996). Constructivism: A psychological theory of learning. In C. W. Fosnot (Ed.), *Constructivism: Theory, perspectives, and practice* (pp. 8–33). New York: Instructors College Press.

Gallego, M., & Hollingsworth, S. (1992). Multiple literacies: Teachers evolving perceptions. *Language Arts, 69,* 206–213.

Gavelek, J. R., & Raphael, T. E. (1996). Changing talk about text: New roles for teachers and students. *Language Arts, 73,* 182–192.

Gould, J. S. (1996). A constructivist perspective on teaching and learning within the language arts. In C. Fosnot (Ed.), *Constructivism: Theory, perspectives, and practice* (pp. 92–102). New York: Teachers College Press.

Graves, D. H. (1983). *Writing: Teachers and children at work.* Portsmouth, NH: Heinemann.

Greene, M. (1988). *The dialectic of freedom.* New York: Teachers College Press.

Gruender, C. D. (1996). Constructivism and learning: A philosophical appraisal. *Educational Technology, 36* (3), 21–29.

Hutchings, P. (1993). Principles of good practice for assessing student learning. *Assessment Update, 5* (1), 6–7.

Johnston, P. H. (1992). *Constructive evaluation of literate activity.* White Plains, NY: Longman.

Kroll, L. R., & LaBoskey, V. K. (1996). Practicing what we preach: Constructivism in a teacher education program. *Action in Teacher Education, 18* (2), 63–72.

Labbo, L. D. (1996). A semiotic analysis of young children's symbol making in a classroom computer center. *Reading Research Quarterly, 31,* 356–385.

Labbo, L. D., Reinking, D., & Mckenna, M. G. (1995). *Incorporating a computer into the classroom: Lessons learned in kindergarten* (Instructional Resource No. 20). Athens, GA: National Reading Research Center, Universities of Georgia and Maryland.

Leu, D. J. (1996). Sarah's secret: Social aspects of literacy and learning in a digital information age. *The Reading Teacher, 50,* 162–165.

Leu, D. (1997). Caity's question: Literacy as deixis on the Internet. *The Reading Teacher, 51* (1), 62–67.

Leu, D. J., Jr., & Leu, D. D. (1997). *Teaching with the Internet: Lessons from the classroom.* Norwood, MA: Christopher-Gordon.

Leu, D. J., Jr., & Reinking, D. (1996). Bringing insights from reading research to research on electronic learning environments. In H. van Oostendorp & S. de Mul (Eds.), *Cognitive aspects of electronic text processing* (pp. 43–76). Norwood, NJ: Ablex.

Means, B. (Ed.). (1994). *Technology and education reform: The reality behind the promise.* San Francisco: Jossey-Bass.

Moll, L. C., & Greenberg, J. B. (1990). Creating zones of possibilities: Combining social contexts for instruction. In L. C. Moll (Ed.), *Vygotsky and education: Instructional implications of sociohistorical psychology* (pp. 319–348). Cambridge: Cambridge University Press.

Morra, L. G. (1995, April). *America's schools not designed or equipped for the 21st century.* Washington, DC: Health, Education, and Human Services Division. (ERIC Document Reproduction Service No. ED 381 153)

Morrison, G. R., Lowther, D. L., & DeMeulle, L. (1999). *Integrating computer technology into the classroom.* Upper Saddle River, NJ: Merrill.

National Council of Teachers of English & International Reading Association. (1996). *Standards for the English language arts.* Newark, DE: Author.

Piaget, J. (1970). *The science of education and the psychology of the child.* New York: Basic Books.

Reinking, D. (1992). Differences between electronic and printed texts: An agenda for research. *Journal of Educational Multimedia and Hypermedia, 1* (1), 11–24.

Reinking, D. (1994). *Electronic literacy* (Perspective in Reading Research No. 4). Athens, GA: National Reading Research Center, Universities of Georgia and Maryland.

Reinking, D. (1995). Reading and writing with computers: Literacy research in a post-typo-graphic world. In K. A. Hinchman, D. J. Leu, & C. K. Kinzer (Eds)., *Perspectives on literacy research and practice, 44th yearbook of the National Reading Conference* (pp. 17–33). Chicago: National Reading Conference.

Reinking, D. (1996). Reclaiming a scholarly ethic: Deconstructing "intellectual property" in a post-typographic world. In *Literacies for the 21st century: Research and practice, 45th yearbook of the National Reading Conference* (pp. 461–470). Chicago: National Reading Conference.

Reinking, D. (1997). Me and my hypertext: A multiple digression analysis of technology and literacy (sic). *The Reading Teacher, 50* (8), 626–643.

Ryder, R., & Graves, M. (1996–1997, December–January). Using the Internet to enhance students' reading, writing, and information-gathering skills. *Journal of Adolescent & Adult Literacy, 40* (4), 244–254.

Tittle, C. K. (1991). Changing models of student and instructor assessment. *Educational Psychologist, 26* (2), 157–165.

Vygotsky, L. S. (1978). *Mind in society: The development of higher psychological processes.* Cambridge, MA: Harvard University Press.

Willis, J. W., Stephens, E. C., & Matthew, K. I. (1996). *Technology, reading, and language arts.* Needham Heights, MA: Allyn & Bacon.

Wolffe, R. (1997). The constructivist connection: Linking theory, best practice, and technology. *Journal of Computing in Teacher Education, 12* (2), 25–28.

# TEACHER
# AS FACILITATOR
# IN THE ELECTRONIC
# CLASSROOM

"Elma, have your students used Make-a-Book-Now to publish their classroom books?"

"No, Lacy, at least not in my class. I use BookIt because I got a free copy. I'm not particularly happy with BookIt, but at least it didn't cost me anything."

"What's the problem with BookIt?" Lacy asks.

"Well, for one thing," Elma says, "it's hard for the students to import anything but very simple graphics. When we use the scanner to import a graphic of any complexity, BookIt makes a mess of it, especially if we're trying to use a four-color picture. So BookIt really limits what students can produce." Elma pauses, thinking about Lacy's question, and asks, "Are you planning on having students publish their work?"

"I'd like to," Lacy responds, "but there seems to be such a bewildering array of software programs that I'm not sure which one to use. You can't imagine the time I've spent just trying to select a program that will work, given my hardware."

"I know what you mean," Elma says with a chuckle. "I remember spending hours and hours preparing a report on software for my principal when I taught at Eastwood. I called vendors to get copies of software packages, previewed software at the District Office's Software Clearing House, and used all kinds of graphic capabilities to prepare a very professional report, if I do say so myself." Elma pauses. Her eyes have that faraway look.

Lacy, after waiting for what seems like several minutes, asks tentatively, "So . . . what happened?"

"Nothing," Elma says flatly. "It turned out that the district didn't have the money to fund any of my proposals, even the least expensive one, which asked for memory upgrades so that we could run programs like BookIt. Your hardware may not have sufficient memory to use all of BookIt's features."

"Someone else said the same thing," Lacy notes. "So what can I do?"

"You have several options. One, you can write a Teaching Technology grant for the Hughes Foundation. They have been very generous to teachers. Two, you can ask the principal for technology money. She's been very supportive of technology and might have a few bucks to help you. Three, you can dig into your own pocket and buy a software package that fits your hardware."

"And don't forget a fourth option," Lacy says with some excitement. "I can borrow money from you!"

Elma laughs and responds, "That's considered a very short-term loan for a very small amount of money. By the way," Elma continues, switching to a more serious mood, "we need to talk about collecting dues for the Teachers Technology Association so that we can prepare a budget for the conference this spring."

"Oh, that's right," Lacy says. "I'd almost forgotten about the spring conference. Hey, maybe we can get a plenary speaker to talk about software evaluation . . ."

"And software money," Elma interrupts; then, with a twinkle in her eyes, she says, "including loans for software and hardware."

# THE TEACHER'S VARIOUS ROLES

The scenario with Elma and Lacy highlights a secret that is not well known beyond the teaching ranks: Teachers spend a significant amount of time preparing to teach and engaging in activities to support their teaching, such as attending meetings, maintaining gradebooks, and communicating with parents. Although most students have a limited perspective of teaching because they see their instructors almost exclusively in a classroom context, teachers actually spend countless hours outside the classroom ensuring that their time in front of the class is effective. And there is a variety of supporting roles they must fill to be effective in the electronic classroom (Morrison, Lowther, & DeMeulle, 1999). Even though this entire book is dedicated to helping teachers learn how to use computer technology to promote literacy, this chapter focuses on the supporting roles teachers fulfill to use computer technology effectively in promoting literacy.

Before discussing those roles, we stress the importance of teachers remaining focused on their primary role as guardians of literacy standards. They should not become so enamored with technology per se that they forget the ultimate purpose of technology in the classroom: to enable students to gain facility with language so that they can enjoy reading, speaking, and writing—not only for their personal benefit but also for the value their literacy skills can provide society at large. Therefore, technology proficiency cannot be an end in itself. The consummate facilitator is one who values technology because it is a means for the end of increasing students' literacy skills and helping students use those skills to promote their own literacy and, primarily in the work force, the welfare of others. With this caveat about the purpose of technology in mind, we discuss teachers' supporting roles in relation to computer technology.

First, we provide a Computer Classroom Snapshot that gives insights into the teaching of keyboarding skills. Although not every K–8 teacher will find it necessary to teach keyboarding skills, they are essential if students are going to use computers efficiently.

Second, teachers can integrate the curriculum so that students have access to a wide variety of computer technologies as they develop literacy skills. In the role of curriculum integrator, the teacher is an architect of the computer classroom because he or she is providing a framework for facilitating students' learning. To explain how to integrate the curriculum, we provide a model that can be used to develop integrated literacy units. In addition, we offer an example of an integrated literacy unit so that you can see how the model works.

Third, the teacher needs to develop assessment instruments to evaluate the processes and products involved when students use computer technology. We have chosen to discuss assessment as one of the teacher's subsidiary roles because we believe that assessment has two purposes. The purpose of *formative assessment* is to help students improve the works they produce. We believe that teachers should devote the major portion of their evaluation efforts to formative assessment. The purpose of *summative assessment* is to provide a grade. Summative assessment is an administrative function and probably has little to do with helping students learn. Thus, we focus on formative assessment and promote the use of rubrics and the use of self-, peer, and teacher assessments.

Fourth, the teacher can use technology to maintain records and prepare documents that support the classroom teaching mission and curriculum goals (Zorfass & Remz, 1992). Documents include flyers about special events, newsletters to parents, and so forth. This role is particularly important because teachers not only need to maintain good records but also must provide interested parties outside the classroom with professional-looking documents about the computer classroom.

Let's begin by considering Carol Ann Brown's experience in facilitating students' learning of keyboarding skills.

## COMPUTER CLASSROOM SNAPSHOT

### *Context*

As a former classroom teacher and school media specialist, I have observed children's enthusiasm when using a computer to write stories or reports. There is increased motivation for producing error-free work, and students will "stay with" an assignment longer when word processing or using a desktop publishing program. In the school where I worked with children in grades 1 through 6, motivation was high, but parents were concerned that their children were not learning keyboarding skills to match the enthusiasm. They asked what effect the hunt-and-peck system would have as their children moved from elementary school assignments to writing and word processing at the high school and college level. "Would they have to unlearn the invented keyboarding?" they asked. They also had concerns about the time "wasted" during the slow, laborious process of hunting for keys as they typed their stories and reports. Many parents expected their children to enter the work force as skilled typists and hoped for training to begin even at the elementary school level.

Because I was teaching at a private school with students from an upper socio-economic level, many of the children had home computers. Access was not the problem; however, parents did not have the time or the know-how for teaching their children keyboarding. Many parents asked that I include keyboarding as part of their regular classroom activities. They asked for recommendations on drill-and-practice programs and other suggestions for training at home. Keyboarding, like playing the piano, they learned, required disciplined practice—every day.

### What I Did and Why

I knew that my first and second graders were still developing fine motor skills. I also knew they were working to master alphabet letters and symbols. Typing, like many psychomotor skills, requires daily practice; therefore I planned to combine alphabet and symbol recognition with daily drill-and-practice. The first question to answer was how to provide keyboarding practice for all children with only three available computers. I also needed to find a method for helping the students become familiar with the keyboard through repeated exposure to the QWERTY keyboard (QWERTY refers to the standard typewriter keyboard). Young children seem to learn better if they can see, hear, and touch interactively during the learning process. Therefore, I planned an activity in which they would use all three senses.

Each student was given a sheet of drawing paper and told to use a marker or crayon to outline his or her left and right hand. I placed the students in pairs so partners could help each other during this task. Once their hands were traced, I explained that each finger had a name and each had its own special job when typing on the computer. Using a large outlined hand on the chalkboard, I identified the left or right pinky, the ring finger, the tall finger, the pointing finger, and the thumb. The second task, then, was to automatically identify each finger by name.

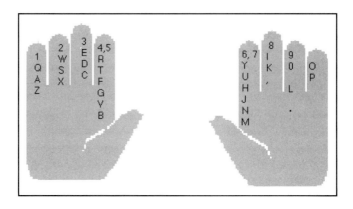

Next, I explained that the right and left thumbs would only have one job: to use the space bar. I had prepared a large simulated keyboard and placed this over the chalkboard. I created my own keyboard from colored cardboard squares and press-on letters, but I know that these can be purchased ready-made. Following this, I explained that the left pinky finger has the job to press the 1, Q, A, and Z keys. I instructed the children to carefully write in these letters on the left pinky of their traced hands. They were instructed to use my enlarged chalkboard example as a guide and to find the 1, Q, A, and Z keys on the large simulated keyboard that had been placed above the chalkboard. Each finger, in turn, was identified and the corresponding letters and symbols assigned. The students were told that this was their official typing guide and that they should place it in their notebooks because they would use it again and again.

I used more than one activity with the hand guides. For instance, as a whole class activity, I would drill the students on a particular letter or symbol. I called a letter while they responded in unison, "Left pinky! Right pointing! Thumb!" and so on. Sometimes, however, we had team competitions for speed or accuracy. The students also worked in pairs as one student called the drill and the partner would respond. The caller was responsible for checking the accuracy of the response.

In a follow-up activity, I duplicated simulated keyboards from a teacher's resource book. This activity works best with partners. The caller drills with letters and symbols while the partner presses the appropriate key. Once again the caller is responsible for monitoring for accuracy. He or she must watch closely to see which key the other "presses" on the paper keyboard. I also used this activity as a way to review for spelling tests and content area vocabulary words.

As another method for review and drill, I removed one or more of the keys from my enlarged simulated keyboard that had been on display. Students were to identify which key(s) were missing. Speed and accuracy are important for this activity because their responses should be automatic by the end of several weeks of drill-and-practice activities.

### What I Learned

The second graders were motivated to participate in the game-like drills for learning the keyboard. Even without access to a lab and a computer for each child, we were able to learn the keyboard and keyboarding skills using all 10 fingers and touch typing on the traditional QWERTY keyboard. The icing on the cake was when I discovered that my students could learn keyboarding while practicing spelling and vocabulary skills. These gamelike activities helped reduce the drudgery usually associated with learning both the keyboard and vocabulary words. I also think that the kinetic activity linked with the visual and auditory input from the simulated keyboards and partner drills enhanced the learning experience. The younger first graders were not as successful with learning the keyboard, but it was a good beginning. In addition, there was valuable practice for identifying letters and numbers and for learning left and right hand orientation. Once the simulated keyboard was prepared and displayed, there was little preparation for me as the teacher. I had only to facilitate as the students tutored one another during their practice! Drills are not always the best strategy for classroom instruction, but in this example I found them to be most valuable for learning a skill that must become automatic and stay with the learner as he or she progresses through elementary and secondary school.

# FACILITATING INTEGRATED LITERACY UNITS

Many teachers are currently using integrated units, so the purpose of this section is to provide a model integrated literacy unit that uses computer technology. At the outset, we want you to know that we are in no way suggesting that whatever you have done without the help of computers to use integrated literacy units is obsolete. Rather, we suggest that technology can help you provide integrated literacy units that will give your students more opportunities to integrate their literacy skills as well as foster critical thinking about content and concepts (Wepner, 1992). The model integrated literacy unit we recommend has several components that need to be planned before the literacy unit is used in your classroom.

## The Integrated Literacy Unit Model

*Topic:* What will be the focus of the unit?

*Major Concepts/Goals:* What new information do you want students to learn while doing this unit?

*Content Areas:* Which content areas will be integrated into the unit: reading, writing, social studies, science, math, health?

*Audience:* With whom will students share their final products: parents, other classes, keypals, senior citizens, siblings, significant others, or community citizens?

*Purpose/Problem Statement Given to Students:* Because the unit focuses on a problem that needs to be solved, when introducing the unit to students on the first day, what will you tell them they are trying to accomplish?

*Rationale Given to Students:* Why investigate this purpose or problem? Teachers must explain to students why a unit is important when it is introduced.

*Time:* How long will the unit last?

*Technology Tools:* Which technology tools will you use in this unit: database, spreadsheet, word processing, HyperStudio, e-mail, Internet, PowerPoint, CD-ROM, Web pages, etc.?

*Procedure:* What problem-solving activities will students engage in, and how will they complete the activities? Will there be whole group, small group, and independent activities?

*Assessment/Outcomes:* How will you include teacher, self-, and peer evaluation in the unit?

## *Example of an Integrated Literacy Unit*

Following is an example of an integrated literacy unit based on the components previously listed.

*Topic:* Touring the United States

*Major Concepts/Goals:* Appreciate geographical and cultural diversity in the United States; learn to manage money; learn to research; examine the relationship of geography to daily life; identify major tourist attractions in the United States; learn how to plan a vacation

*Content Areas:* reading, writing, social studies, science, math in grade levels 3–8

*Audience:* Keypals in schools in other states

*Purpose/Problem Statement Given to Students:* What can you learn from your keypals in other schools across the United States that isn't widely known? What are the major attractions in the vicinity of these schools? If you were to visit your keypals, what would you need to consider before going there?

*Rationale Given to Students:* (Teachers can use the following rationales.) Visiting friends and relatives in faraway places can be fun, but as parents know, a lot of planning is involved. How much time is to be spent away from home? What are the expenses such as gas, food, lodging? What is the distance in miles traveled? What will the weather be like? What do we pack for the trip? These questions, when answered through proper planning, help ensure that a new travel adventure really is exciting—and not frustrating because, for instance, the traveler packed summer clothes for a December trip to Vermont.

*Time:* Approximately three weeks

*Modified Version of Unit:* This unit could be modified by establishing keypals in other countries and making similar plans to visit those countries.

*Technology Tools:* Database, spreadsheet, word processing, e-mail, Internet, PowerPoint, HyperStudio, printer, CD-ROM.

*Procedure:* All units have problem-solving activities. Students have to collect data, manipulate the data, analyze the data, and report the data using the technology tools. In this unit, students working in small groups will research a specific region of the United States. They will find two or three keypals in schools in states within the region they are researching and make simulated plans to visit them and see local attractions. Students will conduct travel research on the Internet, record expenses, and create a list of places using databases and spreadsheets. The student groups will report their study to the class using a HyperStudio stack or PowerPoint presentation. A word processed report should be included in a group portfolio.

*Assessment/Outcomes:* Both teacher and students will develop and use a rubric to assess each group's presentation on its specific region of the United States. In addition, the teacher and students will develop a self/peer assessment rubric to evaluate individual student contributions during the group project. As a starting point, the following broad rubric for this kind of group project is suggested:

- 25% effort/participation
- 25% data collection
- 25% presentation
- 25% written report

In addition, students can become involved in a peripheral, but important, assessment tactic: Three Stars and a Wish (3SW). After each group makes a presentation, class members write down three things they liked (positive) about the presentation and one thing they wish had happened differently (negative) during the presentation. Each group receives the 3SWs the class writes. The 3SWs are not shared with the class.

### Facilitating the Unit Model

The project we have just outlined needs the teacher's facilitation in order to run smoothly, and teacher facilitation involves proper planning. For instance, students will need to know how to make e-mail contact with schools within the region. The teacher can show students how to use the Internet to make e-mail contact. In addition, students will need guidance in developing questions to ask keypals, so the teacher should lead a brainstorming session at the beginning of the project in which students create a list of generic questions. The teacher also might list projected items for the database and spreadsheet, such as travel time, distances, various expenses, and places to visit. In fact, conducting a class discussion about expenses is a good way to help students calculate the myriad costs of traveling.

As facilitator, the teacher has the responsibility to keep students on track and engaged in activities related to the overriding themes (Wepner, 1993). He or she should ensure that each member of a group has an assignment and makes a contribution to each group session. The teacher also needs to have planned, productive activities for groups that complete their project ahead of other groups.

## FACILITATING ASSESSMENT

The group project requires assessment, which can include anything from making an initial assignment to putting a letter or numerical grade on a student's final product. In fact, assessment refers not only to the teacher's evaluation of students' learning but also to teachers' evaluation of their own assignments. This section focuses on the teacher's assessment of students' projects. For more information about classroom assessment, a number of sources are available (e.g., Anderson & Speck, 1998; Angelo & Cross, 1993; Applebee, 1984; Banta, Lund, Black, & Oblander, 1996; Greenberg, 1988; Harp, 1993; Henning-Stout, 1994; Peterson, 1995; Speck, 1998a; Tierney, Carter, & Desai, 1991; White, 1985; White, Lutz, & Kamusikiri, 1996;

Zak & Weaver, 1998). Because of the various uses of the word *assessment,* we give the outlines of a philosophy of assessment before discussing the types of approaches teachers can use.

## A Philosophy of Assessment

Assessment is a complex activity that may seem capricious. For instance, a student or parent can challenge a grade, asking how the teacher derived it. The teacher's explanation may seem strained if he or she simply says, "In my judgment . . ." Those who challenge a grade may not be willing to bow before the authority invested in a teacher and accept his or her judgment as valid. Indeed, challengers may ask for evidence beyond professional judgment. Although the teacher does indeed need to provide such evidence (and thus keep good records), what challengers may not understand is that teacher judgment is central to assessment. Even adding up scores to determine a final grade involves deciding how much weight to give to a particular component of an assignment. Thus, teacher judgment is central to assessment (Speck, 1998c).

This does not mean, however, that teacher judgment is absolute and indisputable. After all, teacher judgments may contradict each other. For instance, two or more teachers might give a full range of grades to the same student's business letter (Dulek & Shelby, 1981; Wilkinson, 1979) or other written projects (Edwards, 1982). Thus, their formal authority as teachers cannot be the sole justification for the assessments they give. (By the way, the problem of reliability among teachers' grades when assessing students' products suggests the benefit of talking to each other in formal ways about grading. Teachers can mark one or two student papers independently and then get together to discuss their approaches to and reasons for marking as they did. Out of a dialogue about assessment teachers can begin to develop local standards.)

In appealing to formal authority—which is granted to teachers as representatives of an educational institution—teachers should ensure that their professional judgments, which are somewhat subjective, are in line with more objective measures. There should be evidence of how a grade was derived, and part of that evidence should include various types of grading instruments (which we discuss shortly). Our philosophical position requires teachers to share their authority with students, not to establish themselves as the sole authority in the classroom. Rather, they are facilitators of authority. They help students learn how to use authority effectively by ensuring that students participate in the grading process (Speck, 1998b).

The notion that students should participate in the grading process may be a bit frightening because traditionally teachers have been the sole proprietors of grading, from producing assignments to giving a final grade for a course. However, the traditional approach fails to consider the need for students to participate actively in the education process, including assessment. Students have to internalize evaluative standards so that they can apply them not only to their own work but also to that of their peers and, later in life, their subordinates. Indeed, if one of the primary purposes of evaluation is to promote improvement, those being evaluated must be able to understand not only what has to be improved but also how it can be improved. The evaluation process, therefore, should be open to investigation by colleagues, students, parents, and other interested parties.

Openness can be promoted in two ways. First, the bulk of evaluation can focus on formative assessment. Second, teachers can actively engage students in the entire evaluative process, both formative and summative.

How can formative assessment promote openness in the assessment process? Formative assessment generally involves evaluations leading up to a final evaluation or grade. The purpose is to give students feedback on their work so they can improve that work. Thus, formative assessment provides the teacher an opportunity to function as a coach, the person who helps students learn how to be effective (Laney, 1993). The teacher as coach is on the same team as the students. She is interested in giving the students every benefit of her expertise by making the process of evaluation transparent. For instance, she might say, "Lillian, as a reader, I like very much the way you describe the cabin you and your family go to during the summer, but as I read your description I keep wondering about the neighboring cabins and the town close by. Can you tell me more about the location?" The teacher is not directly saying, "Lillian, you'll be evaluated on the depth of detail you give and on how well you anticipate readers' concerns"; instead, she is showing Lillian what a real reader—not just a teacher seeking to provide a grade— looks for (Elbow, 1993). By modeling real readers, you can instill in your students the desire to revise their writing to satisfy real readers' needs.

Formative assessment, however, can be much more concrete by including standards that are applied throughout the process. For instance, at the beginning of a project, students should be made aware of the standards that will be used to evaluate it when it is finally due. Those standards should be reinforced throughout formative evaluation at each stage of the evolving products students prepare in response to the initial assignment. This philosophy requires the teacher to be involved in the process of assessment. The old model of assignment, product, and summative assessment is inappropriate. Rather, we endorse the new model of assignment, draft 1, draft 2, draft, 3, and so on, and then summative assessment, giving students time to apply evaluative standards to various drafts.

Openness in evaluation can further be promoted when teachers involve students in the entire evaluative process, both formative and summative (Belanoff, 1993). When students become active participants in the evaluation process, they reflect on and apply evaluative standards to their own work and that of their peers. This approach has several advantages. First, students have an opportunity to articulate evaluative criteria. As a class, for instance, students can negotiate evaluative criteria and consider what is appropriate for a particular assignment. Second, students have an opportunity to apply the criteria so that they can see whether the criteria work and so that they can understand that the application of criteria requires judgment. Then they begin to see that assessment is not merely a matter of the objective application of criteria but that it requires some subjective judgments.

# *Rubrics*

The philosophy of assessment we have outlined here suggests that students should (1) participate in the development of assessment instruments, (2) use the instruments to evaluate their own work and that of their peers, and (3) judge their assessments in the light of teacher and peer assessments. In this regard it is necessary to discuss rubrics—scoring guides that clearly delineate criteria and corresponding rating values to evaluate students' performance—and explain how they foster teacher, peer, and self-evaluations.

Rubrics can provide transparent evaluative standards at the beginning of an assignment, throughout the formative assessment process, and during summative assessment. A rubric establishes the evaluative criteria when an assignment is introduced to students—or shortly thereafter—and then becomes the instrument the teacher and students use for assessing not only progress during the project, but also the completed project. A rubric can be developed at the outset of a project *or shortly thereafter* because sometimes students may need to become involved with the project before they have an adequate understanding of how it should be evaluated. We are not saying, however, that teachers should develop new rubrics for every assignment. Students can be profitably involved in developing a rubric, but they also can use one that was developed, say, last year. Indeed, they can amend an existing rubric and thus save time in developing a new one, a process that could take a significant amount of class time.

It is important to underscore the importance of inviting students to help develop a rubric, which represents grading standards. For instance, students can provide input on what to include: a list of necessary components for an assignment, generally with corresponding weights for measuring a student's success in fulfilling the requirement for each component. In the following section we provide an example of an assignment—a student-produced picture book—and explain how students can be enlisted to produce a rubric for that assignment.

## A Student-Produced Picture Book

The grade level for this assignment is second to third grade. In a class of 18, the students are divided into six groups of three. Each group is responsible for writing six sentences (two for each student) of the text (narrative) on a central theme. Above the text, each group will create an illustration, or drawing, related to the theme developed in the text. Group members do this using the software Paintbrush function.

The six pages of illustrated text are published as one unit. The teacher might want to generate an overall theme so the pages are related. Such a theme might be "Houses on our block," "Fruit we like to eat," or "Our favorite fast food."

Students will probably note that illustrations and text are the two major components of the book. Then the teacher can ask what counts for effective pictures. Students might respond that neatness counts, or that matching of the picture with the text counts, or that color counts. Thus, the teacher can use the overhead projector and write the following on a transparency for the entire class to view:

**ILLUSTRATIONS**

*Neatness:* Is the object clear? Are its dimensions crisp?

*Fit with text:* Is the illustration an appropriate match with the text?

*Color:* Do the colors do justice to the object, or, say, is the orange too blue?

Then the teacher might ask what weight each component should be given. How much should pictures count when the final picture book is being evaluated? Let's say that the students want the pictures to count for 50% of the grade for the final book. Then you need to find out how much each component under the category Illustrations should count. As the students consider weighting, they may come up with other categories, such as creativity. An example of a rubric for the picture book is shown in Figure 2.1.

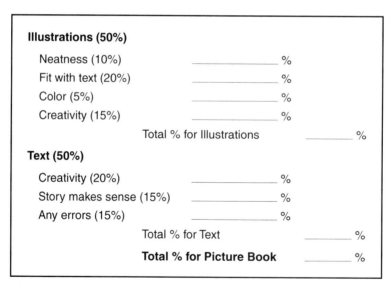

**Illustrations (50%)**

Neatness (10%)                         _____ %

Fit with text (20%)                    _____ %

Color (5%)                             _____ %

Creativity (15%)                       _____ %

         Total % for Illustrations          _____ %

**Text (50%)**

Creativity (20%)                       _____ %

Story makes sense (15%)                _____ %

Any errors (15%)                       _____ %

         Total % for Text                  _____ %

        **Total % for Picture Book**           _____ %

**Figure 2.1**   A Rubric for a Student-Produced Picture Book

Certainly, the rubric in Figure 2.1 can be refined. In fact, students will need to articulate more carefully what constitutes creativity, and they should discuss what constitutes an error. As they begin to use the rubric during formative assessment—as a guide for creating their own picture book—they will raise questions about evaluation. When answered, these questions will help make the criteria for the assessment process more transparent.

## Student Self-Assessment/Reflection

Rubrics are particularly valuable at the outset of a project because they make apparent the criteria students can use to achieve a quality product. This use of the rubric suggests that one thrust of evaluation is to enable students to internalize criteria and become good self-assessors. Not only is the rubric valuable for making criteria transparent, but it also can be used to foster self-evaluation.

We recognize that students may be reluctant to evaluate their own work or that of others. In fact, we have heard teachers say that even though they believe it is important for students to engage in self-assessment, their students don't have the skills to do it. For instance, when students are asked what they learned from completing a project, they often say, "I learned a lot." Such an evaluation is so general that it is practically worthless. But when students are invited to evaluate their work according to a rubric with specific evaluation criteria, they can learn how to make more careful and critical evaluations.

We also acknowledge that involving students in the evaluation process can be controversial. Should students grade other students? Are they really "expert" enough to make judgments on other students' work? In some ways, these questions are a legacy of the old model of teacher-only evaluation because they assume that students cannot be effective evaluators because they are not teachers. This assumption, however, does not take into consideration the teacher's responsibility to help students become effective evaluators. We believe that the teacher does have the responsibility to show students how to assess their own work and that of their peers, so we advocate balancing peer, self-, and teacher assessments. How can this be done?

As already noted, rubrics specify exactly what is required for an assignment to be effective. Thus, one way to balance assessments—both formative and summative—is to have each party use the rubric to evaluate a student's product. Figure 2.2 shows how this might be done.

One virtue of comparing self-, peer, and teacher evaluations is that differences among the evaluations can be discussed and the students can begin to see that assessments must be substantiated by well-grounded reasoning. It is not sufficient to appeal to authority or personal preference. Students need to see that well-intentioned people can have different opinions but that those opinions must be backed up by good reasons. Assessment becomes an exercise in critical thinking; students discover that it entails both the application of objective standards and subjective professional judgment.

In addition to using rubrics, a teacher can engage students in both verbal and written reflection about their work on a daily basis. This may be as simple as asking each student to share with a partner what he or she learned from a specific lesson. Or you might end each day with the students reflecting on it and writing down the most important thing they learned that day. You can encourage students to learn how to reflect on their work by sending home a worksheet (with their completed work) on which parents write down what their children have learned. This fosters discussions between parents and child as well as communication between school and home.

| Illustrations (50%) | Self | Peer | Teacher |
|---|---|---|---|
| Neatness (10%) | _____ % | _____ % | _____ % |
| Fit with text (20%) | _____ % | _____ % | _____ % |
| Color (5%) | _____ % | _____ % | _____ % |
| Creativity (15%) | _____ % | _____ % | _____ % |
| Total % for Illustrations | _____ % | _____ % | _____ % |
| **Text (50%)** | | | |
| Creativity (20%) | _____ % | _____ % | _____ % |
| Story makes sense (15%) | _____ % | _____ % | _____ % |
| Any errors (15%) | _____ % | _____ % | _____ % |
| Total % for Text | _____ % | _____ % | _____ % |
| Total % for Illustrations | _____ % | _____ % | _____ % |
| **Total % for Picture Book** | _____ % | _____ % | _____ % |

**Figure 2.2**   A Rubric for Self-, Peer, and Teacher Evaluation of the Picture Book

# FACILITATING RECORD KEEPING AND EXTERNAL COMMUNICATION

Although the teaching of integrated units may not be required of every teacher in K–8 classrooms, record keeping and external communication are essential functions. This section focuses on the primary record-keeping activity teachers are engaged in—grading—as well as the important role of communicating with parents.

## Grading

One of the great efficiencies of computer technology is that the computation of recorded grades can be automated. A teacher can record a student's grade on a particular assignment, and the computer instantly calculates the student's current class grade. Figure 2.3 shows several examples of Camille's class grade being automatically updated as the teacher inputs the grade for a particular assignment.

Although it is possible to use a database or spreadsheet to create a gradebook, in fact gradebooks often come as part of software already installed in the computer, such as Windows 98. In any case, an electronic gradebook can save a great deal of time and headache when the teacher calculates grades.

A word of caution: A common objection to electronic gradebooks is that they might be erased and then the teacher would have no record of students' grades. First, the problem of "erasing" a gradebook is not unique to electronic media. Teachers lose paper gradebooks all the time. Second, the unbending rule of backup is the solution to the problem of erasing a gradebook. If a teacher happens to "lose" an electronic gradebook, she can retrieve it by using the backup. Of

**CAMILLE grades %**

| | Last name | First name | | Assign #1 | Assign #2 | Assign #3 | Assign #4 |
|---|---|---|---|---|---|---|---|
| | A | B | C | D | E | F | G |
| 1 | Last name | First name | | Assign #1 | Assign #2 | Assign #3 | Assign #4 |
| 2 | Acara | Gari | | 99 | 99 | 98 | 98 |
| 3 | Abler | Mo | | 88 | 89 | 100 | 90 |
| 4 | Horton | Sarah | | 75 | 98 | 88 | 85 |
| 5 | Hicks | John | | 92 | 88 | 90 | 93 |
| 6 | Mosen | Wendy | | 85 | 85 | 80 | 82 |
| 7 | Vanderman | Wade | | 100 | 88 | 87 | 86 |
| 8 | Ward | Heather | | 60 | 65 | 90 | 75 |
| 9 | Wilson | Yolanda | | 87 | 90 | 100 | 95 |
| 10 | | | | | | | |
| 11 | Total | | | 686 | 702 | 733 | 704 |
| 12 | Average | | | 85.75 | 87.75 | 91.62 | 88 |

**CAMILLE grades %**

| | Last name | First name | | Assign #1 | Assign #2 | Assign #3 | Assign #4 |
|---|---|---|---|---|---|---|---|
| | A | B | C | D | E | F | G |
| 1 | Last name | First name | | Assign #1 | Assign #2 | Assign #3 | Assign #4 |
| 2 | Acara | Gari | | 99 | 99 | 98 | 98 |
| 3 | Abler | Mo | | 88 | 89 | 100 | 90 |
| 4 | Horton | Sarah | | 75 | 98 | 88 | 85 |
| 5 | Hicks | John | | 92 | 88 | 90 | 93 |
| 6 | Mosen | Wendy | | 85 | 85 | 80 | 82 |
| 7 | Vanderman | Wade | | 100 | 88 | 87 | |
| 8 | Ward | Heather | | 60 | 65 | 90 | |
| 9 | Wilson | Yolanda | | 87 | 90 | 100 | |
| 10 | | | | | | | |
| 11 | Total | | | 686 | 702 | 733 | 448 |
| 12 | Average | | | 85.75 | 87.75 | 91.62 | 89.6 |

**Figure 2.3**  Camille's Class Grade Being Automatically Updated

course, she can only retrieve the latest copy that was backed up, so it is important to do consistent, frequent backup.

### Parent Communication

In addition to making the recording and computation of grades easier than it would be using a paper gradebook, computers provide the opportunity for teachers to communicate professionally with parents. When we use the word *professionally,* we are talking about appearance. No word processing program we are aware of can create the text of a communication. Teachers need to be proficient writers so that their communications are not marred by the errors that they profess to eliminate in their students' writing. For most of us, creating texts that can stand the scrutiny of many parental eyes requires that we ask colleagues to proofread and edit our work and that we return the favor when those colleagues need our assistance.

However, word processing can give the text a professional appearance and a variety of professional formats. Indeed, it can help personalize communications to parents.

## Mail Merge

The Mail Merge function allows you to personally address communcations to parents and students. When you receive a letter from a company that you never heard of and the the letter is addressed to you, with your name inserted in strategic places, you are witnessing the product of Mail Merge. Essentially, a database with all the names (and, perhaps, addresses) is merged with the letter (or mailing label) you wish to create. Thus, you create a database with the names of all your students' parents, and then you instruct the computer to take the first name in the database (and perhaps the address for that name) and place it at a designated place in a letter (the inside address). After the computer prints that letter, which now is addressed to the first name in the database, it places the second name in the designated place in the letter before printing the second letter. The computer ultimately prints a letter for each student's parents and addresses each letter to each student's parents. The computer can create a list of labels by using the same process. Mail Merge saves lots of time and allows you to produce letters (or a list of labels) addressed to each parent individually.

## Flyers and Newsletters

The computer can also produce professional flyers and newsletters. For instance, you may want to generate a flyer inviting parents to a parent night and enlist your students' help.

The first issue to consider is document design. How should documents look so that they can be read most easily? This question is important because those who produce documents have so much to choose from: all kinds of fonts and type sizes; lines, boxes, and any number of graphics. With this array of choices, some who create documents go wild. In their enthusiasm they use so many fonts and graphics in one document that it becomes an exercise in overkill. It does not communicate effectively with an audience. Figure 2.4 is an example of a flyer that is much too "busy" to be effective. By analyzing the flyer in Figure 2.4, we can develop principles of effective document design.

First, determine the central message of the document and ensure that every part of the document elucidates it. In the ineffective flyer in Figure 2.4, the reader has trouble determining the central message because it's so hard to find. Is the flyer inviting parents to a field day or asking them to bring snacks for the field day?

Second, use a generous amount of white space that does not have text or graphics. White space is important because it can emphasize the essential message of the flyer. The person who designed the ineffective flyer in Figure 2.4 left little white space on it, so we are left a bit dizzy, wondering what exactly the central message is.

Third, limit the use of fonts and graphics. The rule for document designers is not to use more than three different fonts on any flyer. The ineffective flyer in Figure 2.4 uses seven fonts! It also has so many graphics that the reader has trouble determining which graphic to focus on.

**Figure 2.4**   Example of an Ineffective Flyer

Fourth, realize that color is a powerful design tool that can be used for drawing attention, setting a mood, or brightening a page. However, producing documents in color is more expensive than black and white. Ask yourself what page elements you want in color. Will you use color illustrations and a color from the illustration for the headings in the text, or will you just use a large capital letter balanced by a horizontal rule in the same color? Do not use too many colors; you run the risk of overpowering the message. Two colors can make a big impact in a document, and it is much cheaper than full color. You may want to choose a color scheme. A safe way to do this is to choose colors that are adjacent to each other on the color wheel. These tend to create a unified look. Another safe combination is colors that are equidistant from each other on the color wheel. An example is red, blue, and yellow. They generally look good together.

Fifth, make sure you lead the readers through the document. They should not have to wonder how to read it. They should see that they start at the top and logically follow the text from top to bottom. Headings in a newsletter, for instance, can act as signposts, telling the reader what is coming up next.

Using these principles we've created an effective flyer in Figure 2.5 with a software package specifically designed for flyers.

You can also create newsletters using a standard word processing package or specific software packages. We recommend that you use your students' help as

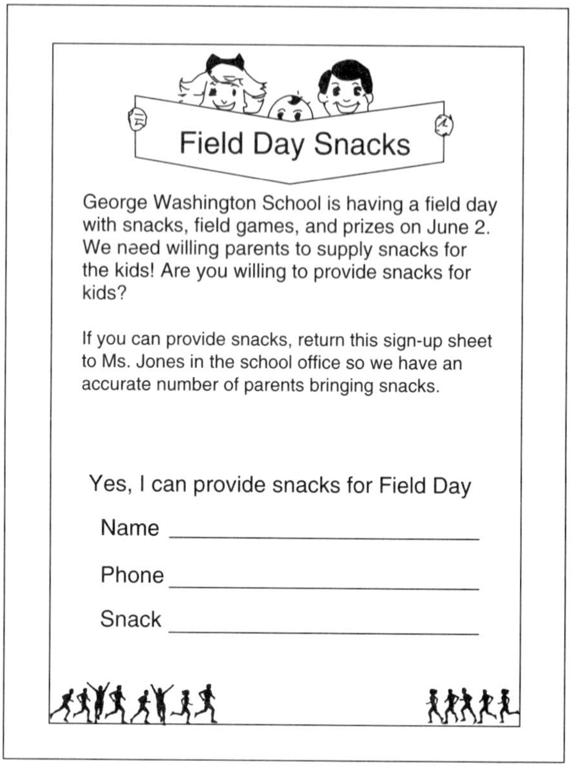

**Figure 2.5** Example of an Effective
Flyer

### Field Day Snacks

George Washington School is having a field day
with snacks, field games, and prizes on June 2.
We need willing parents to supply snacks for
the kids! Are you willing to provide snacks for
kids?

If you can provide snacks, return this sign-up sheet
to Ms. Jones in the school office so we have an
accurate number of parents bringing snacks.

Yes, I can provide snacks for Field Day

Name _____

Phone _____

Snack _____

much as possible. Scan in their work. Ask them to create text. Make the production of a flyer or newsletter a class project, and ask two or three students to be the editors in charge. Parents might be more interested in a newsletter that their children create than in one that the teacher creates. Besides, a student-produced flyer or newsletter can be an example of teaching effectiveness if it has a professional look.

## COMPUTER CLASSROOM EXAMPLES

### *Getting the Genie Out of Genealogy*

**Grade Level:** 6–8

**Objective:** TLW (The Learner Will):

1. become aware of human migratory habits.
2. establish a personal relationship with the past.
3. develop a different sense for history.
4. have fun researching a non-academic topic using the Internet.
5. think more about families and family values.
6. develop a keener self-awareness.
7. search for and maybe find new relatives.
8. find that the Internet can generate personal information.

**Time:** 50 minutes (*Note:* This lesson plan is for day one of a longitudinal project intended to last about two weeks, give or take a couple of fire drills and/or pep assemblies.)

**Problem to Be Solved:** How far back can you trace your family?

**Materials:** Computers on line
Printer
List of Websites
World map
Handout

**Steps:**

1. Students are shown pictures of early hominids, such as Neanderthal or Cro-Magnon. The teacher asks if there are any guesses to who or what they are.
2. When this is established, the teacher announces probable origins, locates site on map, and then asks if any student is aware of his or her own actual ancestry, or at least ancestral country.
3. Then the teacher (very enthusiastically) announces that the students are going on line to search for and discover where they came from (genealogy—but don't ask them to spell it). Students should be told this is a fun assignment and that participation and effort are a main source of their grade.

*First Day Activities:*

1. Divide into groups of three or four. Friends are okay and encouraged.
2. The teacher demonstrates a Website devoted to genealogy; also locates a search engine, such as Alta Vista, and types in the word *genealogy* to see where it goes.

## COMPUTER CLASSROOM EXAMPLES (*CONTINUED*)

3. After being encouraged to help each other and to share in equal time amounts, groups go to the computers and are off and running to pursue ancestral information.

4. The teacher has provided a handout identifying what this information should be and how to organize it. Students should also look for clues as to when and how their family migrated to its present location and speculate as to the reason it did so.

5. Before the bell rings, the teacher asks randomly for a progress report and states that such reports will be a normal routine on subsequent days as more information is researched.

**Assessment:** Did the students participate and make an effort?

And/or: Brief oral report on *anything* found; a written summary for inclusion in a porfolio.

Rubric for expanded assessment:

25% Participation
25% Data Collection
25% Oral Report of Findings to Class
25% Written Report for Portfolio Inclusion

### *Balking in the Balkans*

**Grade Level:** 8

**Objective:** TLW (The Learner Will):

1. develop a sense of teamwork to solve problems and complete projects.
2. gain insight into unfamiliar social and political issues.
3. be able to converse on line with people in other countries.
4. come to a greater appreciation of his or her own country.
5. provide an outlet for Balkan residents to share feelings.

**Time:** 50 minutes (*Note:* This lesson plan is for day one of a longitudinal project intended to last about two weeks for the field work and several more days for report preparation.)

**Problem to Be Solved:** What's happening in the part of Europe known as the Balkans?

**Materials:** 6 or more computers on line
Printer
List of e-mail Websites
Map
Handout

## COMPUTER CLASSROOM EXAMPLES (*CONTINUED*)

**Steps:**

1. Students are shown gruesome pictures of refugees from Kosovo Province (overhead, or on large screen) and pictures of American soldiers in uniform. The teacher does not say they are Kosovo people but asks the class for a probable identity.

2. Question by question, the teacher finds out how much students know about the Balkan situation, such as place names, map location, U.S. involvement, and the like. This serves as a pre-evaluation. Extra credit to anyone making contact within the former Yugoslavia.

*First Day Activities:*

1. Formation of groups, called teams, in accordance with model description.
2. Teams are assigned a country: Yugoslavia (Kosovo or Serbia), Bosnia, Albania, Macdeonia. They should be made aware that computers are in short number in Kosovo.
3. Students are given a primer by the teacher on accessing e-mail Websites and chat rooms.
4. Class expectations are explained verbally and with handout. Students should ask questions about changes in school life, sports, after-school and weekend activities, whether things are improving or worsening.
5. The teacher provides general guidelines on writing proper questions. Questions and answers tend to be self-generating, but actual questions are written by the team.
6. Remaining time is to be spent collecting initial questions or getting on line.
7. The teacher re-emphasizes the need to go outside the local circle and comfort zone to establish contact with the rest of the world and learn more about important world issues from nontraditional sources.

**Assessment:**
25% List of events happening in Macedonia, Bosnia, Albania, Yugoslavia (Serbia)
25% Data collection: e-mail contacts, information
25% Oral report of findings
25% Written report for inclusion in portfolio

# TECHNO-TEACHER TIPS

### Developing Rubrics

One concern that teachers have about developing rubrics is, ironically, the amount of classroom time it takes to create one time-saving tip. Even when you want students to have input in the process, share an existing rubric and ask them to help you modify it. You can create the rubric yourself, borrow one from a colleague, or use one from the previous year as a model. This enables students to have a voice in the assessment process within a short period of time.

### Assessing Technology Products

The students will have varying degrees of success producing spreadsheet and database products. We recommend grading these as parts of a whole—either as data collection, or as effort and participation, or both. Few teachers themselves are competent in all areas of computer technology, and such limitations should be acknowledged in the students as well.

## FREQUENTLY ASKED QUESTIONS

1. **I have been using integrated units in my classroom for the last five years. I'm not sure how to start using the computer in my units. Do you have any suggestions?**

   Ask yourself the potential ways to begin:

   - "Are my students producing a piece of writing?" If so, have them word process their stories.
   - "Will my students share their writing or other information they have learned during the unit?" The Internet provides many ways for students to share their work with the outside world. For instance, they can create a chat room or in-house presentations using tools such as PowerPoint, Hypermedia, and spreadsheets.
   - "Are my students engaged in collecting information on the specific type of study?" The Internet is an excellent resource tool. In addition to having students read textbooks, tradebooks, magazines, and the like, introduce them to Websites related to your type of study. You will be amazed by the students' motivation and excitement.

2. **I am concerned about giving students a group grade for projects they complete during integrated units. Do you any suggestions?**

   We recommend that you provide two grades for each project. The first grade is for the final product, determined according to the rubric developed for the project. Each person in the group receives the same grade for the product. The second grade is an individual grade based on a rubric that assesses the contribution, attitudes, and effort made by each student. Each person in the group completes a one-page rubric that evaluates himself or herself and each member in the group according to criteria such as: completed their part/role on time, got along well with everyone, and helped other team members.

# REFERENCES

Anderson, R. S., & Speck, B. W. (Eds.). (1998). *Changing the way we grade student perform-ance: Classroom assessment and the new learning paradigm.* (New Directions for Teaching and Learning, No. 74). San Francisco, CA: Jossey-Bass.

Angelo, R. T., & Cross, K. P. (1993). *Classroom assessment techniques* (2nd ed.). San Francisco, CA: Jossey-Bass.

Applebee, A. N. (1984). *Contexts for learning to write: Studies of secondary school instruction.* Norwood, NJ: Ablex.

Banta, T. W., Lund, J. P., Black, K. E., & Oblander, F. W. (1996). *Assessment in practice.* San Francisco, CA: Jossey-Bass.

Belanoff, P. (1993). What is a grade? In W. Bishop (Ed.), *The subject is writing: Essays by teachers and students* (pp. 179–88). Portsmouth, NH: Boynton/Cook.

Dulek, R., & Shelby, A. (1981). Varying evaluative criteria: A factor in differential grading. *Journal of Business Communication, 18* (2), 41–50.

Edwards, D. (1982). Project marking: Some problems and issues. *Teaching at a Distance, 21,* 28–35.

Elbow, P. (1993). Ranking, evaluating, and liking. *College Composition and Communication, 55* (2), 187–206.

Greenberg, K. L. (1988). Assessing writing: Theory and practice. In J. H. McMillan (Ed.), *Assessing students' learning* (pp. 47–59). (New Directions for Teaching and Learning, No. 34). San Francisco, CA: Jossey-Bass.

Harp, B. (Ed.). (1993). *Assessment and evaluation in whole language programs.* Norwood, MA: Christopher-Gordon.

Henning-Stout, M. (1994). *Responsive assessment.* San Francisco, CA: Jossey-Bass.

Laney, R. (1993). Letting go. In K. Spear (Ed.), *Peer response groups in action: Writing together in secondary schools* (pp. 151–61). Portsmouth, NH: Heinemann.

Morrison, G. R., Lowther, D. L., & DeMeulle, L. (1999). *Integrating computer technology into the classroom.* Upper Saddle River, NJ: Merrill.

Peterson, R. (1995). *The writing teacher's companion: Planning, teaching, and evaluating.* Boston: Houghton Mifflin.

Speck, B. W. (1998a). *Grading student writing: An annotated bibliography.* Westport, CT: Greenwood Press.

Speck, B. W. (1998b). The teacher's role in the pluralistic classroom. *Perspectives, 28* (1), 19–44.

Speck, B. W. (1998c). Unveiling some of the mystery of professional judgment in classroom assessment. In R. S. Anderson & B. W. Speck (Eds.), *Changing the way we grade student performance: Classroom assessment and the new learning paradigm* (17–32). (New Directions for Teaching and Learning, No. 74). San Francisco, CA: Jossey-Bass.

Tierney, R. J., Carter, M. A., & Desai, L. E. (1991). *Portfolio assessment in the reading-writing classroom.* Norwood, MA: Christopher-Gordon.

Wepner, S. (1992). Using technology with content area units. *The Reading Teacher, 45* (8), 644–646.

Wepner, S. (1993). Technology and thematic units: An elementary example on Japan. *The Reading Teacher, 46* (5), 442–445.

White, E. M. (1985). *Teaching and assessing writing.* San Francisco, CA: Jossey-Bass.

White, E. M., Lutz, W. D., & Kamusikiri, S. (Eds.). (1996). *Assessment of writing: Politics, policies, practices.* New York: Modern Language Association of America.

Wilkinson, D. C. (1979). Evidence that others do not agree with your grading of letters. *The ABCA Bulletin, 42* (3), 29–30.

Zak, F., & Weaver, C. C. (1998). *The theory and practice of grading writing: Problems and possibilities.* Albany: State University of New York Press.

Zorfass, J., & Remz, A. (1992, May). Successful technology integration: The role of communication and collaboration. *Middle School Journal,* 39–43.

# USING THE INTERNET
# TO TEACH LITERACY

As Mr. Brownlee watches the students in his fourth-grade class use the Internet, he marvels at their eagerness to find information. There's Sara, who didn't know much about computers at all until 6 weeks ago, showing Sandi how to access a Web page that will provide information both of them can use for their report on the customs of a small tribe in central Africa. Josh and Mason are accessing links on the White House homepage to gather data about homeless legislation that was recently passed. And Belemy is listening to Jerome as he provides Ziegler with the address of a Website in New Zealand that has information about the kiwi. Ziegler was surprised that the kiwi couldn't fly and wanted to find pictures of the bird that he could download for his article in the class newsletter.

Unfortunately, not everyone is having such success at using the World Wide Web. Kreston, who is absent again today, doesn't seem very interested in computers. Part of the problem may be that Kreston's parents don't have a computer at home and Kreston's friends don't have computers, so the only time he can use one is during class. Another absence will not help him become more familiar with computers and the Web, and Mr. Brownlee wonders what he can do to help Kreston so that he doesn't fall hopelessly behind the rest of the class. Kreston seems to like Blaine, so Mr. Brownlee decides to pair them up in class the next time Kreston comes. Maybe Blaine would be willing to help Kreston after school.

Mr. Brownlee looks at his watch. It's just about time for the next period, so he reminds the students to begin preparing for the bell. Michele says, "We never have enough time on the computer," to which Zach adds, "Yeah, especially time for the Web." Mr. Brownlee smiles broadly, asking no one in particular, "How did you survive before the classroom was wired for the Net?"

"You mean in the 'good old days' before CDs?" Michele asks playfully.

Suddenly the bell rings and the students hustle to leave, laughing and talking about the 'good old days' before CDs. Mr. Brownlee continues to smile, not only at Michele's comment but at the pleasure of working with a community of students who are enthusiastic about learning.

# What Is the Internet?

In dry terms, the Internet is simply the vast world of computers that have the ability to store information and communicate with each other.

In more colorful terms, the Net is a hive of wild anarchy buzzing with chat rooms, newsgroups, bulletin boards, and e-mail messages; with traders buying, selling, and negotiating. It bristles with art, color, graphics, and links of the ingenious World Wide Web. It is on the one hand a priceless source of invaluable, easily accessed research material, and on the other a certifiable rubbish heap of useless facts and misinformation. It has thus far been a remarkable testimony to free speech and free enterprise, with all their attendant difficulties. No governing body distinguishes the good guys from the darkside demons. In a place where anything goes, it usually does.

This is how it's done: Individual computers are linked together by modems, phone lines, and service providers. The modems convert the digital chunks of computer information into fluid analog information such as sound waves, that can be carried over phone lines to service providers (i.e., AOL, MSM), which for a fee make connections to the Internet.

# Why Use the Internet to Teach Literacy?

The gift horse you're looking at, the Internet, might be a thoroughbred. There are hundreds of Websites devoted to all fields of education, sporting all kinds of helpful information. The venerable *New York Times,* for example, has a daily offering of lesson plans in most fields of study. The site enables teachers to upgrade older lessons by providing new information. Or teachers can take a scroll through the pages of the Judi Harris Website and scan myriad lesson plans that make use of Internet technology. There are lots of possibilities here to see how others have been successful at using the Net as a teaching tool.

Building lesson plans is only part of what the language arts teacher can do for a block of literacy instruction. Using the Internet as a research tool, a teacher is able to access the world of literature ranging from children's to adult, short stories, novels, and poems—items not found in class texts or small school libraries.

Now that we have generalized some obvious advantages of the Internet, we will bring forth the heavy educational artillery of jargon and research. Scholars such as Mike (1997) and Ryder (1996–1997) argue that the Internet benefits students because it promotes (1) higher level thinking, (2) a sense of audience, (3) authentic literacy purposes, and (4) cooperative learning. Reinking (1997) adds that when teachers use computers to teach literacy they (1) help teachers do what they have always done, (2) better prepare students for the digital future, and (3) transform literacy instruction. Once a costly and complicated endeavor, the Internet has become increasingly accessible and affordable, and teachers are finding it an exciting and invaluable teaching tool (Blanchard, 1995; Leu & Leu, 1997) that has been shown to increase student interest in reading and writing (Stuhlmann, 1996). As mentioned in Chapter 1, the constructivist paradigm guides our use of the Internet to teach literacy. In particular, the Internet promotes literacy development through the following two constructivist principles: (1) problem solving, and (2) cooperative learning.

## The Internet Promotes Problem-Solving Skills

When students are engaged in problem-based learning, they use the Internet to search, sort, organize, and evaluate information. Specifically, the Internet promotes higher level thinking skills such as "(1) setting purposes for reading, (2) adjusting the reading rate, (3) evaluating text content for relevant and significant information and ideas, and (4) synthesizing textual information" (Brozo & Simpson, 1999, p. 365).

The Internet expands learning beyond the traditional classroom into an international arena because it enables students to access information throughout the world. A student in Missouri can connect with a publishing house in Argentina and find out what books it sells. A student in Arizona can use the Internet to read students' writing in Germany. The Internet is a transnational means of communicating with people in other cultures and learning about those cultures.

The Internet also has the virtue of providing current information. For instance, government documents are regularly posted on the Internet. Companies provide current information about their products. Universities throughout the world regularly update information about their campuses. Scholars create and update Web pages with links to their particular academic specialty and to other Web pages related to the same specialty. Libraries regularly revise the the listings of their holdings posted on the Internet. These examples, and myriad others, provide students with current, up-to-date information that they can use to solve real-life problems.

## The Internet Promotes Cooperative Learning

The Internet provides multiple ways for students to communicate. For instance, through online discussions, they share information, gain multiple perspectives, and learn from one another. In addition, students often collaborate in small groups when working on Internet tasks (Kimball, 1995). Group work is consistent with a constructivist classroom in which students are responsible for helping one another learn. In fact, in the following snapshot a sixth-grade teacher explains how she used the Internet to provide group learning opportunities for her students.

## COMPUTER CLASSROOM SNAPSHOT

### Context

My name is JoAnne Lancaster, and three years ago I was basically computer illiterate. My peer teachers had failed to talk me into using CLASSMASTER, a Claris-Works program that functions as an electronic gradebook. My arguments against using CLASSMASTER were: I just like having my regular gradebook (it can't get "lost" or "deleted"), I don't have a computer at home or in my classroom (it's too inconvenient), and I don't have time to learn anything else new. Then two years ago, when I took an Introduction to Micro Computing class as part of my graduate studies for the Education Specialist degree, I began to understand the powerful potential computer technology held for improving education. Consequently, I began to use CLASSMASTER and loved it. I also applied what I learned in that micro computing class when I had to teach basic computer skills for three weeks to my sixth-grade English classes.

Through my limited computer training I vaguely knew about the Internet, but I had not used it. The main reason for my lack of practical knowledge of the Internet was access: Our school had only one online computer in the library. Even in the spring of this year I was virtually Internet illiterate, using it only once a week during a university class I was taking. However, the more I learned about its potential to enhance literacy in the classroom from guest speakers for the university class and from the literature I was reading, the more I longed to be able to use Internet with my sixth-grade students.

My chance to use the Internet with my students materialized in late March of this year when my principal announced that at last our computer lab was wired and online. I nearly jumped out of my seat and hurried to sign up for lab time during the week of T-CAP testing. (T-CAP is a state standardized test used to measure achievement.) I was motivated to try some of the projects I had learned about in my graduate classes.

Before telling you what I did, let me tell you about my school. I teach at a suburban middle school in western Tennessee. The school of about 1,000 students serves a community made up mainly of single family homes and one apartment complex. The ethnic makeup of the student body is 92 percent Caucasian, 5% black, 2% Asian, and 1% Hispanic. In 1994–1995, about 48% of the sixth graders were above average academically according to the SACS (Self Improvement Committee) study. Scores in language arts skills ranged from 61% to 90% mastery in 1996–1997, according to T-CAP.

### What I Did and Why

During the last week in March 1998, the week of T-CAP testing in our district, I began teaching my students about the Internet by giving each class a brief explanation about the Internet. About 60% of the students had used the Internet before, so I did not spend an inordinate amount of time on the basics. I showed the students our school's homepage and explained the purpose of a homepage. Then I showed students the location field on the homepage and explained how to enter

1. **Dan and Ann's Scavenger Hunt**
   <http://www.athena.ivv.nasa.gov/curric/general/scavhunt.html>
2. **World Wide Web Scavenger Hunt**
   <http://www.cs.rice.edu/~sboone/Lessons/Titles/hunt/hunt.html>
3. **Study Webb** <http://www.studyweb.com>
4. **Idiom of the Day (Cobuild)** <http://titania.cobuild.collins.co.uk/Idiom.html>
5. **The White House for Kids** <http://whitehouse.gov/WH/kidshome.html>
6. **Monarch Watch** <http://www.keil.ukans.edu/~monarch/>
7. **Weekly Reader** <http://www.weeklyreader.com/>
8. **Night of the Comet** <http://quest.arc.nasa.gov/comet>
9. **Live From Antarctica** <http://quest.arc.nasa.gov/antarctica/index.com>

**Figure 3.1**  Website Reference List

an address, noting the necessity of accuracy when entering addresses. I explained the basic rules for Internet use. For example, students were not to "surf the Internet" and were to use the "Back" button if they accidentally got on an inappropriate site. I also warned of the loss of computer privileges if they broke the basic rules. I picked up that warning from a guest speaker in one of my graduate classes who stressed the importance of being in control of what kids do on the Internet and enforcing consequences.

Earlier in the semester, I had had students pick friendship computer pairs. These pairs were assigned to specific lab computers (someone had advised me to assign computers to have better control over the content students used). I made a seating chart and found that a boy pair–girl pair arrangement helped cut down on the noise level. Now that we were ready to begin, we started with a simple search on the Website entitled The White House for Kids (Figure 3.1). I gave each pair of students a worksheet, and they were to find answers to questions and write the answers on the worksheet. Although the worksheet limited them to one site, they gained practice by using links to find information. Most students completed this activity in one class period of about 45 minutes. For the next two days we worked on Dan and Ann's Scavenger Hunt (Figure 3.1). This activity was very organized and controlled. Students were able to work with each other to find all the items on the Scavenger Hunt. As some students were completing the hunt, others explored sites from the reference list, especially Weekly Reader (Figure 3.1). At the end of the six-day period, I asked my students to complete a questionnaire about their computer experiences.

### What I Learned
Upon analysis of the questionnaires, these themes emerged:

1. Students like using the Internet better than the other computer activities they've experienced in school this year.

2. Students like least the word processing and the art activities in comparison to other computer activities.

3. Students prefer working with a partner to working alone on computer activities.

4. Students' main suggestion for improvement of computer activities is to have more time on computers in general.

5. Students recommend continuing next year the Internet projects as well as most other computer activities.

I learned that students need some explicit instruction about what the Internet is and how to begin to access Internet information. I learned that it is helpful to use a frame or graphic organizer to give students something definite to do with the information they find. I also learned that a few strategic instructions are essential, and next time I will make a handout with steps to follow as well as use experienced students as helpers the first few times on the Internet.

I am excited about the future and my role in helping prepare students for productive lives that require all kinds of visual literacy. This small experiment with the Internet has given me confidence to keep "driving," to keep "traveling" on the Information Superhighway. Fear of the unknown no longer haunts me. My principal has already asked me to share what I've learned with other teachers at my school. As one of my students said, "Most students want to spend more time on the computer. I think this really shows the changing age." Yes—we are in a new age of literacy development, and I am finally excited to be a part of it.

## WHAT TYPES OF INTERNET SERVICES ARE USED BY LITERACY TEACHERS?

JoAnn's experience of using the Internet and teaching her students how to use it highlights the ease with which people can gain Internet fluency. Such fluency is important because the Internet provides the latest information through a variety of services. For a list of Internet services most frequently used by teachers, see Figure 3.2. Let's look at each of these services.

**Figure 3.2**   Internet Services That Teachers Use

World Wide Web (WWW)

E-mail

Listservs

Newsgroups

Chat forums

FTP & Gopher

Emerging technologies

## World Wide Web (WWW)

The World Wide Web (WWW), or Web, is an interactive system that offers quick access to the information on the Internet. One reason the Web is the most popular Internet service is that it has unique multimedia capabilities. It links text, colorful graphics, sound, and video in a captivating manner. You can jump from one link to another in a fraction of a second by pointing and clicking, and as a result you can view and hear a great deal of information in an engaging and short timespan. Teachers use the Web in a variety of ways, and there are many popular Websites to visit (Dyril, 1996; Engst, 1995; Etchinson, 1995; Johnson, 1995; Kendall, 1995; Maring, 1997; Munson, 1996; Rosen, 1997). See Figure 3.3 for one example. In addition, Figure 3.4 provides definitions of key terms useful for understanding how the Web works. To learn how you can build your own Website, see the appendix at the end of this chapter.

Be advised of the ever-changing nature of the web. Sites disappear and move regularly. Your server, which connects you to the Web, will tell you when this happens. If a site has disappeared, you probably didn't want it anyway. If it moved, it's probably been upgraded.

Another important aspect of the Web is browsers. The Web is equipped with user-friendly software called *browsers* that enable you to view Web pages and access applications. The two most common browsers are Netscape Navigator and Microsoft Internet Explorer.

**Figure 3.3**   Example of World Wide Web Page

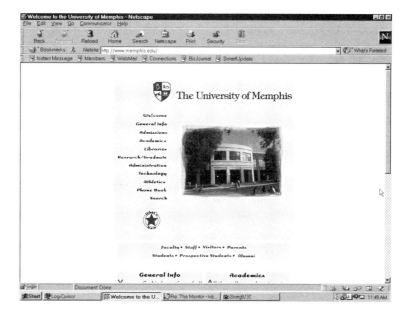

---

**Bookmark.**   Similar to using a bookmark to indicate a specific page in a book, an Internet bookmark enables you to mark a WWW page that you want to travel to at a later date. Bookmarking eliminates having to enter the WWW address (URL) again. Some Microsoft programs use the word *Favorites*.

**Browser.**   A browser is software that allows you to read the Hypertext Markup Language (HTML) of Web pages. It decodes HTML and enables you to see images on the Web, rather than just text, by following menu items or other links.

**Downloading.**   The process of receiving files from another computer and transferring them to your own computer.

**File Transfer Protocol (FTP).**   A program that enables you to transfer files from one computer to another across the Internet, especially for the purpose of retrieving files from public archives. Examples include educational software, electronic books, journal articles, and graphic files.

**Homepage.**   The initial menu page of a Website that you can "visit" to obtain information. Individuals, schools, organizations, and your own classroom can have homepages. An example of a homepage appears in Figure 3.3.

**Hypertext.**   A special language on the Web that enables you to link text with keywords. For instance, by clicking on words, phrases, or icons you automatically connect to new information.

**Hypertext Markup Language (HTML).**   The language of codes and links used to create Web pages. Recent authoring software programs are WYSIWYG (What You See Is What You Get), eliminating the need to learn HTML for Web publishing. You probably will not have to learn this to create your own Web page.

**Hypertext Transfer Protocol (HTTP).**   The program that enables hypertext documents to be transferred over the Web (Lemay, 1995). HTTP is the URL prefix that indicates a Web page address.

**Search Engines.**   Tools that enable you to search for information on the Web.

**Uniform Resource Locator (URL).**   An address at which you can find data on the Web. These addresses have prefixes such as http, ftp, gopher, or telenet: for example, URL <http://english-server.hss.cmu.edu/>

---

**Figure 3.4**   Important World Wide Web Definitions

## *Electronic Mail (E-mail)*

E-mail, a commonly used feature on the Internet, allows you to send and receive messages from individuals who have access to the Internet. In addition, you can send messages to groups of people by using systems such as bulletin boards and listservs. As Ryder and Hughes (1997) discuss, e-mail is a flexible tool that "can be used as an instructional tool for students, as a communication tool for the teacher, and as a communication tool for the school and the community" (p. 53). Students have success forming electronic "literature partners" (Harris, 1992) along e-mail lines; teachers use e-mail to give and receive assignments and to promote class-wide communication (Parson, 1997).

**PENPAL-L** <listserv@unccvm.uncc.edu>: Online penpal exchange

**TAWL** <listserv@listserv.arizona.edu>: Discussion of whole language teaching

**MIDDLE-L** <listserv@postoffice.cso.uiuc.edu>: Discussion of middle school–age children

**ATEG** <listserv@miamiu.acs.muohio.edu>: Assembly for the Teaching of English Grammar

**Figure 3.5** Listservs for Teaching Literacy

## Listservs

Listservs provide a forum for individuals who are interested in the same topic to have online discussions. Listservs can be educational, social, or informational, and they can be open to the general public or only to specific members. A variety of literacy-related listservs are applicable to teachers and students (Figure 3.5).

Listservs have one e-mail address to join the group and another e-mail address for sending messages. Figure 3.6 provides a screen from the RTEACHER listserv, a discussion group on issues related to literacy and technology. Currently there are over 300 educators throughout the world who participate in these discussions. You can review previous conversations at: <http://listserv.syr.edu/archives/rteacher.html.>

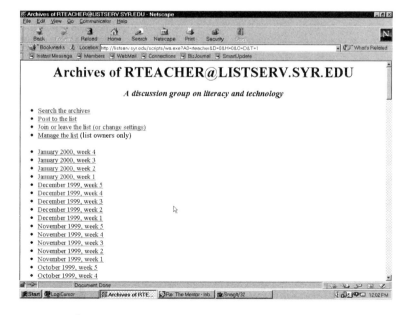

**Figure 3.6.** Listserv for RTEACHER

## *Newsgroups*

Newsgroups are similar to listservs in that they provide a forum for exchanging ideas on a variety of topics. Messages on newsgroups, however, are posted to an electronic bulletin board instead of sent as an e-mail message so that more than one individual can respond to a specific message. For example, Figure 3.7 shows an example of a newsgroup message from <k12.lang.art>. Although students may engage in newsgroups, currently they are more popular with teachers. Examples of newsgroups of interest to teachers include the following: <k12.chat.teacher>—discusses K–12 instructional issues, including language arts; <k12.lang.art>—discusses the language arts curriculum in K–12 education; and <k12.chat.elementary>—discussions by K–5 students.

## *Chat Forums*

Chat forums (also known as chat rooms) allow users to engage in "chat," or talk, in real-time. Similar to a telephone call, chat forums enable users at different computers to talk to one another. When one user enters text into the computer, it is immediately viewed on others' screens and they in turn can respond. One of the more popular means of chatting for educators is a MOO. A MOO (Multiple user dimension Object Oriented) is a computer program, accessed via Telnet, in which multiple users located anywhere in the world can simultaneously interact with each other (DeMeulle, Anderson, & Johnston 1996). Another free and easy chat forum is Global Chat at <http://arachnid.qdeck.com/chat/schedule.html>.

## *Emerging Technologies*

Prior to the WWW, the Internet only used text and did not have multimedia capabilities as it does now. Multimedia capabilities, as Ryder and Hughes (1997) point out, make possible three areas of new Internet technology that are especially promising for teachers: (1) audio conferencing is available by using RealAudio from Progressive Networks at <http://www.realaudio.com/index.html>, (2) virtual reality software gives the illusion of operating in three-dimensional space, and (3) video conferencing allows users to see each other as they communicate. For instance, CU-SeeMe is a video software program that allows a user to broadcast images of himself or herself over the Internet. In addition to the video software, an

```
Janice wrote:
  >Does anybody know of chat room appropriate for >elementary school
  kids?
  >Thanks in advance.

The Kidlink organization runs an excellent, kid-safe chat network. You
can find information on Kidlink at http://www.kidlink.org
Peace,
Lisa
```

**Figure 3.7**   Example of a Newsgroup Message From <k12.lang.art>.

inexpensive video camera is mounted on top of the computer that enables users from all over the world to see each other when they communicate with one another. For additional information, see <http://www.gsn.org/> or <http://cu-seeme.cornell.edu.>.

# HOW DO YOU USE THE INTERNET TO TEACH LITERACY?

Primarily, teachers use the Internet to teach literacy by (1) publishing, (2) accessing information, and (3) communicating and collaborating.

## Publishing

The Internet is a powerful and innovative tool for publishing students' work (Iannone, 1998). Through desktop software, students can publish their written texts in forms such as newsletters and brochures. In addition, the Internet provides an innovative forum for students to publish their written text for audiences in other locations. Thus, students have authentic purposes for their writing. Further examples of how to integrate publishing in the curriculum are provided in Chapter 6.

## Accessing Information

The Internet opens doors for teachers and students to easily access a wealth of information. Multimedia information in the form of text, graphics, and sound can be obtained from libraries, businesses, and governmental departments around the world. Many users claim such broad access is the greatest educational strength of the Internet because it provides new sources of information for students and assists teachers in developing instructional materials (Descy, 1993, 1994; Tomaiuolo, 1996; Wehmeyer, 1996; Zorn, 1996).

### Searching the Web

The Internet contains tremendous volumes of information. The problem is finding the information. There are several tools that you can use to search the Web: subject directories, search engines, and metasearches. In addition, you need to plan how to organize your search.

*Subject directories* organize the Web by categories. These sites start with a few categories and then branch out into subcategories, topics, and subtopics. Directories are good if you do not have a clear idea of what you are looking for. They help in finding general information about a subject. Two subject directories are Yahoo! <http://www.yahoo.com> and Looksmart <http://www.looksmart.com>.

*Search engines* are different from subject directories in that they enable you to search for very specific items. To use a search engine you type keywords in a box or field. The search engine looks in its database and then returns the links to

Websites that contain the keywords. Sometimes you get thousands of results. Examples of search engines are Alta Vista <http://www.altavista.com>, Infoseek <http://www.infoseek.com>, HotBot <http://www.hotbot.com>, and Excite <http://www.excite.com>.

Specific search engines called multi-threaded engines do *metasearches*. Some of these engines are Dogpile <http://www.dogpile.com>, which seaches 14 engines; Cyber411 <http://www.cyber411.com>, which searches 16 engines, SavvySearch <http://www.savvysearch.com>, which searches 5 engines at first but includes the option to search more engines, and MetaCrawler <http://www.metacrawler.com>, which searches 9 engines.

**Organizing Your Search**

Many search engines have advanced ways to conduct a search. This advanced search lets you use the boolean operators (words that refine your search). Boolean operators are **and, or,** and **not.** A search using **and** might be **whales and dolphins.** This search would list sites containing both the words *whales* and *dolphins*. An example of a search using **or** might be **hotcakes or pancakes or crepes.** Sites containing information about hotcakes, pancakes, or crepes would be listed. A search using **and not** might be **cats and not musicals.** This search would eliminate sites referring to the musical *Cats* but would list sites that have the word *cats*. Note: Some search engines use the plus sign (+) for the word **and** and the minus sign (−) for **and not.** You can use phrases to search. The phrase must be enclosed in double quotes, such as **"collaborative learning"** or **"Walt Disney World".** You can use parentheses to define the order in which the boolean operators are read. For example, a search for **(aquanauts or astronauts) and journals** will give results on aquanauts and journals as well as astronauts and journals.

You can also do title searches. In the search box you would type **title:** and the title or keywords you are looking for. The search engine will list Websites that have the keywords in the title.

Domain searches are another way to search for information. A domain search might look like **domain:uk and Sir Walter Raleigh** or **domain:edu and manatees.** The first domain search would take you to the United Kingdom and bring results on Sir Walter Raleigh. The second would look at education sites for information on manatees.

It is also helpful to follow these steps in organizing your search:

1. Write a sentence or two stating what information you want from the Internet.

2. Find the main words or phrases that you can use for the search.

3. Identify synonyms for the words.

4. Try combinations of the words or phrases. Write these down and check them off as you do the search.

## *Communicating and Collaborating*

One reason the Internet is such a powerful and exciting tool for teaching literacy is that it enables teachers and students to communicate and collaborate in new ways. Expanding beyond individual classrooms, students connect with other schools, experts, and the global community. In particular, the Internet is an exceptional tool for supporting communication and collaboration through project-based learning experiences, publishing students' work, communicating with keypals, fostering discussion groups, and reading in content areas.

- *Project-based learning experiences.* Essentially, project-based learning experiences are integrated Internet units of study with classrooms around the world (Leu & Leu, 1997). This integration of classrooms provides an authentic audience for students' writing. Not only do students publish their work on a classroom homepage, but a variety of sites are available on which students can publish. (See Chapter 6.)

- *Publishing students' work.* Students also use the Internet as a tool for online conferences about their writing, via asynchronous bulletin boards, chat rooms, newsgroups, and e-mail. By giving and receiving feedback from one another, students engage in process writing and gain responsibility for and ownership of their writing. In addition, many online writing competitions and contests are available.

- *Keypals.* Currently, numerous classrooms around the world are engaging in keypal exchanges. Many benefits are associated with keypal projects. Students are engaged in a meaningful and purposeful literacy experience, and generally they are highly motivated to read and write to their keypals. A keypal exchange is a natural entrée into studying a different country and gaining insights into a new culture. See Figure 3.8 for a listing of potential keypal sites.

---

- **Classroom Connect** <http://www.gsn.org>
- **Global SchoolNet Foundation** <http://www.gsn.org>
- **Intercultural E-Mail Classroom Connections**
  <http://www.stolaf.edu/network/iecc/>
- **National Geographic for Kids** <http://www.nationalgeographic.com/kids/kids/>
- **Pitsco's Keypals** <http://www.pitsco.com/p/keypals.html> or
  <http://www.keypals.com/p/keypals.html>
- **Scholastic Center** <http://www.gsn.org>
- **WeNet Keypals**
  <http://www2.waikato.ac.nz.educationa/WeNET/key/keypals.html>

---

**Figure 3.8** Keypals: Websites for Connecting to Students, Classes, and Schools Around the World

- *Discussion groups.* Many teachers and students find great value in having online discussions with people around the world. Students' discussions often focus on books they are reading. Teachers often discuss project ideas and current educational issues.

- *Reading in the content areas.* The Internet affords a unique opportunity for students to seek advice from authors and experts about what they are learning. These discussions can be built around any topic of study. They can be one-time questions or an ongoing collaboration. See Figure 3.9 for a listing of expert sites.

**Using the Internet for Professional Development**

In the past, it was often difficult for teachers to collaborate with other like-minded teachers. Today, teachers have access to online sources for engaging in literacy discussions. For example, three teachers used a teacher chat room to discuss issues related to students' lack of motivation when reading informational text (Lapp, Flood, & Martin, 1998). "Technological advances like the Internet offer teachers numerous opportunities to expand their personal visual literacy skills and become adept at accessing and using electronic mail and undertaking Web searches. These advances also provide a new avenue for teachers to share and enhance their professional knowledge about teaching" (p. 705).

---

- **Ask a Mad Scientist**  <http://128.252.223.239/~ysp/MSN/>
- **Ask an Expert**  <http://www.askanexpert.com/askanexpert/index.html>
- **Ask Dr. Math**  <http://forum.swarthmore.edu/dr.math/dr-math.html/>
- **Children's Story Books Online**  <http://www.magickeys.com/books>
- **Classroom Connect's Teacher Contact Database**  <http://www.classroom.net/contact/>
- **The Global Schoolhouse Projects Registry**  <http://www.gsh.org/gsh/class/projsrch.html>
- **Kidproject**  <http://www.kidlink.org:80/KIDPROJ/>
- **The Mad Scientists Network**  <http://www.med-info.wustl.edu/~ysp/MSN/MAS.scilist.html/>
- **Monarch Watch**  <http://www.keil.ukans.edu/~monarch/>
- **NickNack's Telecollaborative Learning**
  <http://www.1.minn.net:80/~schubert/NickNacks.html#anchor100100>
- **The Scoop**  <http://www.friend.ly.net/scoop/adventure/index.html>
- **The Word Wizard**  <http://www.wordwizard.com>

---

**Figure 3.9**  Websites for Seeking Advice From Authors and Experts

## COMPUTER CLASSROOM EXAMPLES

### *Introducing the World Wide Web*

**Grade Level:** Adaptable for K–8

**Objective:** Students demonstrate the basic navigational techniques for using the WWW. Students identify and use common WWW terms.

**Time:** 2 hours

**Problem to Be Solved:** What's in the world?

**Materials:**
Computer with Internet access
Projection device for entire group
Journals
Pencils
Predetermined Website

**Steps:**

1. Begin by asking the students what they know about the Internet and the World Wide Web (WWW).

2. Use these comments and descriptions to structure your introductory lesson.

3. If your students have no knowledge of the Internet, begin by describing it as a network of computers. These computers are linked to each other from all over the world. Messages, in the form of computer text, can be posted on the Internet and read by anyone with a computer.

4. Using the computer and a projection device, travel to a Website that will interest the students. It is a good idea to have your site bookmarked ahead of time.

5. Model locating and accessing your bookmarks.

6. Once you reach the desired WWW page, describe the process of going back and forth between pages of text.

7. Have the students practice going backwards and forwards on the large projection device.

8. After learning three new terms, record these in journals. Include a definition of each term.

9. Familiarize the students with hypertext. This is the highlighted, underlined text on a Web page that enables you to travel to another linked page. Practice clicking on interesting hypertext links.

10. Depending on the level and ability of the students, introduce them to highlighting, cutting and pasting, printing, and downloading files.

11. To end the lesson, show the students how to log off the Internet and close all open screens.

## COMPUTER CLASSROOM EXAMPLES (CONTINUED)

### Introducing the World Wide Web (Continued)

**Assessment:** Ask the students to describe, orally or in writing, what they know about the WWW and the Internet. Travel to a Website and access several hypertext links. Find something of interest on one of the linked pages. Develop a travel guide that will lead students to the interesting object. Group students to complete the WWW puzzle. Give the groups an allotted amount of time to complete the guide and find the object. Discuss navigational strategies and searching techniques.

### Writing a "Netiquette" Guide

**Grade Level:** Adaptable for K–8

**Objective:** The students learn the rules for using the Internet by creating a book of "Netiquette."

**Time:** 4 hours

**Problem to Be Solved:** When you go to a foreign country, you need to know the rules of that country. The Internet is like a foreign country, so you need to know the rules for using the Internet. Help your classmates make a book of "Netiquette" by finding some rules for the proper use of the Internet.

**Materials:** Internet Connection
Computer
Internet Browser

**Steps:**
1. Go to Internet to <http://www.yahoo.com> and type the word "Netiquette" in the search field. Then, a bunch of sites are listed.
2. Visit each one of the sites and then write down the rules for using the Internet.

**Assessment:** Each student will develop five rules for proper use of the Internet.

### Learning About the World Through Keypals

**Grade Level:** Adaptable for K–8

**Objective:** The students learn how to write letters and use effective communication. The students learn effective inquiry skills. The students also learn about another country.

**Time:** 2 hours

**Problem to Be Solved:** You are planning a trip to a country you have never seen before. Before you go there, you want to know about the people, holidays, etiquette, and customs. Travel brochures tell you some of this, but you want the information from someone who lives there and is close to your age. What are you to do?

**Materials:** Computer with Internet access
World Map

## COMPUTER CLASSROOM EXAMPLES (CONTINUED)

### *Learning About the World Through Keypals (Continued)*

**Steps:**
1. Ask students to describe a penpal.
2. Discuss penpals and writing letters in a whole group environment.
3. Use a map of the world, and discuss areas of interest to the students.
4. Ask the students to imagine communicating, or having penpals, with children in an area of the world that is new to them. Discuss these areas.
5. Lead discussion of the similarities and differences in their environment and the environment of the interesting areas. Discuss the people, holidays, and customs of these areas.
6. Introduce the concept of keypals to the students. Keypals are penpals that communicate through e-mail. Discuss how keypals and penpals are alike and different.
7. Tell the students they will be traveling to a Website full of students interested in becoming keypals. Ask the students to think about what type of keypals they would like to communicate with.
8. Travel to Pitsco's keypals using this URL: <www.pitsco.com/p/keypals.html>.
9. Browse through the information categorized according to age, topics of interest, and collaborative project interests. Choose a group of students to communicate with.
10. Contact the students with an initial class e-mail expressing interest.
11. Decide if the class will compose one e-mail or communicate individually with the students.
12. E-mail the students and wait for responses.
13. Read the responses and enjoy.

**Assessment:** Students will write a report about the country they have researched.

### *A Virtual Tour of Washington, D.C.*

**Grade Level:** 2–8

**Objective:** Learn about Washington, D.C. Students demonstrate their creativity by designing an original monument. Students develop their writing skills by writing about the significance of their new monument.

**Time:** 1 week

**Problem to Be Solved:** You have been commissioned by the federal government to design a new monument for the District of Columbia. How will you do it?

## COMPUTER CLASSROOM EXAMPLES (CONTINUED)

### *A Virtual Tour of Washington, D.C. (Continued)*

**Materials:**
Computer
Netscape
Spiral-bound journal
Pencil
Large white paper (11 × 14 or posterboard)
Colored pencils
Black pen
Chart paper
Map of the United States

**Steps:**

1. Locate Washington, D.C., on a map of the United States. Show and discuss the areas where the White House, the Capitol, and the Supreme Court are located.

2. As a group, complete a KWL (What You Know, What You Want to Know and What You Learned) chart about Washington, D.C. Record the chart on large paper for future reference.

3. In small-group settings or as an individual assignment, use Netscape to take a virtual tour of Washington, D.C. Use the following URLs: The White House at <www.whitehouse.gov> and Old Executive Office Building at <www.whitehouse.gov/WH/Tours/OEOB/>.

4. Instruct students that they are to look for information and pictures of important buildings and monuments in D.C. while using Netscape. Require that each student keep a learning log documenting URLs and important monuments sighted. Allow each student sufficient time to search the Internet.

5. Consult the KWL chart completed in Step 2. Using learning logs, ask students to fill in what they have learned about Washington, D.C., on the chart. Discuss the chart and student findings. Discuss Websites and hyperlinks for documenting findings.

6. Ask the students to design a new monument for Washington, D.C., based on the information they found using Netscape. Allow students to brainstorm and work with a partner.

7. Rough drafts with name of monument and its historical significance will be completed before final illustrations are begun. Have students complete these in their learning logs.

8. Use large white paper and colored pencils for the illustrations of the monuments.

9. Have students write the significance of their new monument underneath the illustrations.

## Computer Classroom Examples (Continued)

### A Virtual Tour of Washington, D.C. (Continued)

**10.** Create a book of the monuments for placing in the classroom library. Have students re-create their drawings on book-sized paper. Laminate and bind the pages. Share completed monuments in a class celebration. Ask students to describe, from memory, a new monument that was just introduced.

**Assessment:** Have students created, designed, and written about their monument?

## Techno-Teacher Tips

### Navigational Problems

There are several navigational issues related to the Internet. Reinking (1997) points out that students often encounter navigational problems when they (1) click on keywords that take them away from their original concept, and then (2) have difficulty returning to their original site. A similar navigational issue relates to students who jump from one site to another without reading in depth. Indeed, the downside of the Internet being such an engaging mechanism is that you can navigate, or "surf" for hours on end. Thus, it is critical to teach students appropriate navigational strategies such as those outlined in this chapter.

### Copyright Issues

Although the information on the Internet is technically copyrighted, the copyright is not visible with the work, and it is not entirely clear as to what can be copied freely off the Internet (Futorian, 1995). Crawford (1993) provides guidance in this area, noting that the "fair use" law of copyrighted material covers educational uses. Morrison, Lowther, and DeMeulle (1999) suggest that it is alright to download and/or use free Internet software materials such as (1) shareware (as long as you pay the shareware fee if you continue using the application after the demonstration period), and (2) icons and/or graphics specifically offered for downloading.

The following are examples of copyright infringement:

- placing another person's graphic or photograph on your Web page;
- copying text and including it in curriculum materials from which you or others gain profit, and
- copying icons not specifically created to be shared publicly (Morrison, Lowther, & DeMeulle, 1999, p. 229).

### Treasure or Trash: Evaluating Websites

There is no censorship of the Internet. Essentially, the material on the Internet is unrestricted, making the accuracy and reliability of the information questionable

(Hittig, 1995). Most school districts have in place an Acceptable Use Policy (AUP) that in broad terms allows students access to the Internet only to further educational goals. Often students and parents are required to sign such a document. In reality, however, when a student goes online there is little to prevent him or her from accessing objectionable sites, especially those termed pornographic.

Certain software programs called "filters" help deny access to a major portion of pornography sites, but they have serious limitations. Filters do not pick up sites that have innocent-sounding names. Others that filter by use of keywords, such as *breast,* filter out medical sites dealing with important issues such as breast cancer. Moreover, advanced users are able to skirt around almost any block.

Teacher/parent supervision is still the best method to keep students engaged productively. If teachers set forth strict rules of engagement and are willing to peer into a myriad of screens, problems can be kept to a minimum.

A particularly good strategy for rudimentary Internet research is for teachers to hand out a list of acceptable sites applicable to a given project. Differing URLs (Internet addresses) are easy to spot on the monitors. This takes some teacher planning, but in addition to keeping students on safe sites it will speed up their information gathering.

To maintain a measure of flexibility and to encourage initiative, the teacher might want to adopt the "Hey, teach, check this site out" principle with students who have found alternative, relevant sites.

Websites for popular Internet filters include:

<www.cyterpartrol.com>

<www.netnanny.com/netnanny>

# FREQUENTLY ASKED QUESTIONS

### 1. How do I help my students have good manners when working on the Internet?

*Netiquette* is the term used to discuss the proper way of interacting on the Internet. Although there aren't any clear-cut rules for appropriate behavior, there are some suggestions (e.g., Don't type a message in all caps because it is considered screaming). It is important that you discuss Netiquette with your students and let them help formulate classroom rules based on what is currently known about working on the Internet. If you teach young students, you might want to post the class-generated rules.

**2. Do I have to get parental permission for my students to work on the Internet?**

This is a good question to ask the principal, because most schools and districts do indeed have a policy about parental permission and students' use of the Internet. For instance, many schools require parents to sign permission slips, and many will not publish students' photographs or will publish photographs but withhold students' names.

# REFERENCES

Blanchard, J. (1995). Technology in middle school. Reading education: opportunities to transform the classroom. *Computers in the schools, 11* (13), 79–85.

Brozo, W. G., & Simpson, M. L. (1999). *Readers, teachers, learners: Expanding literacy across the content areas* (3rd ed.). Upper Saddle River, NJ: Prentice Hall.

Crawford, T. (1993). *Legal guide for the visual arts.* New York: Allworth Press.

DeGroff, L. (1990, April). Is there a place for computers in whole language classrooms? *The Reading Teacher,* 568–572.

DeMuelle, L., Anderson, R. S., & Johnston, J. (1996). Exploring MOO environments for self-study. In *Empowering our future in teacher education: Proceedings of the first international conference on self-study of teacher education practices* (pp. 147–152). East Sussex, England: The Self-Study of Teacher Education Practices Special Interest Group of the American Educational Research Association.

Descy, D. (1993, November–December). Tools to ease your Internet adventures. *Technical Trends,* 19–20.

Descy, D. (1994, March). That wonderful Gopher! *Technical Trends,* 15.

Dyril, O. (1996, October). The educator's ultimate World Wide Web hotlist. *Technology and learning,* 44–48.

Engst, T. (1995, October). From the web press to the web. *MacUser,* 117–118.

Etchinson, C. (1995, November). A powerful web to weave—developing writing skills for elementary students. *Learning and Leading with Technology,* 14–15.

Futorian, G. (1995). The Internet as a K–12 educational resource: Emerging issues of information access and freedom. *Teaching and Teacher Education, II,* 229–234.

Harris, J. (1992, August–September). Electronic treasures by electronic mail. *The Computing Teacher,* 36–38.

Hittig, J. (1995, July). Free speech or online slime? *PC Novice,* 74–79.

Iannone, P. (1998, February). Just beyond the horizon: Writing-centered literacy activities for traditional and electronic contexts. *The Reading Teacher, 51* (5), 438–443.

Johnson, D. (1995). The Mankato schools Internet project. *Electronic Networking Applications and Policy, 5* (1), 46–55.

Kendall, D. (1995, November–December). Quick and easy online projects. *Creative Classroom,* 60–62.

Kimball, L. (1995, October). The ways to make online learning groups work. *Educational Leadership,* 54–56.

Lapp, D., Flood, J. (Eds.) & Martin, D. B. (1998). Teachers online: Using personal visual literacy skills to enhance professional teaching knowledge. *The Reading Teacher, 51,* 702–705.

Leu, D. J., & Leu, D. D. (1997). *Teaching with the Internet: Lessons from the classroom.* Norwood, MA: Christopher-Gordon.

Maring, G. (1997, November). Using the World Wide Web to build learning communities: Writing for genuine purposes. *Journal of Adolescent and Adult Literacy, 41* (3), 196–207.

Mike, D. (1997). Internet in the schools: A literacy perpective. *Journal of Adolescent and Adult Literacy, 40,* 4–13.

Morrison, G. R., Lowther, D. L., & DeMeulle, L. (1999). *Integrating computer technology into the classroom.* Upper Saddle River, NJ: Merrill.

Munson, K. (1996, June). World Wide Web indexes and hierarchical lists: Finding tools for the Internet. *Computers in Libraries,* 54–57.

Parson, T. (1997, April). Electronic mail: Creating a community of learners. *Journal of Adolescent and Adult Literacy, 40* (7), 560–565.

Reinking, D, (1997). Me and my hypertext: A multiple disgression analysis of technology and literacy (sic). *The Reading Teacher, 50* (8), 626–643.

Rosen, L. (1997). The World Wide Web: Taking on the pedagogical challenge. *Html,* 1–4.

Ryder, R. (1996–1997, December–January). Using the Internet to enhance students' reading, writing, and information-gathering skills. *Journal of Adolescent and Adult Literacy, 40* (4), 244–254.

Ryder, R. J., & Hughes, T. (1997). *Internet for educators.* Upper Saddle River, NJ: Prentice Hall.

Stuhlmann, J. (1996, June). Whole-language strategies for integrating technology into language arts. In *Call of the North, NECC '96. Proceedings of the 17th Annual National Educational Computing Conference,* Minneapolis, Minnesota. Minneapolis: NECC.

Tomaiuolo, N. (1996, June). An analysis of Internet search engines: Assessment of over 200 search queries. *Computers in Libraries,* 58–62.

Wehmeyer, L. (1996, September). Teaching online search: Techniques your students can use. *Syllabus,* 52–56.

Zorn, P. (1996, May–June). Searching: Tricks of the trade. *Online,* 15–27.

# APPENDIX: CREATING WEB PAGES

Simple Web pages are easy and fun to create. A Web page is a text file with "tags" that tell your browser what to do and where to go. That text file is in a format called HTML (Hyper-Text Markup Language.) When you go on the Web, the browser reads the text file and formats the page according to the instructions given to it by the tags. The browser, not the page, determines how the page will look.

You can use the Notepad (Windows) accessory, or SimpleText (Mac) processor to create the text files. You may buy special software, called Web page editors, that will create the tags for you. FrontPage (Win.), PageMill (Win. or Mac), and Claris-Homepage (Mac) are some editors. To view your Web pages, you will need a browser. Netscape and Microsoft Explorer are popular Web browsers. Netscape Communicator has a composer function that is a Web page editor and can create tags for you.

For this instruction you are going to be using Notepad as the text editor to create the HTML documents, and you will be typing in the HTML code. As a teacher you will find it easier to troubleshoot your students' Web page documents if you know the HTML code. For example, if students are using a Web page editor to create Web pages and they make a mistake or the document does not display properly in the Web browser, you can use your knowledge of the code to find the error.

## Basic Information About HTML

Before starting your HTML, you will need to know some basic information. The following table shows characters that are used to write HTML.

| Character | Function |
| --- | --- |
| < > | These are brackets. Codes are always placed inside brackets. Any text outside of brackets is considered text that is to be shown on the screen. |
| ". . ." | Quotation marks are used to make a specific reference to an image file, color, or URL. |
| / | The forward slash is used in the closing tags. The forward slash is included inside the bracket. |
| Returns, spaces, and tabs | HTML does not recognize the spaces in between code. For the space to be recognized by the browser, you need to use <P> for paragraph break and <BR> for a return. |

The code for a simple Web page would look like the following:

```
<HTML>
<HEAD>
<TITLE>Renee's Page </TITLE>
```

```
</HEAD>
<BODY>
<H1>Renee Weiss' Home Page</H1>
</BODY>
</HTML>
```

To see what these codes create, please refer to the figure.

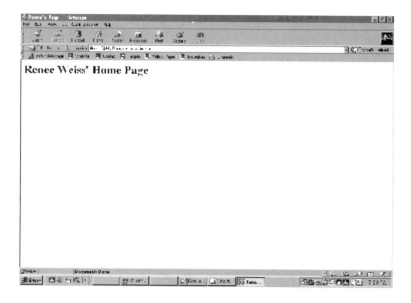

Now, let's talk about what these commands do:

The command <HTML> begins and </HTML> ends the HTML document. The <HEAD> command tells the browser to place codes in the head of the document. Notice that the title "Renee's Page" is in the Title bar of the window of the browser. It is the <TITLE></TITLE> command that does that. The <BODY> command begins and </BODY> ends the body of the document. All commands for the content of the Web page are to be located between these two tags.

With just a few lines of code, a simple Web page can be created.

Now it's your turn.

## Getting Started

1. Launch your word processing software or use Notepad (Win.) or Simpletext (Mac) and get a new page.

2. Type the following:

```
<HTML>
<HEAD>
<TITLE>Renee's Page</TITLE>
```

```
</HEAD>
<BODY>
<H1>Renee Weiss' Home Page</H1>
<H2>Where do I live?</H2>
I live in Cordova, Tennessee. It is a suburb of Memphis.
<H2>What school do I go to?</H2>
I go to the George Washington School. It is an old school but it is
    really neat.
</BODY>
</HTML>
```

**3.** Under the File menu of your word processor, Save As. A dialogue box appears.

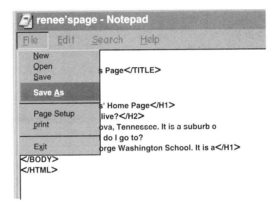

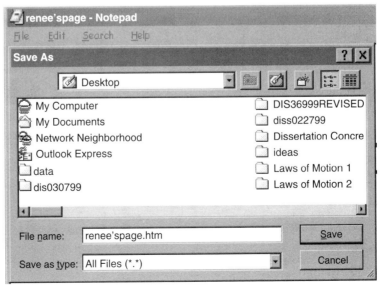

4. Type the name of the file **renee'spage.htm** in the **File name:** field.

5. Select **Desktop** in the **Save in:** field.

6. Single-click the **Save** button.

7. Start the browser. This will be either Netscape or Microsoft Explorer. (These instructions use Netscape) You do not need to log on to the Internet. All you want to do is view the page in the browser to see what it looks like. After the browser has fully started, open the HTML file that you just saved to the desktop.

8. From the browser's File menu, select **Open Page.** A dialogue box appears.

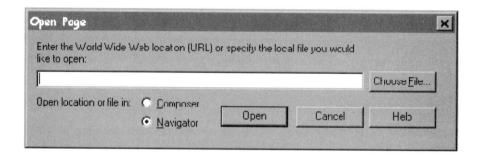

9. Single-click the **Choose File. . .** button. The **Open** dialogue box appears.

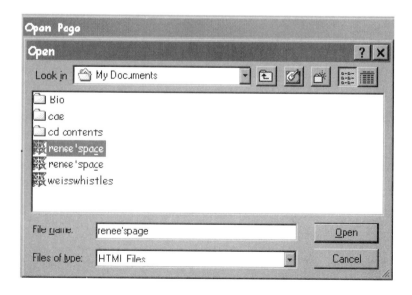

**10.** Select the **renee'spage** file or the file that you saved as HTML. Notice that the **Files of type** field shows HTML files.

**11.** Single-click the **Open** button. The **Open Page** dialogue box reappears.

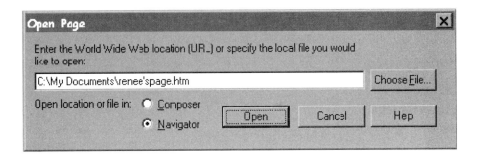

Notice the **Navigator** button is selected. You want to look at this in the Web browser rather than the editor, which is Composer.

**12.** Single-click the **Open** button. You should see the Web page you created.

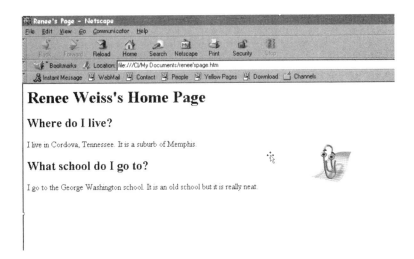

The <H2> command made headings that were smaller than those made by the <H1> command. The Heading command can be <H1>, <H2>, <H3>, <H4>, <H5>, or <H6>. Even though we did not put in special breaks, the text is placed nicely below the headings. We could have used the command <BR>, which would place a line break in the text.

You have learned how to create a title, the commands for beginning and ending an HTML document, and two different headings.

## *Centering the Text and Horizontal Rules*

You should still have your word processing document open. The following text is displayed:

```
<HTML>
<HEAD>
<TITLE>Renee's Page</TITLE>
</HEAD>
<BODY>
<H1>Renee Weiss' Home Page</H1>
<H2>Where do I live?</H2>
I live in Cordova, Tennessee. It is a suburb of Memphis.
<H2>What school do I go to?</H2>
I go to the George Washington School. It is an old school but it is
    really neat.
</BODY>
</HTML>
```

1. At the end of the line **<H1>Renee Weiss' Home Page</H1>** type **<HR>**. The <HR> command creates a horizontal rule.

2. Place the cursor before the <H1> command and type **<CENTER>**. Close the command by typing **</CENTER>** after the </H1> and before the <HR>. Your text should look like the following:

```
<HTML>
<HEAD>
<TITLE>Renee's Page</TITLE>
</HEAD>
<BODY>
<Center><H1>Renee Weiss' Home Page</H1></Center><HR>
<H2>Where do I live?</H2>
I live in Cordova, Tennessee. It is a suburb of Memphis.
<H2>What school do I go to?</H2>
I go to the George Washington School. It is an old school but it is
    really neat.
</BODY>
</HTML>
```

Follow steps 3 through 12 of the previous section to save and open the saved HTML in the browser, just like you did before. Your screen should look like the one in the figure at the top of page 71.

Notice that the heading is centered in the window and there is a horizontal rule under the heading.

You have learned to center the text and make a horizontal rule.

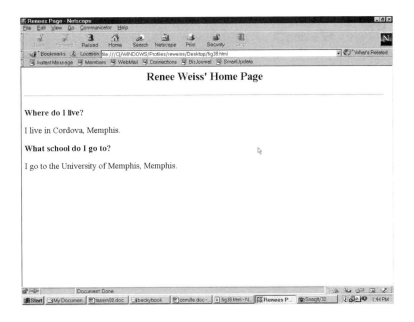

## *Creating Paragraphs*

So far the text has been very short—just one sentence. If you want to create a paragraph, you need to use the paragraph command. The command <P> is used at the beginning of the paragraph and </P> is used at the end of the paragraph. Let's go back to the Web page we are creating.

Go to your HTML document in the word processor.

1. Place the cursor after the sentence **It is an old school but it is really neat.** and press the Enter key.

2. Type the following text:

   **<H2>About Me</H2>**
   **<P>I have a keypal in Mexico. Mexico is really a wonderful place. They have big buildings like the pyramids that were made by the Incas. Mexico City is like big cities in the United States.</P>**
   **<P>I play the piano. I have been taking lessons since I was 5 years old. In the beginning I didn't want to practice but now I really like it. I am getting ready for a recital next month.</P>**

   Now your text should look like the following:

   **<HTML>**
   **<HEAD>**
   **<TITLE>Renee's Page</TITLE>**

```
</HEAD>
<BODY>
<Center><H1>Renee Weiss' Home Page</H1></Center><HR>
<H2>Where do I live?</H2>
I live in Cordova, Tennessee. It is a suburb of Memphis.
<H2>What school do I go to?</H2>
I go to the George Washington School. It is an old school but it is
    really neat.

<H2>About Me</H2>
<P>I have a keypal in Mexico. Mexico is really a wonderful place. They
    have big buildings like the pyramids that were made by the Incas.
    Mexico City is like big cities in the United States.</P>

<P>I play the piano. I have been taking lessons since I was 5 years
    old. In the beginning I didn't want to practice but now I really like it.
    I am getting ready for a recital next month.</P>
</BODY>
</HTML>
```

**3.** Save the document as you did before and open it in the browser. Your screen should look like the one in the figure.

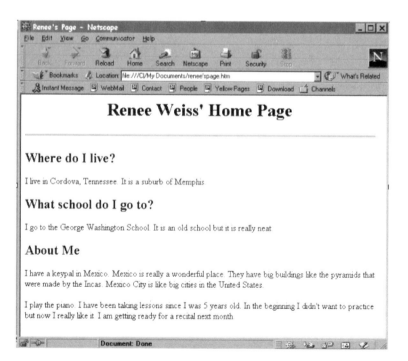

Notice there is space between the paragraphs.

## *Inserting a Picture*

You can put a single picture or many pictures on your Web page. The most common graphic file types are GIF and JPEG. These graphic file formats are relatively compact in size. The empty tag you use to put an image in the HTML document is <IMG SRC= "name and/or location of image">. IMG is the tag that stands for image. SRC means source and refers to the location of the image. An example of an image tag is the following: <IMG SRC= "mydog.jpg">. This tells the browser to locate the "mydog.jpg" image. Another example is <IMG SRC= "images/mycat.gif">. In this example the HTML instructs the browser to look in the images folder and get the "mycat.gif" image.

Let's add a picture to the Web page we are developing. Let's insert the picture after the paragraph about the piano lessons.

1. Place the cursor after the closing paragraph mark belonging to the piano paragraph. Press the Enter key two times. (We just want space to see what we are doing.)
2. Type **<H2>My Dog</H2> Here is a picture of my dog, Skippy. He is a silky apricot poodle. We have lots of fun together. <BR><BR><BR>**.
3. Press the Enter key once.
4. Type **<IMG SRC= "skippy.jpg">**.
5. Type **<BR>** and press the Enter key.
6. Type **<BR>** once again and press the Enter key. The <BR> tag inserts space. **Note:** The picture that you want to display must be in the same folder as the HTML files.

Your code should look like the following:

```
<HTML>
<HEAD>
<TITLE>Renee's Page</TITLE>
</HEAD>
```

```
<BODY>
<Center><H1>Renee Weiss' Home Page</H1></Center><HR>
<H2>Where do I live?</H2>
I live in Cordova, Tennessee. It is a suburb of Memphis.
<H2>What school do I go to?</H2>
I go to the George Washington School. It is an old school but it is
    really neat.

<H2>About Me</H2>
<P>I have a keypal in Mexico. Mexico is really a wonderful place. They
    have big buildings like the pyramids that were made by the Incas.
    Mexico City is like big cities in the United States.</P>

<P>I play the piano. I have been taking lessons since I was 5 years
    old. In the beginning I didn't want to practice but now I really like it.
    I am getting ready for a recital next month.</P>
<H2>My Dog</H2>Here is a picture of my dog, Skippy. He is a silky
    apricot poodle. We have lots of fun together.<BR><BR>
<IMG SRC= "skippy.jpg">
</BODY>
</HTML>
```

Open the file in your browser. You should see the picture. Remember, the pictures must be in the same folder or directory as the HTML files.

## *Linking to Related Pages*

You may want to create more than one page for your Website and link one page to another. Next you will learn how to do this. Let's make a link to a poem.

The HREF argument allows you to jump to an HTML document. You would type <A HREF="name of the html"></A>. Notice you use the link tags <A> and </A> to open and close the link.

1. Place the cursor after the last <BR> just under the code for the inserting a picture. Press the Enter key once.

2. Type **<H2>My Poem</H2>** and then press the Enter key.

3. Type **<A HREF="poem.html">Click here to read my Halloween poem.</A>**

4. Save the text just as you have done before.

The text should look like the following:

```
<HTML>
<HEAD>
<TITLE>Renee's Page</TITLE>
</HEAD>
<BODY>
<Center><H1>Renee Weiss' Home Page</H1></Center><HR>
<H2>Where do I live?</H2>
I live in Cordova, Tennessee. It is a suburb of Memphis.
<H2>What school do I go to?</H2>
I go to the George Washington School. It is an old school but it is
    really neat.

<H2>About Me</H2>
<P>I have a keypal in Mexico. Mexico is really a wonderful place. They
    have big buildings like the pyramids that were made by the Incas.
    Mexico City is like big cities in the United States.</P>
<P>I play the piano. I have been taking lessons since I was 5 years
    old. In the beginning I didn't want to practice but now I really like it.
    I am getting ready for a recital next month.</P>

<H2>My Dog</H2>Here is a picture of my dog, Skippy. He is a silky
    apricot poodle.
We have lots of fun together. <BR><BR>
<IMG SRC= "skippy.jpg">
<BR>
<BR>
<H2>My Poem</H2>
<A HREF="poem.html">Click here to read my Halloween poem.</A>
</BODY>
</HTML>
```

You should see the words **Click here to read my Halloween poem** in a different color from the rest of the text. In this browser it is in blue.

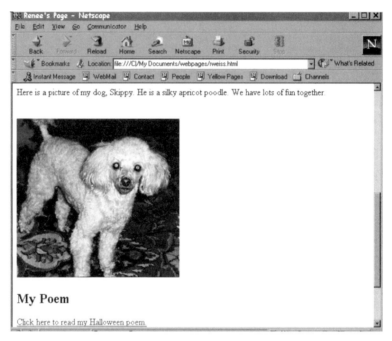

If you click on the blue text, you will go to the page that has the poem.

As you can see from the screen, the link to the page with the poem was successful. **Note:** At the top of the page there is a link to the homepage. To link, you would use the same HREF code as you used to link to the poem page—with one exception. You would type the homepage file name in quotations. In this case the code would look like the following:

### <A HREF="reweiss.html">Back to Home Page</A>

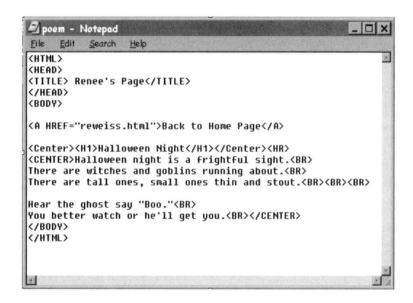

```
poem - Notepad
File   Edit   Search   Help
<HTML>
<HEAD>
<TITLE> Renee's Page</TITLE>
</HEAD>
<BODY>

<A HREF="reweiss.html">Back to Home Page</A>

<Center><H1>Halloween Night</H1></Center><HR>
<CENTER>Halloween night is a frightful sight.<BR>
There are witches and goblins running about.<BR>
There are tall ones, small ones thin and stout.<BR><BR><BR>

Hear the ghost say "Boo."<BR>
You better watch or he'll get you.<BR></CENTER>
</BODY>
</HTML>
```

## *Links to Outside Pages*

Now that you know how to link to related pages on your site, you will learn how to link to pages outside of your Website.

Linking to sites on the Web is very much like linking to pages on your site. In the quotation marks you would type the URL of the site you want to link to. The code for this is the following: <A HREF="http://www.reading.com">My Favorite Reading Site</A>.

Let's add a link to my favorite Web site to the homepage. Open the homepage document in the text editor that you are using.

1. Place the cursor after the **</A>**.
2. Type **<BR><BR>** and press the Enter key.
3. Type **<H2>My Favorite Web Site</H2>**. Press the Enter key.
4. Type **<A HREF="http://volcano.und.nodak.edu/vwdocs/kids/ kids.html>Volcano World's Kids' Door</A>**.
5. Save the document as HTML and open it in the browser. Your screen should look like the one in the figure. At the bottom of the picture you will see the link to Volcano World's Kids' Door. The text will be in a different color and underlined.

## E-mail

We are just about finished creating the Web page. It is important for people to have a place to give you feedback. The last HTML code you will learn is the mailto code.

Open your document in the text editor you are using.

1. Place the cursor after the </A> in the Volcano World's Kids' Door link and press the Enter key.

2. Type **<BR><BR>** and press Enter.

3. Type **<HR>** to place a horizontal rule to separate the e-mail section from the rest of the document. Press the Enter key.

4. Type **Email: <A HREF="mailto:reweiss@memphis.edu">reweiss@.memphis.edu</A>.**

5. Save the document as HTML and open it in your browser.

The e-mail address will be displayed at the bottom of the screen. Now people will be able to e-mail you.

Congratulations! You have completed a simple Web page and you didn't need any special software.

The next step is getting your files uploaded to the server. You should ask the person in charge of the server to give you directions on how to do this.

# USING ADDITIONAL ELECTRONIC TOOLS TO TEACH LITERACY

"Lawrence, what did you learn about the Civil War by reading the CD-ROM?" Miss Benson asks.

Lawrence, brows furrowed as he thinks, says suddenly, "Oh, yeah. I remember. The Battle of Gettysburg was a turning point in the war."

"Good point, Lawrence," Miss Benson says approvingly. "Does anyone know why the Battle of Gettysburg was so important?"

Lucinda's hand shoots up, and Miss Benson says, "Yes, Lucinda."

"General Lee lost about 20,000 men, and according to the CD-ROM," Lucinda says while quoting notes she has written, "'he never recovered from such a great loss of soldiers.'"

"Excellent, Lucinda," Miss Benson says enthusiastically, impressed with the knowledge her students have gained by using the CD-ROM. In fact, she is delighted that the students are interested in studying the Civil War. *Isn't it amazing,* she thinks to herself, *how much CD-ROMs have changed the way students have approached their reading assignments.* Then, in a moment of teacher-researcher inspiration, she decides to ask the students to make comparisons between reading books and reading CD-ROMs.

"I'm interested in knowing what you see as the pluses and minuses of reading books to complete your assignments and reading CD-ROMs," Miss Benson says as she goes to the overhead projector, takes out a new transparency, and makes two columns, one headed Books and the other headed CD-ROMs. "Now," she asks, "what are the pluses and minuses of each?"

"For one thing," Daniel says, "CD-ROMs have links, so I can read about the Battle of Gettysburg, and, if I want to learn about other Civil War battles, I can click on a battle's name and find out about that."

"But books have links, too," objects Amy. "For instance, an index or a table of contents are links, sort of."

"So," Miss Benson notes, "both have links or ways to point to related information. Is that right?"

"Well . . ." Eric says, drawing out his response as he thinks, "that's not exactly right. I mean, yes, both have links, but it's not really fair to compare computer links with book 'links.' They're different. For instance, computer links can get you somewhere almost instantly."

"That's right," interrupts Welsch, "and computers make links for you. But you have to do more work to make links in a book."

"These are important points," Miss Benson notes. "What other points of comparison or contrast can we make between books and CD-ROMs?"

"Graphics!" Michel shouts.

"But both books and CD-ROMs have graphics," Amy says, defending books.

"Sure, sure," Michel agrees, "but pictures in books are not animated and CD-ROMs are loaded with graphics. When I read the article in the CD-ROM about Gettysburg, I saw a video of a reenactment ceremony of a Civil War battle and I read an entire article about General Lee that was crammed with pictures of Lee, his family, and other Confederate generals. Most books about the Civil War wouldn't provide a video or near the number of pictures I saw on the CD-ROM."

Miss Benson takes delight in the way her students are exploring the similarities and differences between books and CD-ROMs, and she continues to lead them in a discussion that excites her not only because of the way the students are eagerly participating but also because they are involved in reading in ways they have never been involved before.

## WHY USE ADDITIONAL ELECTRONIC TOOLS TO TEACH LITERACY?

Why indeed? As teachers, we've survived a millennium using books and chalkboards with success, so we can surely survive another. However, that was long before the quantum leaps in technology of the latter 20th century. The printing press and typewriter had their revolutionary days but have been muscled out by computer power. There is a chance now, in education, to attack literacy along a broad front with the same fervor and success that has swept through medicine, business, industry, and science. Education must move our nation's youth into the world where the computer is a functional necessity. Educators must not allow their profession to fall behind.

If we accept the hypothesis that a country remains strong through a high rate of literacy among its general population, then by extension it succeeds in the computer age when its general population is computer literate. We know that the bulk of the population learns to read and write in the lower elementary grades. There is no reason it cannot learn concomitant computer skills. The two are synergetic. With the field of education carrying the responsibility of teaching both kinds of literacy, it is incumbent on the teaching profession to accept the challenge and be successful.

Chapter 3 examined ways in which teachers use the Internet to teach literacy. This chapter extends the discussion to several other electronic tools: hypermedia, databases, spreadsheets, PowerPoint, and CD-ROMs. In addition, the discussion addresses ways to evaluate software. First, Fran Clark shares a classroom story about how she integrated HyperStudio in a meaningful and purposeful way in her literacy curriculum.

## COMPUTER CLASSROOM SNAPSHOT

### Context

In my third-grade classroom I have a multimedia teaching station, five student computer stations, two color printers, and a color scanner. What I really like about having all this equipment in my classroom is that it allows my students to publish their work in a variety of formats. As a culminating activity for a tall tale unit, my students used the HyperStudio software program to create multimedia books. This was a five-day activity that required them to write and illustrate an original tall tale in a cooperative learning group environment.

### What I Did and Why

On day one, I put my students into groups of four and assigned a computer station to each group. In a large group, the students discussed the tall tales that they had been reading and the characteristics of each tale. Then they broke up into groups and brainstormed ideas for characters, settings, and plots that could be used in an original tall tale. Each group member wrote an original tall tale.

On day two, group members shared their original tall tales within the group. They discussed the characters, settings, and plots of each tall tale and choose those elements that they would use in their group's tall tale. As a group, they wrote the rough draft of an original tall tale.

On day three, the groups proofread their rough drafts and met with the teacher to discuss their tall tales. Each group entered the text from their rough draft onto a HyperStudio storyboard. They also drew and colored illustrations on the storyboard.

On day four, the groups entered the text from their storyboards into a Hyper-Studio stack template. While some of the groups entered text, the other groups used the color scanner to scan their illustrations, which were then imported into their HyperStudio stacks.

On day five, each group used the multimedia teaching station to share its tall tale book with the class. Later, these books were shared with the parents at the school's annual open house.

My goals for this project included teaching communication skills, socialization skills, and computing skills. All my goals were met through this project. The students learned how to give and accept constructive criticism. They learned how to work effectively in a diverse group. They learned how to use the HyperStudio program to create a multimedia book.

### What I Learned

This activity helped me realize that my students are not all alike and that each one brings unique strengths to a group. I learned that if my students are given the opportunity to use these strengths, they can not only write and illustrate an original tall tale but also use the computer to publish their writing in a multimedia format. Their tall tale multimedia books were excellent and were a hit at the school's open house that year!

## ADDITIONAL ELECTRONIC TOOLS TO TEACH LITERACY

Chapter 3 indicated that all manner of ready-made lesson plans are free for downloading off the Internet. This should be construed, however, as only a starting point. Such plans offer good ideas from which teachers can craft their own lesson plans to fit their particular styles and circumstances. After all, what works in New York City might not play well in Peoria. Teachers should add and delete and otherwise embellish such plans with their own savoir faire.

Change, of course, implies improvement. And improvement means packaging to attract as many viewers or users as possible. It may sound commercial, but the axiom holds that students won't get tuned in unless they get turned on. The additional technology tools discussed in the following sections will help teachers refine their lesson plans to student-friendly perfection. These applications will help teachers purge the dreaded word *boring* from the class vocabulary: hypermedia, databases, spreadsheets, PowerPoint, and CD-ROMs.

### Hypermedia

As illustrated in Fran Clark's classroom snapshot, hypermedia links a variety of media—including colorful graphics, sound, and video—in a captivating manner (Burns, Roe, & Ross, 1999; Dillner, 1993/1994). In seconds you move from one link to another by clicking and, as a result, viewing and hearing a great deal of information. Multimedia presentations involve many senses; because of this, they draw and hold the greatest level of attention. The World Wide Web is an example of hypermedia. HyperStudio is an example of a hypermedia program that enables students to create dynamic interactive applications such as books, games, tutorials, and presentations. Other popular multimedia programs are Kids Media Magic, Magic Media Slate, and MediaWeaver.

Hypertext is a nonlinear method of organizing material that enables readers to access text in ways that are especially meaningful for them. It is based on the idea that the ways by which readers access text are more meaningful for the readers than the way the author intended the text to be accessed (Shen, 1996).

The concept of hypermedia came from hypertext. It is like hypertext in the way readers can access it, but it adds graphics, animation, audio, and video with the text. HyperStudio uses the metaphor of cards for the small fragments of text or other media. The cards are grouped into stacks, and the learner navigates through the cards and stacks to create meaning from different points of view according to the way the stacks are linked. The links organize the interrelationships among the stacks. The links are usually identified by a button or highlighted text. The learner uses these links to access other information, thereby exploring the text and other media in a way that enables the learner to form associations with the ideas. The result is a rich environment for learning. On the other hand, a downside of hypermedia is navigation. Because hypermedia applications contain many links and stacks, sometimes the learner gets lost.

Hypermedia fits well in constructivist classrooms, where it is best used as a cognitive tool. For example, students can use hypermedia to express their perspective or understanding of ideas, either in collaborative groups or in whole classrooms. Hypermedia promotes the idea of learning as design, not just information relayed from the teacher, because the students and teacher collaborate in designing the knowledge. Moreover, hypermedia involves many skills—not only those of writer and illustrator but also those related to project management, research, organization, and presentation.

## HyperStudio Example

HyperStudio is an easy program for students to use. As previously mentioned, it uses the metaphor of cards and stacks of cards. Let's create a HyperStudio stack of a few cards using Bird Anatomy as the subject.

### CREATING A NEW STACK

**1.** Select **New Stack** from the File menu. A dialogue box appears.

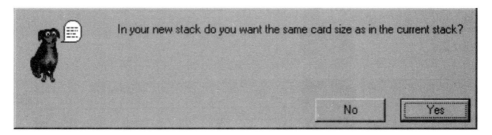

If you choose **Yes,** the card will be the same size as those in the current stack. If you choose **No,** a dialogue box opens giving you choices for card size and colors. The width and height of the card size you select is shown in the fields.

2. Single-click the **OK** button. A blank card appears.

The tools for HyperStudio are indicated in the Tools menu located in the tool bar. You can detach them from the menu and move them anyplace you want by single-clicking the tools palette, holding down the mouse button, and dragging them where you want them.

### CREATING TEXT

1. From the Objects menu, select **Add a Text Object.**

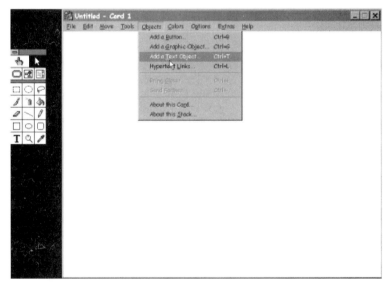

A rectangular box appears. This is a text box that you can resize and drag wherever you want. The cursor turns into a double arrow so that you can change the width or height and length of the box.

**2.** When you have placed the box where you want it, single-click outside of the box to deselect it. The **Text Appearance** dialogue box appears.

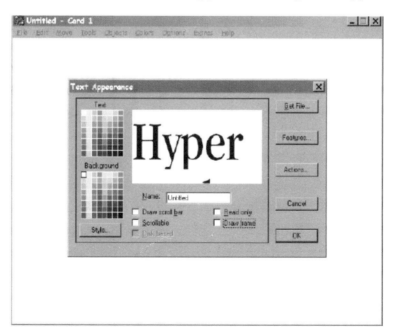

**3.** Deselect the box next to **Draw scroll bar,** the box next to **Scrollable,** and **Draw frame** if they are selected. You would want to select **Draw scroll**

**bar** and **Scrollable** if you were going to place a lot of text on the card. In this example, we do not want to draw a frame around the text box.

4. Single-click the box next to the **Read only** option. This locks the text so that it cannot be edited.

5. Single-click on a tiny red square in the **Text** color grid to make the text color red.

6. Single-click on the tiny yellow square in the **Background** color box. This action makes the background of the text box yellow.

7. Single-click on the **Style** button located below the **Background** selection box. The **Text Style** box appears.

8. You may select a font from the scrolling list. In this example, Garamond Book Condensed is selected.

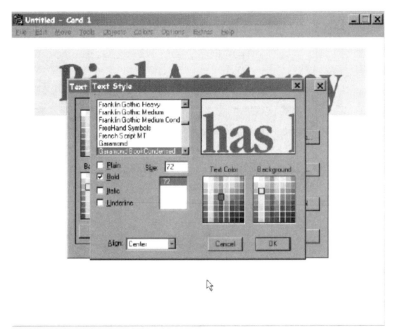

9. Single-click the box next to the word **Bold.** This makes the text bold.

10. Single-click the numbers in the **Size** box to select the numbers, and type **72** in the field.

11. From the **Align** pull-down menu, select **Center.** This action places the text in the center of the text box. When you are finished, click the **OK** button.

12. You will return to the **Text Appearance** box. Next, single-click the **OK** button.

13. Place the cursor in the rectangular text box, and type **Bird Anatomy.**

14. Repeat steps 1 through 10 to create a second text box, this time with a white background and red text.

15. Type your name or your school's name in this box.

**CREATING A BUTTON**

In order for the user to get to the next card, you need to create a button.

**1.** From the Objects menu, select **Add a Button.**

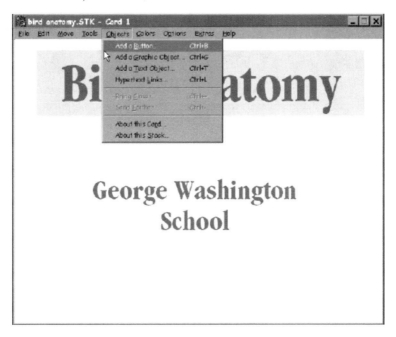

The **Button Appearance** dialogue box appears.

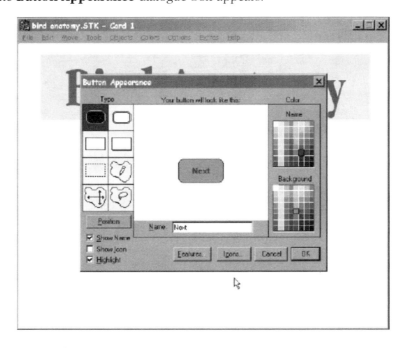

**2.** Type the word **Next** in the **Name:** field. This button will be used to go to the next card.

**3.** Single-click the box next to **Show Name.** Selecting this box will display the name of the button on the button. In this case it is **Next.**

**4.** Single-click the box next to **Highlight.** Selecting this box will cause the button to highlight when it is clicked. The user will have a visual cue that the button has been clicked.

You may change the color of the button and the text on the button by selecting colors in the **Background** and **Name** option boxes. You may also select an icon or picture from a list to go on the button by single-clicking on the **Icons . . .** button.

**5.** Single-click the **OK** button when you have finished making your choices.

**6.** Drag the button where you want it.

**7.** Single-click outside the button. The **Actions** dialogue box appears.

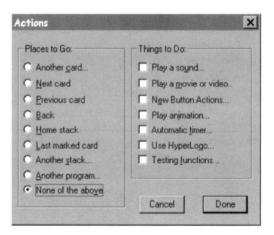

You can select **Places to Go:** and **Things to Do:**.

**8.** For this exercise, single-click on the circle next to **Next card.** The **Transitions** dialogue box appears. See the top of page 91.

On the left side of the screen is a list of the types of transitions that are possible when the user clicks the button. To see what each effect looks like, single-click the **Try it** button. In this case, **Dissolve** is selected and **Fast** is selected.

**9.** Single-click the **OK** button when you have finished. The **Action** dialogue box reappears.

**10.** Single-click **Done.**

**CREATING A NEW CARD**

1. Select **New Card** from the Edit menu. A new card appears.

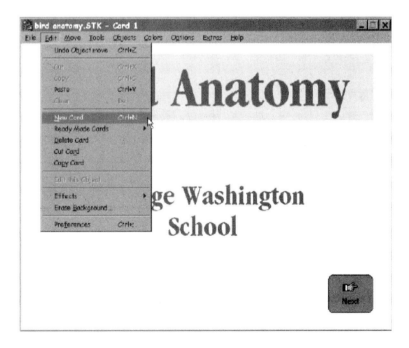

**2.** Repeat the steps for creating a button. This time, select **Previous Card** from the Actions menu. Test the button to see if it takes you to your first card.

### ADDING A GRAPHIC

**1.** From the File menu select **Add Clip Art,** or from the Objects menu select **Add a Graphic Object.** A dialogue box appears.

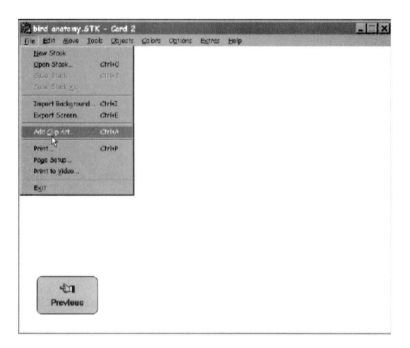

You can get a graphic from a disk, file, digital camera, scanner, or video.

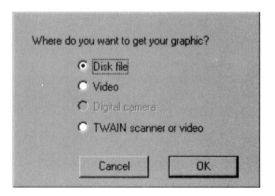

**2.** When you click the **OK** button, you will be prompted to navigate to the file that contains the graphic. When the have located the graphic, a screen will display with the graphic on it.

3. The cursor now changes to a cross. Alternately, you can use the lasso tools to select all the graphic or portions of the graphic.

### CREATING INVISIBLE BUTTONS

One reason for using hypermedia is that the student can navigate through the material as he or she wishes. In this exercise we want to make links from the picture of the bird to cards that have more detail about various parts of the anatomy. An invisible button is placed over each part that you want to link to the card.

1. From the Objects menu, select **Add a Button.** The **Button Appearance** dialogue box appears. There are four options for creating an invisible button. These options are located on the left-hand part of the screen under **Type.** You can choose the marquee, pencil, expanding area, or lasso option.

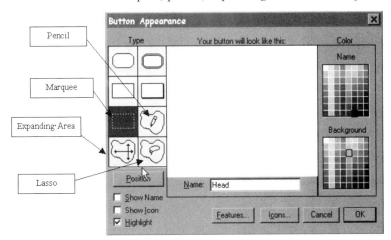

**2.** Drag around the head of the bird with the tool you have chosen. A dialogue box appears.

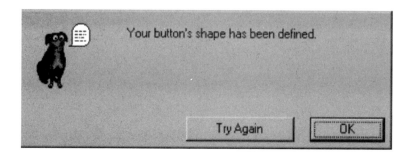

**3.** Single-click the **OK** button. The **Actions** dialogue box appears.

**4.** Single-click the circle next to **Another card.** The **Move to card** dialogue box appears.

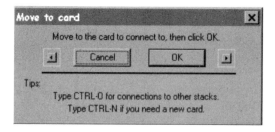

**5.** Use the left or right arrows to go to the card that has information about the head of the bird.

**6.** Repeat the steps for creating invisible buttons for the rest of the anatomy of the bird.

**7.** Save your stack.

Congratulations! You have completed a stack.

## *Databases*

Database software is a management tool that enables you to keep track of large volumes of information in an organized way. The software allows you to sort information by fields or categories. It is helpful to think of databases as index cards with each card representing a record. Each item of information is considered a field or category. For example, if you are keeping records about books that students are reading, then one record would contain information about one book. One field would contain the title of the book, another field would contain the author's name, and another would contain a summary of the book or a description of the main character. The database allows you to manage these multiple records in an effective and organized manner.

Students benefit during literacy instruction when using databases by learning to develop skills in organization, refine vocabulary, compare and contrast information, and discover relationships in the information (Deming, 1990). Because students sort the data themselves, they can create reports on that data and even develop new layouts for their reports (as shown later in this section).

The sets of related information are stored in data files, which are made up of individual records. The individual records are made up of fields or categories. An example is a database of poems that a student has read. The student would have a record for each poem. Some of the fields might be as follows: Title of Poem; Length of Poem; and Description of Poem.

It is important to decide, before setting up the database, the information that is to be in the database. The database function from ClarisWorks is used for the following example.

## Creating Fields

Fields should be limited to one specific item of data. Instead of writing **Author's Name,** it would be better to have **Last Name** and then **First Name** for the author's name. This allows a user to look up the author by first or last name. Information in a database can be sorted by any of the fields.

ClarisWorks displays a dialogue box to prompt you to type the name of the field. Field type can be selected from a pull-down menu. Field type can be text, number, serial number, or multimedia, to name a few choices. Information classified as text usually includes names and definitions. Information classified as numbers involves calculations. Date, time, and phone numbers are not considered numbers; they are text. In the example in the figure most of the field types are text, and only one field type is a popup menu.

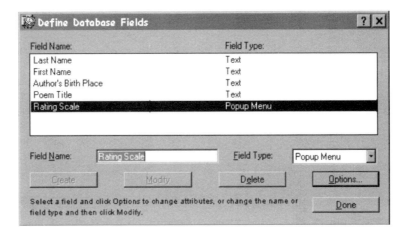

**Entering the Information**

Place the cursor in the first field of the record. Type the required information in this field, or select the information from the list such as the popup menu that is defined in this example. Press the Tab key or place the cursor in the next field to type in that field. The text can be modified as you would in word processing. You may change the font as well as the size and style of the font. You may also change the contents of the fields by deleting, copying, or pasting. The figure shows one example of a predefined list for the field.

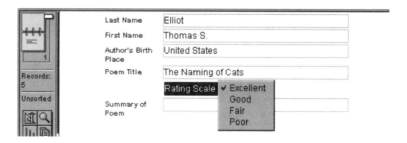

You can view the records in the Browse mode as shown in the figure or in the List mode as shown in the next figure.

You can adjust the size of the columns of the table when you are in List mode. Place the cursor on the dividing lines of the table. The cursor will change to a line with an arrow on each side of it. Click and drag to resize the column.

**Customized Layouts**

Database programs usually have two standard layouts. One is similar to a Rolodex or index card. The entire information of the record is displayed all at once, and you can scroll down through the records.

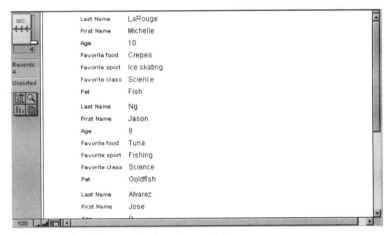

The other standard layout looks like a table.

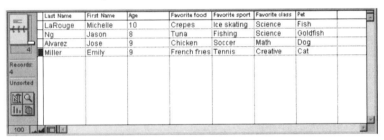

You do not have to stay with these standard layouts. You can create new layouts for most databases. When using the ClarisWorks database program, choose **Layout** from the Layout menu. This takes you to the drawing program, where you

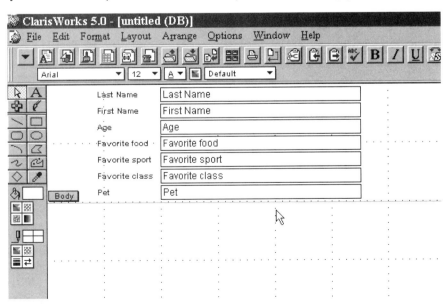

can move the database labels and fields individually. Click on a field to select it. The field becomes a box with little squares at each corner that allow you to resize the box. You can drag the fields and their labels separately to different positions on the screen.

You may not want to use all the fields in this new layout. In that case, you can click on a field or label and delete it with the Delete key. Also, you can add clipart to the layout to make it more interesting. Refer to the next figure to see the new layout that was created for a keypal database.

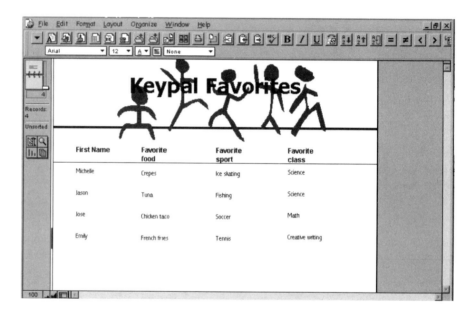

**Examples of Database Use**

You can create a database of keypals much like the one illustrated in this chapter. Have the students decide what fields they want. You may choose to include the number of brothers and/or sisters the keypals have; their age, height, and weight; their pet; their favorite class, sport, or food; and their language, to name a few.

## *Spreadsheets*

The term *spreadsheet* is usually associated with accounting. Numeric information is spread across columns in rows, forming a mathematical matrix. The spreadsheet software calculates, sorts, and creates graphs. Teachers and students use spreadsheets to analyze, graph, and compare and contrast data, and to predict or infer solutions to a problem. Many teachers use spreadsheet software to manage grades. Students can use spreadsheets as a tool to help them evaluate information.

### Components of the Spreadsheet

Most spreadsheets look alike. They are composed of numbered rows and lettered columns that intersect to form cells. You can use the cursor to move around in the matrix. When a cell is selected, a dark outline is displayed around the cell.

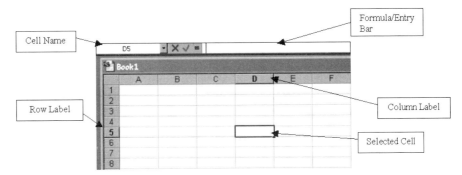

The name of the cell is shown in the left-hand corner of the screen. In this case it is **D5.** Formulas or entered information are displayed in the Formula bar.

### Entering Information

Spreadsheet programs allow you to use numbers, letters, or a combination in the cells. Click in the cell where you want the data or formula. The clicking activates the cell. Next, type the data or formula in the cell. This data is displayed in the Formula bar. For the data to remain in the cell, you must accept the data. Press the Enter key to accept the data. If you want to edit information, highlight the data to be changed and press the Delete key. Next to the Formula bar is a box with an X and one with a ✓. You can click on the ✓ to accept the information in a cell or click on the X to *not* accept the information in the cell.

Sometimes it is necessary to adjust the width of the columns to fit all the text or numbers in the space. To adjust the width of a column, place the cursor over the dividing line of the column heading; the cursor changes to a line with arrows on each side of the line that allows you to click and drag the line to the size you want. In the figure, the Name column was made larger to accommodate the names.

You can change the font as well as the size and style of the font, just as you would in word processing software. Click in the cell that contains the word(s) you want to change. Highlight the word(s) you want to change in the Formula/Entry bar, and select the font, size, and style from the tool bar options.

As stated earlier in this section, spreadsheets are used to manipulate data. The most common functions of the spreadsheet are addition (+), subtraction (−), multiplication (×), division (/), and exponentiation (∧). The spreadsheet comes with a variety of built-in functions that can be used by referencing the function. A few of these are Sum, Average, Minimum, Maximum, and Standard Deviation. The gradebook illustration shows how the Average function can be entered in a cell to calculate the average grade for a student. Follow two simple steps to enter a calculation.

1. Type an equals sign (=) to tell the spreadsheet that a calculation is being entered. Microsoft Works, Excel, and ClarisWorks use the equals sign to start each calculation.

2. Type the formula in the cell where you wish to see the results of the calculation. In this case, it is cell G3. The formula is =AVERAGE(B3:F3). The results are displayed in cell G3. The formula could have been written as =B3+C3+D3+E3+F3/5. This would have given the same answer (37.6).

| Arial | 10 | B *I* U | ≡ ≡ ≡ 圉 | $ % , ⁺⁰⁰.⁰⁰ ⁺.⁰₀.⁰ 鏵 鏵 | ▢ ▾ 🕭 ▾ A ▾ |
|---|---|---|---|---|---|

G3 = =AVERAGE(B3:F3)

for book

| | A | B | C | D | E | F | G |
|---|---|---|---|---|---|---|---|
| 1 | Name | Journal | Book Report | Portfolio | Essay | Poem | Grade |
| 2 | | 100 | 10 | 100 | 10 | 10 | 46 |
| 3 | Addams, Clarissa | 75 | 9 | 90 | 8 | 6 | 37.6 |
| 4 | Applegate, John | 80 | 10 | 98 | 10 | 10 | 41.6 |
| 5 | Baker, Susan | 74 | 5 | 68 | 9 | 10 | 33.2 |
| 6 | Bennett, Gary | 80 | 8 | 85 | 9 | 9 | 38.2 |
| 7 | Dover, Clifford | 80 | 10 | 95 | 10 | 10 | 41 |
| 8 | Mertens, Gabriel | 85 | 9 | 90 | 8 | 6 | 39.6 |
| 9 | Singer, Gloria | 100 | 10 | 98 | 10 | 9 | 45.4 |
| 10 | Smith, Robert | 80 | 7 | 80 | 8 | 8 | 36.6 |
| 11 | Williams, Andrew | 95 | 10 | 100 | 20 | 9 | 46.8 |
| 12 | | | | | | | |

## Creating Graphs and Charts

Another important function of the spreadsheet is the capability of creating graphs. Graphs are easy to make once the spreadsheet has been created. For example, to create a chart of the student name and the journal grade, select cells A3 to B11. In Microsoft Excel, select the Chart function on the tool bar or select **Chart** from the Insert menu.

File  Edit  View  Insert  Format  Tools  Data  Accounting  Window  Help

Arial ... 10 ... B  I  U ... $ % , ... Chart Wizard

B11 ... = 95

for book

| | A | B | C | D | E | F | G |
|---|---|---|---|---|---|---|---|
| 1 | Name | Journal | Book Report | Portfolio | Essay | Poem | Grade |
| 2 | | 100 | 10 | 100 | 10 | 10 | 46 |
| 3 | Addams, Clarissa | 75 | 9 | 90 | 8 | 6 | 37.6 |
| 4 | Applegate, John | 80 | 10 | 98 | 10 | 10 | 41.6 |
| 5 | Baker, Susan | 74 | 5 | 68 | 9 | 10 | 33.2 |
| 6 | Bennett, Gary | 80 | 8 | 85 | 9 | 9 | 38.2 |
| 7 | Dover, Clifford | 80 | 10 | 95 | 10 | 10 | 41 |
| 8 | Mertens, Gabriel | 85 | 9 | 90 | 8 | 6 | 39.6 |
| 9 | Singer, Gloria | 100 | 10 | 98 | 10 | 9 | 45.4 |
| 10 | Smith, Robert | 80 | 7 | 80 | 8 | 8 | 36.6 |
| 11 | Williams, Andrew | 95 | 10 | 100 | 20 | 9 | 46.8 |
| 12 | | | | | | | |

The Chart Wizard appears. The type of chart is selected. In this example, the column icon is selected.

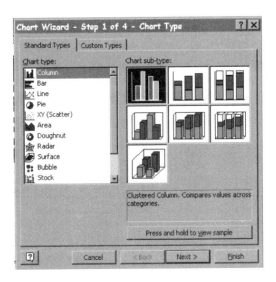

For this example, select **Column.** Single-click the **Next>** button. You are prompted to select **Row** or **Column** for the data in the next screen. Select **Column.** Single-click the **Next>** button. The third screen of the Chart Wizard displays. You will be prompted to label the graph and the x (horizontal) and y (vertical) axes. The title for this chart is Journal, the x axis is labeled Students, and the y axis is labeled Grades.

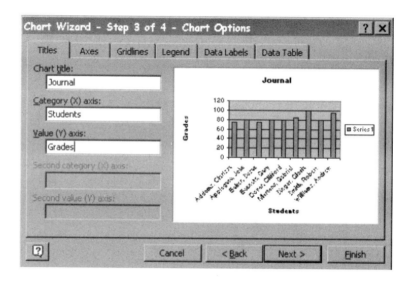

Single-click the **Next>** button. The final step of the Chart Wizard involves selecting where you want the chart placed.

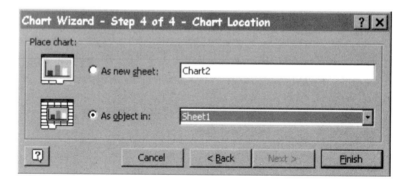

You have a choice to place the chart on a separate page or on the same page as the spreadsheet. In the figure, the **As object in:** option is selected. Single-click the **Finish** button.

Graphs and charts help to illustrate abstract numerical data in a clear and concrete way, showing relationships that would be difficult to express in text alone. Because graphs have the potential to express a bias via the manipulation of scale, it is important that students learn how to interpret graphs. Please refer to the two Book Report graphs that show performance and achievement. One graph has a scale of 0 to 12, and the other has a scale of 0 to 120. The same students do not look as if they performed as well when the scale is 0 to 120.

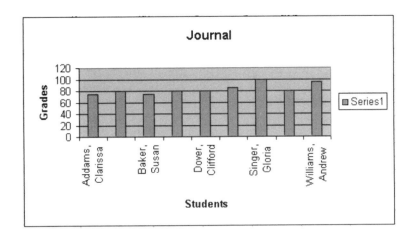

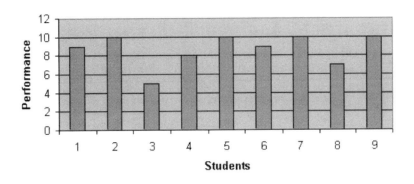

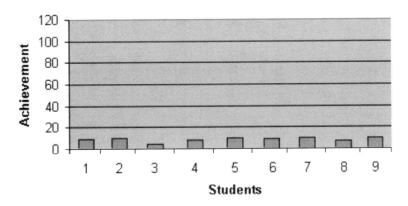

## Styles of Graphs and Charts

There are three main styles of graphs: line, column, and pie chart. *Line graphs* are excellent for displaying trends or continuous information over time. These graphs are very accurate but often are difficult to understand. The figure is an example of a line graph showing the amount of rainfall in inches that occurred in a year.

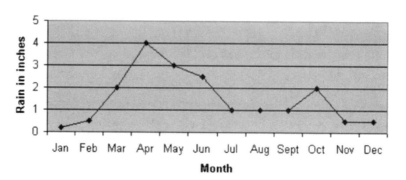

Column graphs (vertical columns) and bar graphs (horizontal bars) do not display continuity as well as line graphs do. They are best used to show changes in one variable over another. An example of this kind of graph is illustrated in the figure of portfolio grades. Notice that the individual student's grade stands out. This is because the columns are distinct; they are not connected.

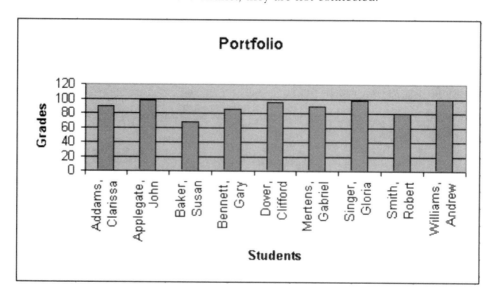

*Pie charts* effectively display percentages. The size of each slice shows the part-to-the-whole relationship. The pie chart in the figure shows the percentage of dogs as pets owned by the students in each grade of an elementary school.

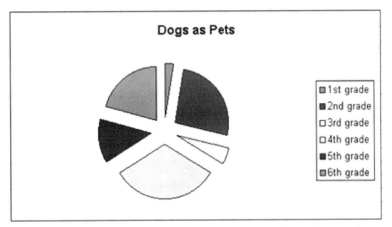

At the end of this chapter, a lesson plan entitled "Who's the Students' Favorite Author?" illustrates how spreadsheets can be used during reading instruction.

## PowerPoint

Students enjoy sharing information through slide shows, and Microsoft PowerPoint is designed to create slides that include text, graphics, sound, animation, and video. Several features of PowerPoint enable you to change text with different fonts, size, styles, and colors; use powerful drawing tools to create your own images; and print handouts and lecture notes.

PowerPoint gives three options to create a new presentation: AutoContent Wizard, Template, and Blank Presentation. Using the Wizard is the fastest way to create a slide show. This is the option to choose if your students have not used PowerPoint before.

**STEPS FOR USING POWERPOINT**

**1.** Select **New** from the File menu. A dialogue box displays.

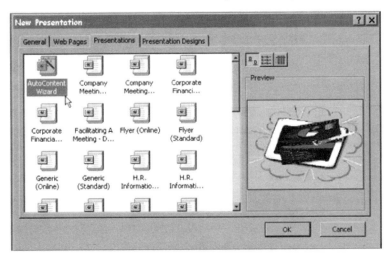

**2.** Select the **Presentations** tab and the AutoContent Wizard. Click **OK.** The
AutoContent Wizard displays.

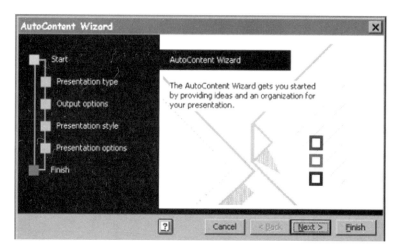

**3.** Single-click the **Next>** button. Another screen displays, allowing you to
select the type of presentation you are going to give.

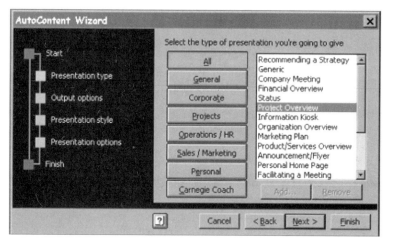

**4.** Answer the promptings of the Wizard, and then single-click the **Finish** but-
ton. When the Wizard creates your presentation, you see it in Outline View.
However, there are five views in PowerPoint: Slide View, Outline View,
Slide Sorter View, Notes Page View, and Slide Show View.

### Slide View

*Students may find it easiest to work in Slide View when placing text on the*
*slides. Slide View shows one slide at a time. This allows you to modify text, add*
*graphics, and create animated text directly on the slide. You can change the*
*layout of the slide by using the Common Tasks tool bar.*

### Outline View

*Outline View is text only. In this view you can add and delete slides, edit text, and rearrange slides. In Outline View you can see a tiny picture of the slide that updates the contents of the slide as you modify it.*

### Slide Sorter View

*This view shows small pictures of each slide. It is easy to rearrange slides in this view. To move a slide, single-click on it to select it and then drag it to the new position. You can delete a slide by selecting it and then using the Delete key to delete it. When you double-click on a slide in this view, the slide opens in Slide View.*

### Notes Page View

*In this view you can type notes that will help you with the presentation. This is the only thing you can do in this view.*

### Slide Show View

*Slide Show View is the slide show itself. This view is helpful when rehearsing the presentation. You can go forward by pressing the Enter key, the Page Dn key, or the right arrow key. You can go backward by pressing the Page Up key or the up arrow key. The Esc key quits the slide show.*

#### ANIMATING TEXT

A feature that is very popular is animating text. It is easy to animate text while in the Slide View.

1. Highlight the text.
2. Select **Custom Animation** from the Slide Show menu in the tool bar. The **Custom Animation** dialogue box appears.

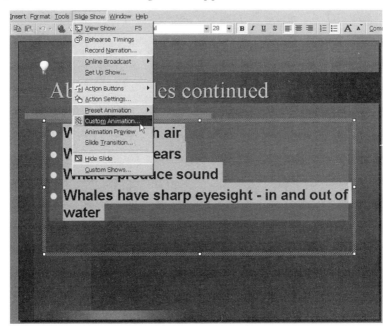

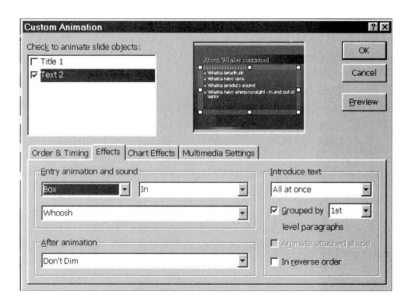

3. The **Entry animation and sound** box contains two fields. One allows you to select animation effects from a pull-down menu. In this case we chose **Box In.**

4. To play sound with the animated text, select a sound from the pull-down menu. In this case **(No Sound)** is selected.

5. Click on the **Preview** button to see the effects.

6. When you have finished choosing the various effects, click the **OK** button. You have created animated text. When you are in Slide Show View, press the Enter key each time you want the text to animate.

### PLACING THE PICTURE ON THE SLIDE

1. From the Insert menu in the tool bar, select **Picture;** and from the sub-menu, select either **Clip Art** or **From File.** In this case, **From File** is used. See the next page.

2. Navigate to where the picture is, and single-click the **Insert** button. The picture appears on the slide. You may move the picture anywhere on the slide by clicking and dragging.

## Presentation on the Web

You may save PowerPoint presentations and place them on your Web page. Select **Save as HTML . . .** from the File menu. PowerPoint will save the presentation ready for the Web.

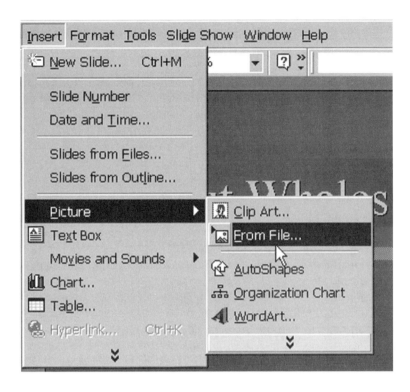

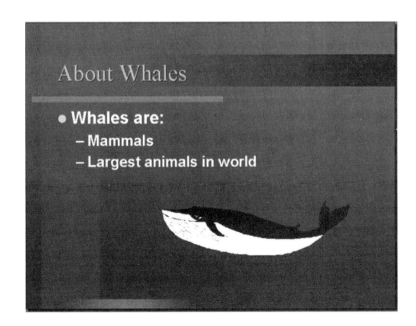

## *CD-ROMs*

A compact disc digital read only memory (CD-ROM) contains data in digital form. CD-ROMs have the capacity to hold great volumes of data that can be retrieved on the computer in a manner similar to accessing information on a floppy disk or hard drive. CD-ROM resources include technology books, the complete set of *National Geographic* magazine, and Encarta and Grolier's encyclopedias; these all take advantage of hypermedia. One example of a good use of a CD-ROM book is included as a Computer Classroom Example at the end this chapter (Ekhalm, 1993); see the activity entitled "Bring a Book to Life."

### Managing CDs

One of the advantages of the CD-ROM is that it takes up very little space and contains a lot of information. Yet because of its size it is easy to misplace. You should store CD-ROMs in a box in a secure place, and you may want to label the box with the contents. It is helpful to keep a database of your CDs. You might include the following types of fields: title, subject, grade level, platform (PC/Mac), amount of memory needed, location of the disks (e.g., classroom closet), type (software or CD-ROM), publisher, location of documentation (e.g., library), license number, number of licensed copies, lesson ideas, and notes about the contents of the CD-ROM.

CDs are easy to use. Just place the CD in the CD-ROM drive of your computer with the reflective side down. Many times the CDs begin automatically. If the CD does not automatically start and you are using a PC, go to **My Computer** and select either the D or E drive. You should see an icon of a CD on top of the drive.

Double-click this drive to open it. You should see an icon of the program that you want to start. Double-click it to start the program. See the next page.

If you are using a Mac, you should see an icon of the CD on the desktop. Double-click the icon to open the CD. Then double-click the icon of the program to start the program.

Some CDs require an executable file in order to run. Usually the program guides you through the install process. However, many times school computers have a program that is installed to protect the contents of the hard drive from access by students. If this protection software is in place, it may not allow you to install the executable files necessary to run a CD-ROM. In this situation you should check with the person who manages the computers in your school to get permission to install the software for the CD-ROM.

Sometimes a CD-ROM will not run on a particular operating system; for example, if your school is running Windows NT and the software is for Windows 3.1. Some CD-ROMs will not run on Windows NT. When purchasing CDs, be sure to notice how much memory is required to run them; also be aware of the system requirements.

# ELECTRONIC TEXTS

Currently, many teachers are teaching students how to read both electronic and printed texts. Reinking (1992, 1994) points out that electronic texts are different from printed texts because (1) readers and electronic texts can interact, (2) electronic reading can be guided, (3) electronic texts have different structures from printed texts, and (4) electronic texts employ new symbolic elements.

Several series, such as the Living Book and the Discis Books, offer many children's books on CD-ROM. These electronic books have unique features: for example, the story is read in another language, specific words are pronounced, sound effects are heard, and animated pictures are viewed. Although these interactional books can be motivational for students, Willis, Stephens, and Matthew (1996) identify disadvantages, such as the students being depicted as symbolic elements.

An engaging student activity involves a comparison/contrast assignment—the CD versus the book. Find several comparable stories, both on CD and in book print. Have students list strengths and weaknesses (call the lists "what I liked" and "what I didn't like") and engage them in discussion. After doing this on several occasions you'll have your own program analysis.

# EVALUATING SOFTWARE

The primary purpose for educational software is to enhance the learning goals you have established. These goals are dependent on the age, skill level, and needs of your students. The software may be excellent in terms of the accuracy of subject matter and also technically good in that it runs without errors, but if it does not meet the needs of the curriculum then it is not valuable to you (Haughland, 1994). With this in mind, consider the following general guidelines.

Get to know the software thoroughly. Read the documentation and evaluate it for clarity. Notice if the documentation is laid out in a logical manner and if it is easy to find what you are looking for. Pay attention to the way the information is displayed on the screen. Does the program have a good Help function or documentation that replaces the Help function? A desirable feature is the ability to leave the program and pick up where you have left off without loss of data.

If they are used properly, sound, graphics, and animation can aid learning. Sound can illustrate reality, hold the student's attention, and give feedback. But it can be distracting when many students are using the program. Notice if the program allows you to turn off the sound. You may need to have headphones available for students using the software if you cannot turn off the sound.

Many studies have shown that graphics are important to understanding concepts (Anglin, 1985, 1986; Anglin & Stevens, 1987; Duchastel, 1981; Dwyer, 1978; Levin, 1981; Mayer, 1989, 1990). Research shows that the right amount of realism in a graphic allows for the maximum amount of retention, too little realism results in too few visual cues, and too much realism is distracting and results in less learning (Dwyer, 1978). Graphics must support the subject of the lesson.

Animation is very popular in commercial educational software. Although animation can serve a purely cosmetic function, Rieber (1989) suggests five other purposes: attention gaining, motivation/reinforcement, conceptualization, presentation, and interactive dynamics. As with static graphics, animation can be distracting and results in shallow thinking if it is not used properly.

It is helpful if software includes suggestions for use in the classroom. When evaluating software, be sure to check if it comes with good lesson plans and resources that support them.

### Questions to Evaluate Educational Software Programs

*Lesson Content*

❏ Is the topic appropriate for the curriculum?

❏ Is the information correct?

❏ Is the content free of bias?

❏ Are the grammar and punctuation correct?

*Interactivity*

❏ How much student interaction is available?

❏ Is the degree of realism satisfactory?

❏ Does the learner have control over navigation through the program?

❏ Does the learner have control over the level of difficulty?

❏ Does the learner have control over entering and exiting at any place in the program?

*Skills Needed to Use*

❏ How much knowledge is needed to use the program?

❏ Can the learner use the program without help from an adult?

*Performance*

❏ Is the program reliable?

❏ Does it fulfill the promised educational outcome?

❏ Are the educational strategies sound?

❏ Is feedback appropriate for correct or incorrect responses?

❏ Is there effective remediation?

❏ Are graphics, animation, and sound used in an appropriate manner?

❏ Do the graphics, animation, and sound enhance the learning experience?

*Student Data*

❏ Does the program collect and evaluate student data?

❏ Is the student's privacy respected?

❏ Are collected data secured?

*Support*

❏ Does the program include a manual?

❏ Is there technical support via the Internet or telephone?

*Resources*

❏ Does the program have detailed lesson plans and resources?

## Computer Classroom Examples

### *Who's the Students' Favorite Author?*

| | |
|---|---|
| **Grade Level:** | Adaptable for K–8 |
| **Objective:** | Students will increase their reading ability by reading a variety of books. Students will practice their writing skills by writing about their favorite author in their journals. Students will create computer graphs from the results of the spreadsheet exercise. |
| **Time:** | 2 hours |
| **Problem to Be Solved:** | Who are the students' favorite authors? |
| **Materials:** | Many books (grouped by theme, author, or grade level) Paper Pencil Computer Printer Spreadsheet software Writing journals |

**Steps:**

1. Read a variety of books with and to your students before beginning this activity.

2. Type the authors' and students' names in a spreadsheet so that the students can vote for their favorite author.
   **Note:** If the students are young, the teacher will need to create the spreadsheet. See example.

| | | Student's Name | | |
|---|---|---|---|---|
| **Author's Name** | | | | |
| | John A. | Susan B. | Emily R. | Walter P. |
| N. Hawthorne | X | | X | |
| E. E. Milne | | | | X |
| M. LeEngle | | X | | |

3. Have each student locate his or her name and then find the cell under his or her name that corresponds with the name of the favorite author. Then, the student will type an X in that cell.

4. Have each student write the reason for choosing this author in the writing journal. **Note:** This would be a good time to start an electronic journal by using the word processing software. Students could store the journal on their own diskette.

## COMPUTER CLASSROOM EXAMPLES (CONTINUED)

### Who's the Students' Favorite Author? (Continued)

5.　Tally the results.

6.　Discuss the results as a group.

7.　Using a basic spreadsheet program, demonstrate how to create a graph. The type of graph you create (bar, line, pie chart) will depend on the software.

* Type author names in the cells of one column.
* Type the number of student responses in the cells of the third column.
* Use the software tool bar to select the type of graph you want.
* Have each student print her or his graph.

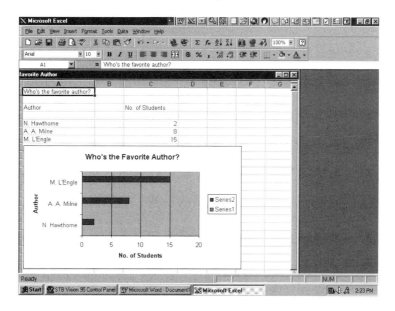

**Assessment:**　Pair students and let them use the spreadsheet to create a graph of their own. Develop a rubric for assessing the graphs and reporting the results. Engage in a culminating session in which the students display and explain their work to their classmates.

### Bring a Book to Life

**Grade Level:**　Adaptable for K–8

**Objective:**　Students will practice their reading skills by reading *Arthur's Birthday* by Marc Brown. The students will explore the *Arthur's Birthday* CD-ROM to search for hidden objects. Students will enhance their writing skills by writing the directions to a hidden object on a specific page.

## COMPUTER CLASSROOM EXAMPLES (CONTINUED)

### *Bring a Book to Life (Continued)*

**Time:**    2 hours

**Problem to**    Someone has hidden objects at Arthur's birthday. Can you find them?
**Be Solved:**

**Materials:**    *Arthur's Birthday* by Marc Brown
*Arthur's Birthday* CD-ROM (Living Books)
Paper
Pencils
Computer

**Steps:**

1. Read *Arthur's Birthday* by Marc Brown to the class.

2. Discuss setting, characters, problem, and resolution with the students.

3. Introduce the class to the *Arthur's Birthday* CD-ROM. Play the "Read to me" version first.

4. Discuss how the book and CD are alike and different.

5. Engage the class in the "Let me play" version of the CD.

6. After reading the text, click on different characters and items on the page. Tell the students that they will be choosing a favorite hidden item to write about.

7. Group the students in pairs.

8. Give the students time to explore the CD on their own. Assign them a specific page in the CD.

9. Ask them to find their favorite hidden object. (On each screen of this CD, there is a hidden party blower with confetti. Students do not have to choose this item. They may select from any of the hidden objects or actions.)

10. Ask the student pairs to plot a course to find their hidden object. You may wish to develop a rubric with the students for this. If not, ask that the students include four or five specific written directions to the object.

11. Have each pair of students exchange directions with another pair of students.

12. Use the CD to travel to the specific page. Follow the directions to find the hidden object.

**Assessment:**    Develop a rubric with the students for writing the directions to the hidden objects. After exchanging directions and completing the activity, have students share their experiences with writing and following directions. Suggest ways of improving writing and listening skills.

## TECHNO-TEACHER TIPS

### Determining Reading Levels

Traditionally when educators determined students' independent, instructional, and frustrational reading levels, students were required to read independently and did not receive assistance when they came to unknown words. However, electronic books provide audio assistance in decoding unknown words. This makes it somewhat confusing in determining students' reading levels because the machine, not the teacher, is helping the student.

### Promoting Your Technology Program

As you gradually integrate a technology design into your classroom procedures, pay particular attention to those most likely to scrutinize your activities—parents and principals. The principal already knows you have the hardware delivery system, but needs to be brought up to date on lesson planning, particularly under the heading of goal setting.

Parents are sometimes skeptical of new approaches to learning old behaviors. Technology won't sell itself at Parent Conference night. You will have to do it. After a general discussion of why you are using the new technologies, provide parents with a handout giving more detailed explanations of the software. It's always a good idea to show examples of student work generated by the software.

## FREQUENTLY ASKED QUESTIONS

1. **I'm afraid that when I teach literacy by using computers I will not cover all the literacy skills my students need. How do I make sure I'm covering everything?**

   It is important to be aware of your local and state grade level scope and sequence guidelines as well as the National Language Arts Standards. The computer is a tool that will help you teach the students, and it in no way changes what you expect them to learn. How your students go about learning will be what changes.

2. **When students are engaged in hypertext, they follow different links based on personal interest. How do I assist my students in reading this form of text?**

   Ask students to be specific about their interest. This helps them select a path they want to explore. Alternatively, you could instruct students to read all titles of links very closely because this will save time in their navigation as well as provide them a road map by which to return. Remember to emphasize that an advantage of hypertext is the ability to freely explore content, which means you do not want a highly structured activity. On the other hand, this does not excuse students from being held accountable for learning new information; they should be able to explain how this information fits in with the rest of the material they are reading.

## REFERENCES

Anglin, G. (1985). *Prose-relevant pictures and older learners' recall of written prose.* Paper presented at the annual convention of the Association for Educational Communications and Technology, Annaheim, CA. (ERIC Document Reproduction Service No. ED 256 305)

Anglin, G. (1986). *Effects of pictures on recall of written prose: How durable are picture effects.* (ERIC Document Reproduction Service No. ED 267 755)

Anglin, G., & Stevens, J. (1987). *Prose-relevant pictures and recall from science text.* Paper presented at the annual convention of the Association for Educational Communications and Technology, Atlanta, GA. (ERIC Document Reproduction Service No. ED 285 524)

Burns, P. C., Roe, B. D., & Ross, E. P. (1999). *Technology for literacy learning: A primer.* Boston: Houghton Mifflin.

Deming, P. (1990, February). Databases: A hidden treasure for language-arts instruction. *English Journal,* 69–70.

Dillner, M. (1993/1994). Using hypermedia to enhance content area instruction. *Journal of Reading, 37* (4), 260–270.

Duchastel, P. (1981). Illustrations and long-term memory. *Programmed Learning and Educational Technology, 18* (1), 11–15.

Dwyer, F. (1978). *Strategies for improving visual learning.* State College, PA: Learning Services.

Ekhalm, L. (1993, November). CD-ROM and the curriculum. *School Library Media Activities Monthly, 10* (3), 42–44.

Haughland S. (1994, Summer). Selecting software that facilitates developmental gains. *Computers and Young Children,* 45–46.

Levin, J. (1981). *Pictures as prose learning devices.* (ERIC Document Reproduction Service No. ED 209 660)

Mayer, R. (1989). Systematic thinking fostered by illustrations in scientific text. *Journal of Educational Psychology, 81* (2), 241–246.

Mayer, R. (1990). When is an illustration worth ten thousand words? *Journal of Educational Psychology, 82* (4), 715–726.

Reinking, D. (1992). Differences between electronic and printed texts: An agenda for research. *Journal of Educational Multimedia and Hypermedia, 1* (1), 11–24.

Reinking, D. (1994). *Electronic literacy* (Perspective in Reading Research No. 4). Athens, GA: National Reading Research Center, Universities of Georgia and Maryland.

Rieber, L. (1989). A review of animation research in computer-based instruction. In *Proceedings of selected research papers presented at the annual meeting of the Association for Educational Communications and Technology.* (pp. 370–489). Ames: Iowa State University.

Shen, V. (1996). The role of hypertext as an interactional medium among fifth-grade students. *Literacies for the 21st century: Research and Practice,* 484–499.

Willis, J. W., Stephens, E. C. & Matthew, K. I. (1996). *Technology, reading, and language arts.* Needham Heights, MA: Allyn & Bacon.

# THE WRITING PROCESS, COMPUTERS, AND YOUR CLASSROOM

Cortez is reading Wanda's writing and making comments in the margin so that he can ask Wanda questions about her essay. Betsy has finished reading Gerald's essay and tells him three things she particularly liked about his writing. Then she says to Gerald, "But I don't understand why basketball players should graduate from college before signing up with the NBA. Wouldn't they lose a lot of money by staying in school another year?" Trisha is explaining to Wilhelm why she first wrote about the history of fashion before writing about current fashions in New York. Wilhelm says, "I just don't see the connection. What has the way people dressed in ancient Egypt got to do with fashion design today?" Other students in the class are responding in similar ways to their peers' writing.

Mrs. Storey, the students' eighth-grade teacher, visits different pairs of students as they peer critique each other's writing; she mainly listens but sometimes answers a question when students ask for her opinion. The peer critiques are an important part of the writing process Mrs. Storey learned about last summer in a writing workshop where she had to write using a word processor. Before attending the workshop she used to give students an assignment, comment on their rough drafts, and then grade the students' final drafts. Now she helps students develop their ideas for a paper, requires them to produce three rough drafts on the word processors in her classroom or in the computer lab, discusses drafts with

**Education Place** <http://www.eduplace.com/hmco/school/>: Lists Internet writing projects in which your class can participate. You can submit your own writing project, or you can engage in a collaborative writing project with classrooms throughout the United States.

**Inkspot** <http://www.inkspot.com/>: Provides resources for students, giving and receiving feedback on their writing. Also provides an electric bulletin board for posting questions about writing and for finding peer-critique partners.

**Outta Ray's Head** <http://www3.sympatico.ca/ray.saitz/>: Provides lesson plans for blending art and writing and a 16-week unit that entails publishing an electronic autobiography.

**University of Illinois at Urbana-Champaign, Writers' Workshop** <http://www.english.uiuc.edu/cws/wworkshop/writer.html>: Provides a writer's technique handbook, a grammar handbook, and links to APA and MLS style manuals. An excellent site to use during editing.

**Wisconsin Department of Public Instruction, Education Resource List** <http://www.state.wi.us/agencies/dpi/www/ed-lib.html>: Provides a list of links to language arts handbooks and lesson plans.

**Writing Instruction in Computer-Based Classrooms:** <http://www.comp.edu.composition>: Discusses issues related to writing electronically.

**Figure 5.1**    World Wide Web Sites Mrs. Storey Has Visited

students in teacher-student conferences, teaches the students how to be effective peer critiquers, schedules ample time for students to revise their peer-critiqued drafts, comments on the revised drafts, provides students time to revise the revised drafts, and grades the final drafts according to a rubric the students helped generate at the beginning of the writing assignment. Mrs. Storey didn't used to require students to type their papers, in part because she herself didn't feel comfortable using a word processor. Now she wants to use computers even more in her classroom—for collaborative writing assignments, for classroom publications—so she is reading books and articles about how to use computers in the literacy classroom. She also has visited several World Wide Web sites to get information about how to help students reach audiences beyond the classroom (Figure 5.1).

## THE WRITING PROCESS: GETTING STARTED

If you're like Mrs. Storey before she took the writing workshop, you haven't received training in the use of computers, so there's no reason you should feel comfortable integrating technology into the curriculum. Maybe you're attempting to help your students learn to write by applying the old behavioral model—assigning five-paragraph themes, requiring students to produce a detailed outline of the theme before any text is created, and forbidding any useful help from peers (that would be cheating, after all). A number of teachers have no qualms about using the behavioral model and hope that their students learn to write well because of it.

Many college professors are stuck with the legacy of students who have been taught to write according to the behavioral model. Our experience as both college professors and authors of this book leads us to make the following observations:

- The behavioral model makes a poor fit with the way people really write (Forman, 1992; Galegher, Kraut, & Egido, 1990; Odell & Goswami, 1985; Spilka, 1993) and does very little to help students create written products typical of academic or work settings. When was the last time you read a five-paragraph theme in a newspaper, magazine, pamphlet, or journal article? In college, we only read them when our new students replicate those artificial high school norms (often unsuccessfully) to fulfill writing assignments.

- If students learn to write according to the behavioral model, they do so despite the model. For instance, some students confide in us that they outline their paper after writing it, even though they produced a feeble outline at the beginning of the writing assignment because they were required to.

- In Chapter 4 we broached the subject of students' nonlinear methods of organizing the information they access from texts (Shen, 1996). The organization of writing works in a similar fashion: The straight-line behavioral method does not take into account the experiential complexities of the individual writer. Each person works from a unique perspective and is perfectly capable of organizing a composition from a nonbehaviorist set of parameters.

This chapter discusses how to shift writing from a behavioral model to a constructivist model by using the process approach to writing. In addition, we discuss how to use the computer as a tool for process writing. But first, let's clarify some literacy jargon. When educators talk and write about infusing writing into the language arts curriculum using technology, what does that mean?

*Infuse* means to put something into something else. Thus, infusing writing into the literacy curriculum means making sure that writing is put into the curriculum. Computer technology, therefore, is a tool for infusing writing into the curriculum.

But infusion means more than just putting A into B. We could drop a cube of sugar into a hot bowl of chili, but the sugar wouldn't be infused until we stir it in. Similarly, writing must be stirred into the curriculum so that the curriculum cannot be separated from it. Indeed, the literacy curriculum is composed of writing and reading and speaking and listening. Take them all away and there is no curriculum. Take even one away and the curriculum is incomplete.

To illustrate use of the computer to infuse writing into the curriculum, we provide a snapshot of a teacher who has used process writing in her classroom. Whitney Miller explains the writing process she uses with her students and also tells how she integrated computer technology into the writing process.

## COMPUTER CLASSROOM SNAPSHOT

### *Context*

My name is Whitney Miller, and I teach second grade at an inner-city school. My school is supported by Title 1 and is the only kindergarten through fourth grade school in a district with 120 elementary schools. My school is a neighborhood school; none of our students come to school by bus. The entire student population is African American, and 95% of our students are on free or reduced lunch. My class is composed of 10 girls and 18 boys, and five of them have repeated first grade. In addition, two resource students are in the class. Because I am a 21st century teacher, I have three computers, a printer, a laser disc player, a scanner, and a large monitor in my room. The majority of my students do not have computers at home. Their only time to use the computers is at school, so their computer experience is limited. Most of their class time is spent using networked software. Minimal work is done on the word processor, but I have done some journal writing on the computer. Although I see the benefits of using computers to help my kids write, in the past I had trouble finding time to integrate technology into my curriculum. Consequently, I took a course in education about using computers in the writing curriculum. I decided to make time to take my students through the entire writing process for the first time and to use computers during the process. In this way, I killed two birds with one stone as I had a project to do for the computer class.

### *What I Did and Why*

I began my project by motivating my students to write by modeling how to produce a whole-group generated story. I conducted weekly and biweekly author studies because I felt they would be of interest to my students. Marc Brown is one of the authors students are extremely fond of, and they especially love his Arthur series, so on the first day I decided to read two of their favorites: *Arthur's Pet Business* and *Arthur's Teacher Trouble*. Following the readings, we brainstormed about the components of a story. We discussed the characters, setting, plot, and endings. The students began to see that all stories had several key components.

Next I brought out Bubba, a toy bear that talks when you squeeze him. The students were familiar with Bubba and were excited to hear him talk. Bubba is like Arthur, so I told my students that we would be writing a class book about Bubba. As a class, we brainstormed possible titles for our book. They came up with over 30 different titles, some very similar to the Arthur titles. After much discussion and an actual vote, we decided to write a story entitled "Bubba's Wedding." It was funny to see how excited students were to be writing about a wedding. Several students actually drafted their own versions that night at home.

During the following day we began to write our story. We first mapped out the setting, characters, and main idea. The students were very involved and loved coming up with the different names for the characters and the setting. We had to vote on some of these, because we came up with so many. Finally, we began our story with the students dictating and me entering the text into the computer. The students could see what I was keyboarding on the large monitor attached to the computer. Next, it was time to revise and edit the story. We added words and sentences. This was a great time to introduce necessary grammar skills as they came up. For example, quotation marks were something that we needed for our story, but they are not usually taught in second grade. The students liked learning about them and actually tried to use them later in their own stories. This also was an excellent time to show students how to indent, underline, and use specific keys on the computer. I showed them how to go back and make changes. Finally, each student illustrated a page. Our first class book was a success.

Our next writing project involved students working with a partner to produce their own "All About Me" books. First, I paired the students with a member of their sex and had them complete a prewriting activity. Together, they had to come up with at least three ways that they are alike and different. Some of them did this easily, and others took longer. After handwriting their three-point list, they typed it on the word processor. The students really seemed to enjoy this activity.

Now it was time to write the team stories. The excitement in the room was evident as each pair of students worked together to hand-write their story. I even had students who would not line up for recess because they wanted to write just one more sentence. One pair of students had difficulty completing their story and decided that they would rather work alone. I allowed them to do this and got two good stories instead of one bad one. I also paired two low-achieving students with behavior problems. They had trouble agreeing during the prewriting activity but actually agreed when it came to writing a story. Amazingly, there were no behavior problems when they were writing the story. When I looked around the room, it was exciting to see how actively engaged the students were. It took about two days to get the drafts done.

After a group finished writing their first draft, they conferenced with me for five to ten minutes. During the conference, in addition to catching spelling and grammatical errors, we made sure that each story flowed, so I also asked them questions about the content of their writing and made corrections on their papers with a blue or black pen so that the errors would not be perceived as negative. (Red is the color of blood, and students can think that you are "bleeding their paper" by using a red pen.) In most cases they were glad to hear my suggestions, because they felt that those suggestions would make their story better.

After a conference, the pairs of students began to word process their stories. They loved this part. I assigned times for the students to work on the computer. The pairs would sit together at the computer and take turns typing. While one was typing, the other one was looking at the keys to identify letters and watch the screen for any errors. Each group had 45 minutes to type their story. After they printed their story, there was another conference. At this time we made final revisions. Together, we decided where to place page breaks. The students then went back to their computer and completed the corrections. This part presented a problem for the students, because they were afraid they might accidentally delete their story. With my help, they moved the cursor and deleted spaces without erasing their stories.

After printing, the students illustrated their stories. While they were illustrating, I called individual groups over to the computer to design their covers using clipart. This was something new for them, and they loved playing with the different fonts and sizes. I felt that it made their books look like real books. I laminated their books and had them bound. All the students and I were very proud of the job that we had done. Then we had an authors' party. We shared our stories with the class, and each person shared something nice about the other group's story. The students were respectful as they listened to and applauded their classmates.

### What I Learned

Initially, I thought it would be difficult for the students to start using the computer because some of them had little or no knowledge of computers. That problem was solved after the first few students typed, because they taught each other. Even drawing was more purposeful; students were concerned with details and did a good job of making the picture go with the words on that page. They were not trying to jump up and ask what they could do next. It was not as stressful as I had imagined it would be. All the students felt that they had worked harder because they knew they would be publishing their stories on the computer. Most of the students said they would rather produce a word-processed story than a handwritten one.

Students benefit from process writing because it engages them in higher-order process writing. In addition, the technology is not only a wonderful motivator but a professional presentation tool also. I suspect that over time the combination of the writing process and technology will greatly improve students' writing skills. I would like to start developing this process at the beginning of the year.

## EXPLAINING THE PROCESS APPROACH TO WRITING

Whitney's snapshot provides a good example of infusing computer technology into process writing. The following discussion offers details about process writing and suggests how it can be wedded to technology.

Imagine yourself taking a graduate class at a local university. The professor enters and announces, "This evening you are going to complete an in-class writing assignment: Explain in lay terms what $e = mc^2$ means. You have 15 minutes to brainstorm, half an hour to write a draft, 15 minutes to discuss your draft with a peer, half an hour to revise your draft, 15 minutes for a formal peer critique, and half an hour to complete a final draft of your paper for a grade." The professor smiles and asks, "Any questions?" What would you feel at that point?

We'd feel trapped, and our first question would be "What does $e = mc^2$ mean?" As educated adults—teachers even!—we should know how to explain that famous formula to a lay audience, but we don't; we don't really know what the formula means. And that's a real problem if the professor expects us to be successful in completing the writing assignment.

Although we may be part of the problem because we didn't study our science well enough, the real problem is the professor's approach to the writing process. Even though she did follow part of a process approach, she failed to understand that a teacher can't use part of the process approach and expect the entire process to work. She has to use the entire process approach, which includes letting students write on things that they know about and are interested in (Calkins, 1990, 1986; Graves, 1994). This does not mean, by the way, that students cannot be challenged to learn things they don't know much about and perhaps don't find very interesting. Rather, it means students go through all stages of the writing process as outlined in Figure 5.2: (1) prewriting activities such as brainstorming, (2) writing a rough draft, (3) revising the draft, (4) peer reviewing the draft, (5) revising the draft based on peer reviewers' comment, (6) editing the draft, (7) proofreading the draft, and (8) publishing the completed work. It is important to note that although the stages of the writing process are presented in a linear fashion, in reality writing is a recursive process. For instance, a student may be at the editing stage of a draft and determine that the conclusion needs to be changed and thus will return to the prewriting stage.

Returning to the physics assignment, we've already stated that we don't know much about the formula $e = mc^2$ (and, to be honest, our interest level in that formula is not very high), but if we are aware of a reason why we should know it, we're willing to learn. We're willing to have someone explain the formula to us,

---

### How to Integrate Process Writing Into the Curriculum

- **Brainstorming:** helping students come up with ideas and narrowing those ideas so that students can write a focused paper
- **Drafting:** scheduling time for students to prepare multiple drafts of a project
- **Revising:** showing students how to shape their writing to meet the needs of particular audiences
- **Peer reviewing:** providing writers with real audiences (their peers) and teaching peers how to respond to the writers' writing, while not correcting grammar, mechanics, and spelling
- **Revising again:** showing students how to sort through peer response and use what's left to prepare a "final" draft
- **Editing:** teaching students how to help each other correct mistakes in grammar, mechanics, and spelling
- **Proofreading:** comparing the next to last draft with the "last" draft to catch errors that were supposed to be fixed but were not
- **Preparing presentation copy for readers:** printing the final copy so that it can be read, shared (or published), and evaluated

**Figure 5.2**  Stages of the Writing Process

answer our questions, work through our uninformed ideas about physics, and get us to a point where we can write sensibly about e = mc$^2$. Then we'd be on the road to fulfilling the professor's assignment. But until we have knowledge about something—not assumed knowledge, that is, the knowledge the professor assumes we have—we're not prepared to write the kind of paper she wants. In fact, even gaining knowledge about something includes forms of writing—lists of questions, notes from readings, thumbnail outlines—that make visible the issues we need to investigate and provide a record of the bits and pieces of knowledge we are gaining as we work toward fulfilling a writing assignment that can be useful to readers both inside and outside the classroom.

The writing process extends to the entire curriculum—from using writing to explore topics, to completing writing assignments for a variety of audiences (Fulwiler & Young, 1982). As teachers, then, we need to use writing throughout the literacy curriculum and with other literacy projects, such as keeping journals for reading assignments and constructing writing projects that fit with course content. Then we need to allow time for students to use the writing process to complete those assignments. Process writing, therefore, is not something just added on to the literacy curriculum; it must be integrated, or stirred, into the curriculum.

## Teacher as Facilitator

In Chapter 1 we discussed the constructivist classroom in which students take an active, not passive, role in their education. We emphasize again the need for such a classroom when we consider integrating writing into the curriculum. The focus of the constructivist classroom is student-centered learning, not teacher-dispensed knowledge. This does not mean that teachers should never present students with background material for a topic, suggest ideas for writing assignments, or respond to students' concerns about their success in meeting requirements for a writing assignment. Teachers should do all those and more, but they should perform their teaching role in the spirit of being a facilitator rather than an authority figure who provides answers to questions (Speck, 1998). In the facilitator role teachers have a great deal of control in shaping the classroom so that students feel comfortable exploring ideas. The teacher, as a facilitator, provides a flexible structure within which students learn about limits but are not merely passive receptors of knowledge. In fact, part of the answer to the question about how to integrate writing into the classroom has nothing to do with technology per se. Teachers can be facilitators without computers. As DeGroff (1990) notes, "It is teachers' beliefs about writing and writing with computers, rather than the technology itself, that makes a difference in how instruction proceeds" (p. 570). Labbo, Reinking, and McKenna (1995) also confirmed this finding in a case study on incorporating the computer into kindergarten—teachers used computers according to their philosophy about how children become literate. Integrating writing into the literacy curriculum has nothing to do with skill and drill exercises, whether used with or without a computer.

### Abandoning Skill and Drill

Writing is not a matter of identifying parts of speech, filling in the proper verb forms in isolated sentences or paragraphs, or identifying the subject and verb in a sentence by putting two lines under the subject and one line under the verb. Such an approach is counterproductive because the focus is on grammar, a technical aspect of language analysis. Indeed, a student may accurately identify subjects and verbs and still not be able to write something that makes sense to an audience. Likewise, a student may not be able to identify parts of speech and still be a good communicator in writing. Skill and drill exercises promote one sort of ability, and writing promotes another.

When language arts teachers truly understand the difference between those two types of abilities, they change the way they teach. They realize that using skill and drill exercises as a way to promote writing may be counterproductive to students' ability to write. Why? Because the time a teacher spends on skill and drill takes away from the time a teacher can spend helping students learn how to write. Of course, certain standardized tests, including state-mandated instruments, use multiple choice questions about writing as a way to test students' writing ability, so teachers might wonder why they shouldn't teach skill and drill to help students prepare for those tests. There are several good reasons.

Teachers should not confuse helping students prepare for such a test with actually helping students learn how to write. A multiple choice test on writing requires students to provide knowledge *about* writing; it does not ask students to demonstrate their writing ability. The scores from such a test reveal nothing about a student's ability to write. This type of test measures the ability to identify language features, and it is not at all clear that a student's ability to identify language features has much relationship to his or her ability to write serviceable prose. Skill and drill is not a productive way to integrate writing into the literacy curriculum, whether the skill and drill takes the form of a pencil and paper test or a computer test.

### Reasons for Integrating Computers Into the Writing Curriculum

If skill and drill should be discarded, how can teachers incorporate computers into the mentoring process regarding writing? We will answer that question after we address teachers' possible objections to joining computers and writing. After all, if teachers don't understand why computers should be integrated into the writing curriculum, then they probably won't see any sense in committing themselves to such integration. For instance, a teacher might ask, "Why must I use technology to infuse writing into my classroom? I really don't have time enough to do what I'm supposed to do without getting involved in technology."

The standard answer to that question is this: "Everything is moving toward computers. Computers already have made a great impact on our lives, and that impact will only increase in the years ahead." This answer, which reflects common wisdom, is insufficient because it assumes that simply because something is, people ought to accept it. Computers are only a tool. They are not a panacea, even if they have become well entrenched in today's world. We suggest four practical reasons why computers are useful in integrating writing into the language arts classroom.

1.  *Computers allow flexibility.* The teacher can encourage students to take chances with their writing because the computer allows so much flexibility in deleting, moving, and correcting text (Macarthur, 1988).

2.  *Computers make revising easier.* Notice we didn't say *easy.* Revising is hard work, but with the computer it is easier than with a typewriter or a pencil and paper. Students don't have to take the intermediate step of writing something out before going to the keyboard. And once they have a document in a file, they can revise it—correcting misspellings, fixing a sentence that doesn't sound right, changing margins, cutting, pasting—without having to retype the entire document.

3.  *Computers widen the concept of audience.* Traditionally, students have written for teachers. Of course teachers are good audiences, but we are only one type of audience; students will have to write for various types of audiences throughout their lives, so we need to provide them with opportunities to write for authentic purposes (Butcheri & Hammond, 1994; Maring, Wiseman, & Myers, 1997; Smede, 1995; Smith, 1995). This means that students need to learn how to write for the audiences they will encounter after their schooling is complete: parents, colleagues, subordinates, bosses, friends, clients, the general public. According to many researchers (Atwell, 1998; Calkins, 1986; Cohen & Riel, 1989; Graves, 1994), when real audiences are involved students' writing has greater depth because they pay closer attention to content, detail, and clarity. Thus, writing assignments should target a variety of audiences. Also, if computers are linked to the Internet, students have lots of opportunities to write for all kinds of audiences, especially using e-mail (e.g., Sullivan, 1998).

4.  *Computers raise the stakes on what it means to produce professional-looking documents.* Computers help you show students what a professional document looks like. When kindergarten students construct books using the computer, they develop models of professional documents that can be reinforced throughout their schooling. Part of our job as teachers is to prepare students to be successful employees and citizens, and one aspect of that preparation is to learn that how a document looks has an impact—negative or positive—on the way others read it. Perception is important. After all, even in the elementary grades a scrawled assignment generally gets a lower grade than a cleanly typed copy of the same assignment (Fuller, 1988; Soloff, 1973).

These four reasons may not satisfy teachers who think they won't be able to learn how to use a computer. We want to allay such concerns and fears. Computers are not that hard to learn about. They do take time (a precious commodity for teachers), and anyone can get irritated when he or she "wastes" time because of a computer glitch that wasn't his or her fault—such as a power failure just when you go to back up a file. But a teacher doesn't have to be able to explain $e = mc^2$ to learn about computers. And we haven't met anyone yet who regretted learning about them, because they really do expand your horizons. For instance, using the World Wide Web adds a new dimension to your personal world of information, and e-mail connects you to this global community instantaneously.

# INTEGRATING COMPUTERS INTO THE WRITING CURRICULUM

Once teachers realize how influential computers can be in helping their students use writing to learn and to communicate with audiences, they will want to use computers in the classrooms. The question then becomes, "How can I use computers effectively to help my students write?" The first step is to assess your resources. Besides yourself and the support from school administrators—including the computer(s) you have access to in school—there are two other sources of support: your students and their parents. Let's begin by assuming that you have a one-computer classroom, including a printer. How can you effectively use your limited access to technology?

## *The One-Computer Classroom*

You need to recognize that you can't have every student go through every step of the writing process for every writing project on the computer. You have to think strategically about what parts of the writing process for which projects you can use the computer. Figure 5.3 outlines one way to use the lone computer for various stages of the writing process. Select parts of the writing process for any project that you want the students to do on the computer, and make use of human resources—students and parents—to help. For instance, group students so that they can help each other (Copeland & Lomax, 1988).

### Grouping Students

We recommend that you begin by grouping students in pairs. You can do this by matching a stronger and weaker student so that the stronger student helps the weaker one. If you don't feel comfortable matching students that way, you can form pairs based on other criteria—friends, gender, similar or dissimilar interests, expertise with computers. The value of such collaborative work is that the students help each other. If one student is more advanced in computer skills than the partner, the more advanced one can teach the partner how to delete or insert text. You can also use parents as a resource. Perhaps they can come to class and give individual or group tutorials on keyboarding (for younger students) or using desktop publishing functions to create pamphlets with graphics (for older students). You can also do cross-age pairing—a younger student with an older one (Sassi, 1990; Zukowski, 1997). In short, make the most of all your resources even when you have very limited access to technology resources. As is true with all group work, students should be assigned roles that rotate on a regular basis. In addition, clear rules for working together should be established and discussed.

**Brainstorming**

- The whole class watches the computer monitor as the teacher or a student types the ideas the class is brainstorming. The list of brainstorming ideas can be printed, with copies distributed to each student. Students can work in groups or individually to select a topic. Students begin a first draft by either writing it out or drafting at the computer.

**Writing and Revising**

- Individually or in groups (if the paper is a collaborative paper) students can begin to type the written draft into the computer or draft at the computer. For instance, as soon as a person or group is ready to type, that person or group may spend 10 minutes on the computer. While individuals or groups are waiting to use the computer, the teacher can involve them in a related activity, such as reading a selection that fits with the topic the class is writing about.

- After a student or group of students uses their 10 minutes, they print their draft and begin rewriting.

- Once students have revised their draft, they have another 10 minutes to make the changes on the computer.

- If time permits the teacher can take the students through another cycle of revision.

**Reviewing**

- Then, the students peer review each other's drafts.

**Editing and Proofreading**

- On the basis of the peer reviews, the students have time to consider what needs to be changed in the draft; they have 15 minutes to make those changes on the computer.

- The final draft is edited by another student or a parent who has good editing skills, proofread by the author(s), and corrected at the computer before it is printed out and submitted to the teacher for evaluation.

**Figure 5.3**  One Way to Integrate the One-Computer Classroom Into the Writing Process

## Scheduling Computer Time

Develop a rotation schedule so that students have a guaranteed time on the computer. This is crucial in the one-computer classroom because there is already limited computer integration to a particular stage of the writing process for a particular project. Thus, if every student group is going to have sufficient time to use the computer for keyboarding a handwritten draft during one week, it is important to determine how much time the students need, develop a schedule, and stick to it.

Let's say that you are starting a collaborative writing project. You talk about the project with the students so that they understand what you're expecting. You show them a rubric that you and they will use to evaluate the project, and you ask them if they believe the rubric needs to be modified for this assignment. You set up a schedule for each group to use the computer to keyboard a rough draft, revise it once, and edit it. If the drafting stage takes a week and there are six groups of four in the class and each group should have 15 minutes on the computer each week, you need to schedule time for the groups. Some days you may want to schedule two 15-minute sessions. Other days you may want to schedule no sessions. Or you may want to schedule 30-minute sessions during the revising stage.

While one group is at the computer, the rest of the class should be working on their drafts. They can peer critique another group's draft or work as a group to revise their draft in preparation for using the classroom computer. You may want to schedule individual group conferences about the draft the group members are developing. You need to determine how much time the assignment will take, how long each part of the writing process will be, and how to keep every group involved in the writing process whether that group is actually using the classroom computer or waiting to use it.

## *The Multi-Computer Classroom That Is Not Networked*

The non-networked, multi-computer classroom is similar to the single-computer classroom, with the advantage that the activities of the single-computer classroom can be replicated simultaneously. Thus, students complete the writing process more quickly. Figure 5.4 provides an example of how a fifth-grade teacher could have her class complete a writing project in one week.

---

**Monday:** As a class, the students brainstorm while the teacher keyboards the brainstorming ideas so that everyone can see what is typed on the monitor. Alternatively, students could brainstorm, web, read, search the Internet, interview others, and so forth to collect information and get ready to write.

**Tuesday:** The teacher divides the class into four groups, one group at each of the four computers. Each group has 30 minutes to prepare a draft. Then each group has 30 minutes to review the draft and revise it.

**Wednesday:** The groups have 30 minutes to make revisions to the draft on the computer, print out a new draft, and pair off (group 1 with group 2) to peer review the drafts.

**Thursday:** The groups have 30 minutes to make revisions to their drafts based on peer reviews, print a new draft, and edit it.

**Friday:** The groups make the edited revisions and compare (proofread) the edited draft with the new draft to ensure that all the changes have been made, make any changes that weren't made earlier, and print a final copy to be read to the class or published and then turned in to the teacher.

---

**Figure 5.4**  A One-Week Writing Project

### *A Networked Computer Classroom/Lab*

The distinction between a multi-computer classroom and a computer classroom/lab is that the computers in the latter are networked; they are linked to each other electronically so that all students can communicate with each other. Thus, students can send their drafts via computer to a peer in the class, and the peer can critique the draft on the computer and send the critiqued draft back to the author. In addition, students can communicate via the Internet with other classes in the same building, across town, or in another state.

One of the significant advantages of networked computers is that students can communicate with each other electronically. As the computer becomes increasingly essential to the writing process, students spend more time not only using it to write but also working through the other stages of the writing process on it (Hoot & Silver, 1988; Le, 1989; Mageau, 1992; Montague, 1990). Networking enables students to work simultaneously on a project and communicate in the networked environment (Anderson-Inman, Knox-Quinn, & Tromba, 1996). We'll talk more about networking and writing projects in Chapter 6 on publishing.

### *Internet Access*

Internet access increases yet again the possibilities for integrating technology into the writing process by providing various audiences for students' work. The Internet offers two basic resources for student writers: (1) audiences (e.g., students can publish their work on the Internet; see Chapter 6 on publishing); and (2) writing resources (e.g., students can get information from the Internet for their writing projects; visit Kids Web, Kids on Campus, EdWeb, etc.).

## COMPUTER CLASSROOM EXAMPLES

Fortunately, as teachers are more frequently using the computer as a tool to teach literacy (Leu, 1997; Rose & Meyer, 1994), more of their stories are being published (Holland, 1996; Iannone, 1998; Leu & Leu, 1997; Stuhlmann, 1996). Some of the following proven classroom examples are taken from the literature. Each example provides opportunities for students to engage in process writing.

### *Holiday Stories*

**Grade Level:**  Adaptable for K–8

**Objective:**  Students will learn about diversity, gain experience in peer review and getting along with others, learn more about the writing process, and get more practice writing.

**Time:**  1 week

**Problem to Be Solved:**  Your school has decided to create a time capsule filled with information about today's society, and your class has been assigned to write and publish stories about their favorite holidays using StoryBook Weaver Deluxe CD-ROM. What kinds of stories can you create?

**Materials:**  Paper
Pencil
Computer
Color printer
StoryBook Weaver Deluxe CD-ROM
Projection device

**Steps:**

1. Engage students in a discussion of holidays. Ask students to define a holiday and give examples. Ask students to describe favorite holidays and customs.
2. In a whole group setting, present StoryBook Weaver Deluxe to the students. This works best using a large television screen as a projection device.
3. Demonstrate starting a new file, opening a file, printing, and quitting the CD.
4. Demonstrate word processing in a new file. Ask for student volunteers. Model adding graphics to a completed (typed) file. Use student volunteers to add backgrounds, music, people, and objects.
5. Have the students begin writing about their favorite holiday. Tell the students that once a rough draft is completed, the story will be published using StoryBook Weaver Deluxe.
6. Use peer conferences and one formal teacher conference to edit the rough drafts.
7. Assign computer time for students to create their holiday essays using the CD. Color print each completed product.
8. Have students take their stories home for parents, siblings, and friends to read.

**Assessment:**  How effectively did students describe their favorite holiday and custom? Have they effectively analyzed other students work?

## COMPUTER CLASSROOM EXAMPLES (CONTINUED)

### *The Dyadic Paper*

**Grade Level:**   5–8

**Objective:**   The student will think critically about one side of an issue and express the position clearly. The student will demonstrate how e-mail can be used to send text. Students will learn to work as a team.

**Time:**   1 week

**Problem to Be Solved:**   Carol, a lawyer, needs help demonstrating both sides of an issue. To help Carol, two students will take opposing positions on a topic and write one paper on that topic.

**Materials:**   Computer

**Steps:**
1. The dyadic paper may be an opinion paper in which students present opposing opinions without research to back up their claims, or the paper may include research (conducted using the World Wide Web). The successful paper represents both sides of an issue equally well. A paper in which one side "wins" is an unsuccessful paper.

2. The format for the paper may vary. It could be a dialogue, a question and answer interview, a play in which characters express viewpoints, or a formal report in which the pro (or con) side presents its case and then the con (or pro) side presents its case.

3. If students use two different computers to write their parts of the paper and then combine the parts to revise and edit the final draft, they will need to know how to transfer text from one computer to another. This could be an opportunity to show how e-mail can be used to send text to another person.

**Assessment:**   Are both sides of the issue expressed equally and completely? Did the students demonstrate they could work well in a team?

### *Electronic Traveling Journal*

**Grade Level:**   Adaptable for 1–8

**Objective:**   Students will communicate and describe their thoughts to an audience unfamiliar with your class environment. Students learn to use a WebBoard. (A WebBoard is a software package, such as WebCT or Web in a Box, that allows for Web-based chat, or real-time conversation on the Internet. It is a place to ask questions, get information, explore problems and share successes. It is a great place to have focused conversations around one topic. It can also serve as a location to post journals, assignments, or tests.)

## COMPUTER CLASSROOM EXAMPLES (CONTINUED)

### *Electronic Traveling Journal (Continued)*

**Time:** One day for each student

**Problem To Be Solved:** Several students in another country are interested in your response to activities in the classroom, so they asked you to keep a traveling journal. A traveling journal offers an opportunity to write personal reactions to a day in the classroom. The journal "travels" from person to person, providing a written history of students' perceptions of the class.

**Materials:** Word processor
Notebook to store daily entries

**Steps:**
1. At the end of each day, one student is responsible for word processing a traveling journal entry for that day.
2. To begin class the next day, the student reads the journal entry aloud. The traveling journal also can be used with a Webboard so that the other students in the class can read an entry and respond electronically to it.

**Assessment:** Did the students clearly describe their perception of the class?

## TECHNO-TEACHER TIPS

### Scheduling

Usually there are more students in a classroom than the number of available computers. This means that computer time should be scheduled and monitored to ensure that all students receive adequate time to complete their projects. Develop a rotation schedule that allows six to eight students to use the computer in one day. Require that all students sign a time log when using the computers. Use a kitchen timer to remind students that their allotted time is over.

### One-Computer Classroom

With only one computer available to a large number of students, try group writing or buddy writing to reduce the time limitations. As students collaborate to compose and publish their work, their writing and keyboarding strategies will improve as they learn from one another.

**Software**

Many excellent software programs have been developed for writing and publishing. These can enhance the writing process with special features such as on-screen spell check, word count, thesaurus, clipart, and graphics. It is not essential, however, to purchase specialized software titles because most computers already have a basic word processing program developed especially for writing.

## FREQUENTLY ASKED QUESTIONS

1. **My students are already engaged in process writing and publishing without the use of technology. Will using computers lengthen this process and add to their responsibilities?**

   Yes and no. Initially it will lengthen the processes because students will find handwriting quicker than word processing. But eventually it will actually shorten writing time. As students learn to compose directly onto a word processor, the need for a handwritten draft is eliminated. The teacher or peers can edit drafts on-screen. Several students can edit a single draft by printing multiple copies. With practice, students (and teachers) can learn to integrate computers into the entire writing process, rather than as the final step.

2. **Should every writing assignment employ the entire writing process?**

   No. Students should be allowed, at times, to choose the piece of writing they would like to revise, edit, and publish. To take every writing assignment through the process would be too time consuming. Some writing assignments, such as reflective journals, are not appropriate for the writing process.

3. **Can this be part of a portfolio assessment?**

   Yes. Some assignments can have a due date that might read, "This writing assignment should be in your portfolio by such-and-such date." The benefit? The teacher isn't swamped all at once with grading papers.

## REFERENCES

Anderson-Inman, L., Knox-Quinn, C., & Tromba, P. (1996). Synchronous writing environments: Real-time interaction in cyberspace. *Journal of Adolescent & Adult Literacy, 40* (2), 134–138.

Atwell, N. (1998). *In the middle: New understanding about writing, reading, and learning* (2nd ed.). Portsmouth, NH: Boynton/Cook.

Butcheri, J., & Hammond, J. J. (1994). Authentic writing makes the difference. *Journal of Reading, 38* (3), 228–229.

Calkins, L. (1986). *The art of teaching writing.* Portsmouth, NH: Heinemann.

Calkins, L. (1990). *Living between the lines.* Portsmouth, NH: Heinemann.

Cohen, M., & Riel, M. (1989). The effects of distant audiences on students' writing. *American Educational Research Journal, 26* (2), 143–159.

Copeland, J. S., & Lomax, E. D. (1988). Building effective student writing groups. In J. Golub (Ed.), *Focus on collaborative learning: Classroom practices in teaching English* (pp. 99–104). Urbana, IL: National Council of Teachers of English.

DeGroff, L. (1990). Is there a place for computers in whole language classrooms? *The Reading Teacher,* 568–572.

Forman, J. (Ed.). (1992). *New visions of collaborative writing.* Portsmouth, NH: Boynton/Cook.

Fuller, D. (1988). A curious case of our responding habits: What do we respond to and why? *Journal of Advanced Composition, 8,* 88–96.

Fulwiler, T., & Young, A. (Eds.). (1982). *Language connections: Writing and reading across the curriculum.* Urbana, IL: National Council of Teachers of English.

Galegher, J., Kraut, R. E., & Egido, C. (Eds.). (1990). *Intellectual teamwork: Social and technological foundations of cooperative work.* Hillsdale, NJ: Lawrence Erlbaum.

Graves, D. H. (1994). *A fresh look at writing.* Portsmouth, NH: Heinemann.

Holland, H. (1996). Way past word processing. *Electronic Learning, 22,* 24–26.

Hoot, J. L., & Silvern, S. B. (Eds.). (1988). *Writing with computers in the early grades.* New York: Teachers College Press.

Iannone, P. (1998). Just beyond the horizon: Writing-centered literacy activities for traditional and electronic contexts. *The Reading Teacher, 51* (5), 438–443.

Labbo, L., Reinking, D., & McKenna, M. (1995). Incorporating the computer into kindergarten: A case study. *Perspectives on literacy research and practice, forty-fourth yearbook of the National Reading Conference,* 459–465.

Le, Thao. (1989). Computers as partners in writing: A linguistic perspective. *Journal of Reading, 32* (7), 606–610.

Leu, D. (1997). Caity's question: Literacy as deixis on the Internet. *The Reading Teacher, 51* (1), 62–67.

Leu, D., & Leu, D. (1997). *Teaching with the Internet: Lessons from the classroom.* Norwood, MA: Christopher-Gordon.

Macarthur, C. (1988). The impact of computers on the writing process. *Exceptional Children, 54* (6), 536–542.

Mageau, T. (1992). When technology meets process writing. *Electronic Learning, 31,* 32–34.

Maring, G. H., Wiseman, B. J., & Myers, K. S. (1997). Using the World Wide Web to build learning communities: Writing for genuine purposes. *Journal of Adolescent and Adult Literacy, 41* (3), 196–207.

Montague, M. (1990). Computers and writing process instruction. *Computers in the Schools, 7* (3), 5–20.

Montague, M., & Fonseca, F. (1993). Using computers to improve storywriting. In J. J. Hirschbuhl (Ed.), *Computers in education* (pp. 80–83). Guilford, CT: Dushkin.

Odell, L., & Goswani, D. (Eds.). (1985). *Writing in nonacademic settings.* New York: Guilford Press.

Rose, D. H., & Meyer, A. (1994). The role of technology in language arts instruction. *Language Arts, 71* (4), 290–294.

Sassi, A. (1990). The synergy of cross-age tutoring: A catalyst for computer use. *The Computing Teacher, 17,* (5), 9–11.

Shen, V. T. (1996). The role of hypertext as an interactional medium among fifth-grade students. In D. J. Leu, C. K. Kinzer, & K. A. Hinchman (Eds.), *Literacies for the 21st century: Research and practice* (pp. 484–499). Chicago: National Reading Conference.

Smede, S. D. (1995). Flyfishing, portfolios, and authentic writing. *English Journal, 84* (2) 92–94.

Smith, C. (1995). Grandparent pen pals: Authentic writing at work. *Teaching PreK–8, 25* (8), 40–41.

Soloff, S. (1973). The effect of non-content factors on the grading of essays. *Graduate Research in Education and Related Disciplines, 6* (2), 44–54.

Speck, B. W. (1998). The teacher's role in the pluralistic classroom. *Perspectives, 28* (1), 19–43.

Spilka, R. (Ed.). (1993). *Writing in the workplace: New research perspectives.* Carbondale and Edwardsville: Southern Illinois University Press.

Stuhlmann, J. (1996). Whole-language strategies for integrating technology into language arts. *Proceedings of the annual National Educational Computing Conference,* Minneapolis, Minnesota. (ERIC Document Reproduction Service No. ED 398 895)

Sullivan, J. (1998). The electronic journal: Combining literacy and technology. *The Reading Teacher, 52* (1), 90–93.

Zukowski, V. (1997). Teeter-totters and tandem bikes: A glimpse into the world of cross-age tutors. *Teaching and Change, 5* (1), 71–91.

## CHAPTER 6

# USING ELECTRONIC TECHNOLOGY TO PUBLISH STUDENTS' WRITING

Bill, a student in Miss Harmon's fifth-grade class, has just talked with Group 1, the Harmonizers, about their contributions to the class book of poetry. Just before he leaves, Jamal asks, "So what you're saying is that we—our group—have to get all our poems on one disk to you by this Friday?"

"That's right," Bill responds, adding, "I just want one disk, rather than trying to fiddle with 17 disks. One disk per group. That makes it easier for my group, because we have to make a draft copy of the entire book for peer review."

"But what if the word processing program I'm using at home doesn't fit the one the rest of the group is using?" Sarah asks, with some concern in her voice.

"Sarah," Bill responds, "your word processor will probably let you 'save as' so that you can save your work in the program the rest of the group is using. By the way, Barbara," Bill says, turning to Group 1's leader, "you remember that the disk you give me should be in Word for Windows 6.0 or later?"

"We've got everything taken care of," Barbara notes, adding, "I'll help Sarah."

"Any other questions?" Bill waits a moment, and seeing that Barbara has things under control, says, "OK, I'll look for your disk this Friday."

Bill then moves to Group 2, the Poe Poets, to confirm the delivery of their disk in the proper format on Friday.

# EXPLORING CLASSROOM PUBLISHING

In the scenario you've just read, the time Bill spent with Group 1 was devoted to one step in planning a class publication. No writing was produced. No instruction on how to write was given. Yet the time students spend in planning classroom publications is critical to the success of those publications. Indeed, the amount of planning that is needed to produce a group publication—especially if the students take responsibility for the publication—is an added dimension to the writing process.

In this chapter we provide a snapshot of a classroom publishing activity, explain why you should incorporate classroom publishing activities into your literacy curriculum, give instructions on how to use a variety of classroom publishing activities, and discuss issues associated with those activities.

## COMPUTER CLASSROOM SNAPSHOT

### Context

My name is John Bauer, and I'm a doctoral student and graduate assistant at the University of Memphis (UM). I was part of a team-teaching research project involving a sixth-grade class at Campus Elementary School, which is operated under the auspices of the university's College of Education, and a senior-level college class. The sixth-grade class was taught by Judith Thomson, who had agreed to allow her class to become the "students" of UM seniors about to graduate into the teaching profession. The college class was taught by Professor Becky Anderson, who also wrote the syllabus, and myself. A requirement for the college seniors was that they spend 10 hours in an elementary school setting. The college class, numbering some 28 students, divided itself into seven groups of four, and the 22 sixth graders were assigned as equally as possible to these groups. Each college group, then, became the collective "teachers" of their younger counterparts.

In the abstract, the goal for both sets of students was to learn how computer technology can be an indispensable tool for teaching/learning content literacy: the college students on how to apply such techniques in future classes; the sixth graders on how to use the technology to do research, how to read data, and how to write results.

### What I Did and Why

It was done this way: Each group was to research a topic and to write a chapter for inclusion in a book entitled *A Young Person's Guide to the City of Memphis*. The book features chapters on history, geography, famous personalities, sports, tourism, and entertainment. For a one-hour time slot each week, the sixth graders met with their new sets of teachers, who were armed with lesson plans designed to guide activities in the most productive manner. After initial brainstorming and planning sessions, the groups did their field research, which for the most part consisted of accessing Internet sites using the university's computer labs. Further computer use entailed correspondence via e-mail between group members during the week.

The end product notwithstanding, the weekly hour each class spent with each other was the critical period for the project. Could the seniors get the kids to work? Would they all get along? Would there be an even division of responsibilities? Would lesson plans be conscientiously prepared so that members knew where they were headed? Could sixth graders maintain a focus serious enough to be important contributing members? We observed the group dynamic closely and arrived at a resounding yes for an answer. The college seniors enjoyed working with the kids immensely, it being the one hour they felt they were gaining good, hands-on field experience working with classroom kids. For the sixth graders, they saw the hour as a break from the norm, a chance to enter the new and lofty realm of the university setting, something they could be proud of in front of peers and family. In addition, they used their youthful enthusiasm to attack computer problems and were excited that their work might be part of a published book. Observing this whole group dynamic at work was for myself an unparalleled educational experience. The entire exercise was stretching the outer limits of content literacy in terms of a constructivist design in a real-world setting. What the sixth graders learned was clear: how to work as a team to set goals, perform tasks, and produce a viable end product in a given period of time. They learned the value of Internet technology as a resource tool, and that e-mail communication can be used as valuable links to team members.

### What I Learned

The college learning coefficient was based more on what effort and enthusiasm the college seniors put into the project. It was, of course, a class assignment, and some were typically not flexible enough to succeed in a nontraditional setting such as this, and thus they allowed stronger team members to take charge. What was clear was that they all learned that there are options in terms of teaching literacy and technology should they be predisposed to initiate similar techniques as new elementary school teachers. As I look back on the class, I see certain important restrictions on this particular model, but endless possibilities as well. To begin with, requisite to the design is the location of a college conveniently close to an upper elementary or middle school, since busing over long distances poses logistical difficulties. Second, up-front cooperation between the college and school administrators, teachers, and most likely the school board may be hard to establish but is nonetheless an absolute necessity. Third, the grade school teacher must be thoroughly involved in and in favor of the project. It is possible to have a school close by whose teachers are reluctant to participate. Fourth, effective motivational talks to both sets of students are needed at the onset so that they can "buy into" the program and make it work. Other factors that may affect outcomes are availability of labs, work areas for groups, and student absenteeism.

On the other hand, the most important element of the model is that it can be put to use in a grade school class without the guidance of a college class. Nothing prevents, say, a fifth- or sixth-grade teacher from accomplishing the same goals in his or her own school setting. Most schools today are equipped with adequate lab facilities to make it happen. In this case, however, the work load in terms of planning and execution falls entirely upon the classroom teacher—not an undaunting task, but one that can be a completely rewarding experience. Even the "publishing" of a book using a school copier can involve students at divergent learning levels, and topics can be tailored to a more localized level than the model's use of a citywide design.

The whole experience of working with the class broadened my outlook on educational possibilities. The flexible nature of the concept allows for success within different parameters. One can pick and choose different elements of the design to fit a number of disparate circumstances. In any case, the use of Internet research remains the important constant, and this is what drives the design and makes it particularly relevant as schools enter the technological millennium.

# WHY USE CLASSROOM PUBLISHING?

In this chapter, we discuss two types of classroom publishing, traditional and electronic, although both types use electronic media. By *traditional publishing* we mean the production of paper products of students' work, emulating traditional book and journal publishing. By *electronic publishing* we mean that students make their work available in electronic form, perhaps even creating a Website so that their work is published on the Internet. Before discussing each type of publishing, we provide reasons why classroom publishing is a useful pedagogical tool.

The major purposes for publishing students' writing are to help students go through the entire writing process and to provide audiences for student writing. In Chapter 5, we discussed the writing process, noting that the process culminates in a written product. Too often, however, students prepare an individual "final" draft for grading, a draft that has yet to undergo the publishing process. That is, either students do not have the opportunity for their individual works to go through the publishing process, or students do not have the experience of compiling their works into a cohesive unit, such as a book or magazine. Working with others to publish an individual text and creating a book or magazine made up of peers' texts can give students insights into the entire process of text production that they do not get when they prepare an individual paper.

In particular, literature on collaborative writing promotes both co-authored works (Comstock, 1993; Long & Bulgarella, 1985; McEachern, 1986; Tsujimoto, 1988; Yanushefski, 1988) and writing projects that include collaborative production of a text composed of students' individual texts (Angeletti, 1993; Doolittle, 1991; Marzano, 1990; Music, 1988; Paeth, 1996; Vincent, 1993). Participation in the development of a composite text mirrors the types of writing activities students will do when they leave school and become employed. In fact, collaborative writing, including the production of books or magazines of students' writing, is not limited to the workplace. Increasingly in higher education, students are asked to participate in collaborative groups to prepare written products, such as reports for engineering classes and research papers for classes in the social sciences, so when K–8 teachers introduce their students to collaborative writing projects, including collaborative construction of books and magazines, they are preparing their students for greater success not only in business and industry but also in future educational endeavors.

In addition, a published book or magazine provides a tangible product that can attract a wider audience beyond the students' classmates and teacher. For instance, parents, grandparents, siblings, friends outside of school, and a host of other people can have access to the final draft of any given project, instead of the writing only their child, sibling, or friend did. Why is it important to broaden the scope of audiences for students' writing? For one thing, a major purpose of writing is to communicate with others; and for writing aimed at a general audience, the more readers the better. In addition, the possibility of more feedback (including praise) is increased when more readers have the opportunity to experience the students' writing. As writers receive more reader responses, such feedback has the potential to teach the value of writing to audiences. In fact, authentic reader responses may have much greater value than classroom lectures.

Of course, the assumption is that readers will respond in helpful ways. Readers, especially those with a filial relationship to the writer, may heap more praise on the writer than the finished text merits. Although the literature on praising writers strongly promotes such cheerleading (Dragga, 1988; Zak, 1990), and although affirmative responses to writers can be a powerful motivater for writing again, it is important to note that helpful response includes more than praise. As a teacher, therefore, you not only have to model a range of responses to students' writing but you also have to teach students how to respond to peers' writing so that the writer wants to write again, but even better next time. See Figure 6.1 for a process by which to teach successful response to writing.

Teaching readers how to help writers improve their work is particularly important when teachers use the publishing process in their classes because the publication of student work raises the ante on quality. When a book or magazine is available for those outside the classroom to read, the quality of learning and teaching becomes public in ways that writing limited to the classroom is not. Thus, teachers have an obligation to prepare students for the higher stakes involved in giving wider audiences access to their written products.

## TRADITIONAL CLASSROOM PUBLISHING

The traditional publishing forms include books, newspapers, newsletters, and brochures. You can use these traditional publishing forms for a variety of projects. For instance, let's talk about using books in the classroom. Your students may be studying history, and you decide to have them interview a family member who grew up at least 30 years ago. You lead the class in brainstorming interview questions (e.g., Where did you live? What was your school like? How much did a loaf of bread or a gallon of milk cost? What did you do for recreation?). Depending on

1. Create effective assignments so that students know what audiences they are expected to address. Effective response depends on identifying the audience for a given piece of writing.

2. Ask students to analyze audiences for their writing. For instance, you can prompt students to analyze their audiences by saying, "Who would want to read what you are writing?" "What kind of people might be interested in your topic?" "How old would a person need to be to understand what you are writing about?" "What would a person need to know in order to understand what you are describing?"

3. Model response by asking questions and making statements. When responding to students' writing in writing groups or in student-teacher conferences, you can say, "I'm confused. Why did the toy bear lose his ear?" "I'm interested in knowing more about why Simon decided to leave home." "Would your audience understand what you're writing about when you use computer terms?"

4. Train students in ways of responding effectively. Modeling effective response is important, but students also need guidelines such as, "The purpose of responding to your peer's writing is to help the peer revise that writing. This means that you *do not* want to argue with your peer. For instance, you do not want to say, 'I don't understand this, and you're a bad writer.' Rather, you want to say, 'I don't understand this and here is why I don't understand it.' Whether the peer takes your suggestions or not is a decision the peer has to make. Your also *do not* want to say, 'Wonderful' or 'Terrible!' Neither one of those helps a person revise. What exactly was wonderful? What exactly in the writing caused you to think it was terrible? Tell the writer what the problem is without telling the writer that his or her writing is terrible. You *do* want to say what you like about the writing and why you like it and what could help the writing become stronger (what needs to be added or deleted). In short, *do* say positive things (including what could help the writer improve the piece of writing) in a positive way, and *do not* say negative things in a negative way. Focus on the writing, not the writer."

5. Construct critique sheets that reinforce the instructions you give students. A critique sheet could ask students to identify the main point of a piece of writing (the thesis); to point out a particularly strong image or metaphor; to suggest two ways to make the piece of writing stronger; to cite one or two errors in grammar, mechanics, or spelling; to identify the audience(s) for the piece of writing; and so on.

6. Determine which group of students in the class does a good job of critiquing, and ask them to model their critiquing in front of the class. Alternatively, you could ask a student to volunteer to have you critique his or her writing in front of the entire class.

7. Conduct student-teacher conferences—even mini-conferences during class—and model effective response.

8. Ask students to critique a piece of your writing.

9. Critique a piece of writing by putting it on a transparency and using an overhead projector or computer monitor; ask the entire class to determine (1) the main point of the writing, (2) gaps the writer has left for the audience to fill, (3) other information readers might want to know, (4) errors that might distract readers, and (5) particularly pleasing aspects of the writing. If you can, use a computer instead of an overhead projector—it gives you more options to demonstrate editing techniques.

10. When you make responses on students' writing, ask questions and make statements. Do not use code words (e.g., "awk," "frag") to cite problems in students' writing. Rather, indicate why you think something in the writing is awkward ("Do you mean to say that all the animals jumped over one another at one time?") or why something is an error ("Where is the verb in this sentence?").

**Figure 6.1** Process for Teaching Successful Response to Writing

the age of the students, you or one of the students can use the word processor to type the final questions and make a copy for each student to use for the interviews. Each student can conduct the interview (and send a thank-you note to the interviewee), write a draft of the results (the class would need to determine the format for the results), and go through the writing process of revising, peer reviewing, revising, and editing, to produce a "final" copy. A group of students can compile the final copy into a book.

## Compatible Software

Clearly, a great deal of planning has to be included in the entire process. For instance, the students need to ensure at the outset that they are using compatible software. If one student is using a Macintosh and another is using an IBM, problems may arise when the student using the Macintosh tries to read the IBM disk on the Macintosh. How do you determine whether students are using compatible software?

First, students can find out whether they have the **Save As** capacity on their computers. Can the student who uses a Macintosh **Save As** save a file so that an IBM can read the file? Sometimes, saving a Macintosh document to an IBM disk is all that is needed to make the Macintosh file readable on an IBM machine.

Second, students should know that later versions of a particular word processing package read files created by earlier versions of the same package. Thus, Word for Windows 7.0 will read documents created in Word for Windows 6.0. However, the reverse is not the case. Word for Windows 6.0 will not read a document produced using Word for Windows 7.0.

Third, students may have to do a test run to determine whether their files are compatible. Students can take an existing document or create a paragraph of prose and find out whether one program will be able to read the files from another program. If the files are not compatible, the students may have to make arrangements to use the same word processing program.

Compatibility is an important issue that should be resolved early in the publishing process. It can be extremely frustrating to produce a "final" draft of a document that is ready to be integrated into a book and then find that the program being used to create the book will not read the disk containing the final draft.

## Style and Format

Putting the book together requires even more up-front planning. Not only should students determine at the outset whether their files will be compatible, but they also should resolve a variety of issues regarding style and format. For instance, what fonts should be used? You might explain to students that using more than one or two fonts is not a good idea because too much variety in type is distracting to readers. If students want to produce documents with variety, they can use the bold, italics, and roman styles of a particular font. In addition, students can use rules (thin lines used either as ornaments, such as the rules at the top of a maga-zine page, or as dividers, such as the rule that separates text), centering, bullets, and a variety of tables and figures to enliven a document and enhance its readabil-ity. (Tables have columns and rows; figures don't. Charts, pictures, and graphs are figures.)

However, you should caution students not to use various word processing func-tions simply for the sake of using them. The purpose of publishing a document is to attract a wider audience than the unpublished document would, so issues of read-ability are extremely important. Jazzing up a book just because you can is one sure way to produce a gawdy and ostentatious publication, one that may unintentionally amuse and confuse audiences. You might be interested in learning more about doc-ument design so that you can provide students with principles for creating effective documents (Baird, McDonald, Pittman, & Turnbull, 1993).

## The Publication Committee

When using classroom publications, it is a good idea to create a publication com-mittee to plan much of the publishing process. We often use the quiz in Figure 6.2 as a lighthearted way to single out those who might have some propensity for publishing. The three or four people with the highest number of True answers to the quiz become members of the publication committee. The purpose of the com-mittee is to work with the class to create instructions on how to plan and put together the publication. Figure 6.3 is an example of the type of instructions the publication committee might produce.

One major purpose of the instructions the publication committee produces is to make more efficient the job of those who will actually produce the book. For example, those who put all the student contributions together do not need to change all the headings in each interview to a particular font style. Each contribu-

---

1. I would rather read than eat.
2. I like to roll words around in my head.
3. Give me a book and leave me alone.
4. My favorite store is a bookstore.
5. I like to spend lots of time watching TV.
6. Words are wonderful.
7. I am good at finding misspellings in writing.
8. If I could, I wouldn't read anything but labels on soup cans.
9. So far this year I have read lots of newspapers, magazines, and/or books.
10. I enjoy writing.

**Figure 6.2**  Quiz for Identifying Possible Members of the Publication Committee

1. Please provide a disk and hard copy of your interview on [date].
2. The disk must be formatted for Word for Windows 98/2000.
3. The paper should conform to the following requirements:
   - Length should be between 1,000 and 1,200 words. [Younger students would have a much reduced word requirement.]
   - Use Times New Roman typeface.
   - Single-space all text unless otherwise noted.
   - Center title in 14-point bold on the first line of the page.
   - Center your name in 12-point bold on the next line.
   - Double-space to the first paragraph of text and introduce the person you interviewed. This introduction should be no longer than three lines.
   - Double-space to the first line of the interview. Type **Interviewer:** and leave two spaces before you type the first interview question.
   - Double-space between each interview question and each response from the interviewee to the question. For example, double-space after the first question and type **Eugene Smith:** (or whatever the interviewee's name is) and leave two spaces before typing the interviewee's response to the question.
   - After you have completed typing the interview, double-space and provide a two-line biographical sketch of yourself.

**Figure 6.3**   Example of Instructions the Publication Committee Might Produce

tor can do that. Imagine, for instance, the work involved in making sure that all the interviews—say, 20 in a class of 20 students—use **Interviewer:** instead of *I:* or *Interviewer:* or some other designation to introduce the questions in the interview. Certainly, technology can make searching and replacing easier than it would be without computer ingenuity, but correcting is something that contributing authors can do before handing in their papers.

So far, we've talked about some of the mechanics of publishing a class book. What needs to be reiterated, however, is that the publishing process includes a heavy dose of the writing process. That is, when students write their interviews (or whatever the assignment might be) for the book, they should be engaged in peer critiques before the individual papers are submitted to the publications committee. Then the committee compiles the papers and goes through the review process again, beginning with the committee members' review of the book in draft form. Once the committee reviews the draft of the book and makes needed adjustments, including editing the text of individual papers, a copy of the book should be printed out for the entire class to review, as well as a copy of each author's contribution. After authors have had the opportunity to review their contributions, making corrections or questioning changes, they return the contributions to the committee so that it can create a final draft. In terms of the cover for the book and possible art for the cover, the committee can enlist a person in the class to create a cover and ask the class for comments. Alternatively, the committee can provide several examples of covers and ask the class to select one.

## *Printing and Binding*

Many schools have equipment for printing and binding students' works. If that is the case with you, then you can photocopy and bind the books students create. However, you will need to inform students at the outset whether there are limitations concerning printing and binding. For instance, can you create color copies of the cover? Are there limits on the number of pages per book and the number of books you can produce? If students want additional copies of a book, can you collect money for those copies and reimburse the school for the copies?

If you don't have the necessary photocopy and binding facilities, including sufficient budget, then you can ask students to create a master copy for the class. The publications committee can determine what a copy costs and make copies for students who agree to pay for them.

These procedures can be adapted to various projects, including newspapers, magazines, brochures, and newsletters. For instance, either the entire class or groups within a class can create a newsletter or a brochure, using standard software packages (e.g., Big Book Maker, Super Print, Toucan Press). Such projects may not be bound individually, but a newsletter, for instance, can be a joint effort by the entire class, with particular articles or sections provided by individuals or groups.

Even though many steps in the publishing process for print materials can be used in electronic publishing, it is not the case that a print document can be automatically and easily translated into an electronic document. This is true for several reasons.

1. People read electronic documents differently from print documents. Electronic documents generally are not designed for sustained reading, so if you want your students to produce a book of interviews for the Web, you must recognize that most readers will not want to read every interview beginning with the first one and ending with the last one.

2. An electronic document has different requirements from a print document. Because Web readers expect to have links to other documents and to have choices about what they can read and in what order, you will need to help your students design a Web document.

3. Designing a Web document requires certain skills and knowledge that are not required for print documents. So let's talk about publishing students' work on the Web.

# COMPUTER CLASSROOM PUBLISHING

In electronic publishing, students make their work available in electronic form and for an electronic forum, such as a Website. Clear rationales have been provided for the value of classroom publishing using the Internet (Bronzo & Simpson, 1998;

Kinzer & Leu, 1997; Leu, 1997; Leu & El-Hindi, 1998; Leu & Iannone, 1998; Leu & Leu, 1997; Maring, Wiseman, & Myers, 1997; Shen, 1996), including a positive effect on students' writing. To help students create electronic forums, essentially you need to know three things: (1) how to create electronic products; (2) how to download information from other forums; and (3) how to post materials to electronic forums.

## How to Create Electronic Products

Although an anthology of student work that has been word processed is an electronic product, it does not take advantage of sound, animation, and video, which are components of multimedia publishing. Certainly, students can post a word processed book to the Web, but the book will not be a multimedia text and therefore will not have multimedia capabilities. However, students can create multimedia books by using authoring tools such as HyperStudio, SuperLink, and Multimedia Scrapbook. In addition, the traditional book, intended as a document that can be read from beginning to end, cannot take advantage of the nonlinear features of hypertext. For instance, in a hypertext, readers can follow one idea throughout a text or linked texts without reading all of the text. Here's an example.

Let's say that your class's book of interviews is constructed as a hypertext document. (Remember that the assignment was for each student to interview a member of his or her family who lived at least 30 years ago.) During the planning stage of the book, students would need to think about how readers access hypertexts. In thinking about readers, students would want to consider ways to link the interviews. This could be done, for instance, by each student developing a list of five to ten index terms for his or her interview. Students would select index terms by considering major themes in their interviews, such as education, leisure activities, cars, clothing, food, and economics. The class or the publication committee would then determine which themes were the most prominent throughout all the interviews. Let's say that the class or publication committee selected education, leisure activities, cars, and family life as the themes most frequently addressed throughout the interviews. Each student would then identify anything in his or her interview related to each of the themes, and the publication committee, using HyperStudio, would create links that enable readers to follow a theme throughout the entire interview book.

Thus, a reader who wanted to know everything the interview book said about family life could start at a designated place (generally the homepage for the class or book) and read every entry on that topic. If the class already has a Web page, one button on the page could be entitled "Thirty Years Ago: Interviews About Life in the 1960s." A reader would click on that button and read a synopsis of the book, including an explanation of the assignment that generated the book. Then the reader could select a button for one of the themes and follow that theme throughout the entire book by clicking on a **Next** button after reading any one entry related to a particular theme. Should the reader want to change themes, a **Go Back to Title Page** button would allow the reader to select a new theme or read the book from the beginning, page by page.

Let's say that the students who create the interview book want to do more than provide interviews; they also want to add video and music. For instance, one theme of the interviews might be the music of the 1960s, so students decide to include parts of a popular Beatles song because one of the interviewees said that he particularly liked a selection from *Sgt. Pepper's Lonely Hearts Club Band*. In addition to providing a few bars from the selection, the class decides to add a video of the Beatles in concert so that viewers will be able to both see and hear the band. Thus, when readers first read about the Beatles in the interviews, they will have access to a button that enables them to see and hear the Beatles. Readers can then return to the theme of music in the interviews. Students also could create video for their presentation. If, perhaps, a student were vacationing in a place with Beatle memorabilia, the student could videotape the memorabilia and use the tape as part of the multimedia presentation. Or students could use a scanner to scan pictures of the Beatles into a file that is incorporated into the interview book.

This type of publishing also can be accomplished by posting or submitting students' documents to other Websites. That is, students do not have to create a Website to publish their work. Indeed, they do not have to produce an elaborate multimedia presentation. Rather, they can post or submit their projects to Websites constructed for the very purpose of eliciting student writing and creating a forum for student writers to view and discuss each other's work. Examples of such Websites are listed in Figure 6.4. Most of the sites explain how to submit or post a contribution to the site.

## *How to Download Information From Other Forums*

We have already suggested that students can use materials from other sources to create a multimedia presentation. Before talking about downloading information from other electronic forums, however, we need to say a word about intellectual property and copyright. Most people do not understand that copyright—the exclusive right to one's work—is guaranteed the moment that work is produced. Thus, the first draft of this very chapter, the moment it was written—in fact, *while* it was being written—was copyrighted. Of course, had other supposed authors pirated the chapter in draft form, cleaned it up a bit, and published it, we would have had to decide whether it was worth our time and money to prosecute them. Even though we legally were granted copyright at the moment of production of the chapter, proving our ownership of the chapter is another matter. The classic way to prove ownership is to file and be awarded a copyright from the U.S. government. Thus, this book has been copyrighted: It displays the copyright sign together with the year the copyright was awarded. The copyright sign and date constitute a formal statement of copyright. In fact, the right of copyright precedes the formal statement of copyright. This means that an author's right to control the distribution of his or her work does not require the copyright sign and date. What has all this got to do with the Internet?

When you download a document from the Internet, it may be copyrighted even though it does not carry the copyright sign and date. We say *may be* because

- **The Book Nook** <http://www.i-site.on.ca/booknook.html>: Publishes book reviews written by students
- **Candlelight Stories** <http://www.candlelightstories.com>: Publishes students' writing and illustrations
- **Children's Voice** <http://schoolnet2Carleton.Ca/english/arts/lit/c-voice/welcome.html>: A listserv that publishes K–8 writing
- **Cyberkids** <http://www.cyberkids.com>: Publishes writing of students aged 7–11
- **Inkspot for Young Writer's** <http://www.inkspot.com/~ohi/inkspot/young.html>: Provides support for writers
- **International Student Newswire** <http://www.umass.edu/SpecialPrograms/ISN/KidNews.html>: Publishes the news written by students
- **KidsPub** <http://www.en-garde.com/kidpub/intro.html>: Publishes all work submitted by students
- **Kid's Space** <http://www.kids-space.org/>: Provides pictures for which students create a corresponding story
- **Mind's Eye Monster Exchange** <http://www.csnet.net/minds-eye/>: Young children exchange writing and illustrations about monsters
- **My View** <listserv@sjuvm.stjohns.edu>: Creative writing exchanges for students
- **The Quill Society** <http://www.quill.net/>: Provides a message board to support young writers and a location to publish writing
- **Realist Wonder Society** <http://www.wondersociety.com/>: Provides hypertext stories written in different genres that students can respond to online; they can even write a different ending to the stories
- **The Scoop** <http://www.friend.ly.net/scoop/adventure/index.html>: Provides stories to which students can write their own ending
- **WAC-L** <listserv@vmd.cso.uiuc.edu>: Focuses on writing across the curriculum
- **Web66: A K–12 World Wide Web Project** <http://web66.coled.umn.edu/schools.html>: Publishes K–12 writing and information about creating a home page
- **Young Author's Magazine Home Page** <http://www.yam.regulus.com/>: Publishes student poetry and short stories
- **Young Writer's Clubhouse** <http://www.realkids.com/club.html>: Provides online chat and bulletin board information about writing contests and advice about writing

**Figure 6.4**   Websites Where Students Can Publish Their Writing Projects

some works—such as government documents—are not copyrighted but are available to the public so that people can photocopy or download them without any concern about copyright violation. However, a Website with instructions about how to evaluate style in writing may very well be copyrighted, and downloading information from that site into your own site or into a document your students are producing could be a violation of copyright. At this point in the legal wrangling about copyright, linking your site to another site is not a violation of copyright, so perhaps the best way to deal with many potential and real problems associated with copyright law is to create a button so that readers can go directly to a related site; in this way you don't have to download information from a site and transfer it to your site.

Nevertheless, you may want to download information that either (1) is in the public domain, or (2) has a disclaimer stating the information can be used freely but needs to be cited or has been approved by the author for public use. Although much classroom use of downloaded information could be covered under the "fair use" provision of the copyright law (meaning that the law allows an individual to copy a certain amount of copyrighted material), you certainly should determine whether your use of such material—especially material that will be distributed outside the classroom—constitutes fair use. The next issue, then, is how to download information.

1. You can print out a copy of the information. You could scan the information into a document you are creating, but a better way is to download the information into a file on the computer's hard drive.

2. You can copy and paste an Internet text into a word processing program. Just highlight the text in the Internet document you want to copy, and go to the Edit menu and click on **Copy.** The text is ready to be pasted in a word processing document or a multimedia presentation you are creating.

3. You can save graphics by clicking on a graphic you want to download and waiting until a pop-up menu appears and gives you the option to **Save this image as . . .** Then save the image to your hard drive.

You must have the appropriate software to download text and graphics, so you should check with your local computer facilitator to determine what you need. The facilitator may talk to you about plug-ins, that is, software that allows you to download certain sites. If you do not know how to load plug-ins, you will need to get help; indeed, you may have to find out how to get a purchase order for certain plug-ins.

## How to Post Materials to Electronic Forums

We have already talked about posting materials to electronic forums, and we mentioned that many of the sites in Figure 6.4 provide instruction on how to post or submit student work for the site. However, one way to post or submit work to a site is to compress a HyperStudio stack, for instance, and send it as a Eudora Mail attachment. Indeed, e-mail, often via attachments, is the way to send materials to sites. One of the difficulties you may face in sending materials to Internet sites is the incompatibility of software packages. A file sent in Hypertext Mark-up Language (HTML) cannot be opened unless your computer has the software to read HTML. Much of the success of publishing on the Internet depends on the compatibility of software, and such compatibility begins when your students make plans to compile a document derived from projects they create using various word processing packages.

## COMPUTER CLASSROOM EXAMPLES

### *A Dictionary of Slang*

**Grade Level:**  Adaptable K–8

**Objective:**  Students identify language changes from one generation to another. Students compile lists of changes. Students gain appreciation for the evaluation of language.

**Time:**  1–2 weeks

**Problem to Be Solved:**  Adults are often unfamiliar with today's slang terms, so students will brainstorm and define slang terms common in everyday speech. Then, students will create a dictionary of slang terms.

**Materials:**  Computer
Printer
Netscape
Microsoft Works or Word
Pencil
Crayons or markers

**Steps:**

1. Engage students in a discussion of language. Discuss the differences in speaking at home and speaking at school. Ask students to think of words or phrases that are considered slang.

2. Provide an example of a slang phrase and a definition to get the students started. For example, *chill out* usually refers to getting someone who is upset to calm down.

3. Group the students into threes to continue brainstorming slang phrases.

4. Use Netscape to travel to the Word Wizard's homepage HYPERLINK <http://www.marleys.com>. Click on **Slang Street** to view the slang terms and definitions.

5. Using HYPERLINK <http://www.marleys.com> as a reference, have the students complete a dictionary of slang terms they commonly use.

6. Using Microsoft Works or Word, have student groups word process their dictionaries.

7. Create the title page of the dictionary. Add clipart if desired.

8. Create remaining pages for slang word entries. Make sure that all slang terms and phrases are defined. Students may add clipart for illustrations or leave blank space for hand drawings.

9. Review slang terms and phrases in a discussion environment. Ask the class to choose one original slang phrase they like best.

10. Submit the phrase to HYPERLINK <http://www.marleys.com>.

11. Compile a list of the 10 most commonly used slang terms from the student dictionaries. Write sentences using the terms, and have students tell the meaning of the sentences.

## COMPUTER CLASSROOM EXAMPLES (CONTINUED)

### *A Dictionary of Slang (Continued)*

**12.** Travel to another class and share the dictionaries with other students. Ask the students to guess the definitions of the terms before telling them.

**Assessment:** Develop a rubric for the slang dictionary with the students. Be sure to include:

**1.** willingness to participate;

**2.** contribution to group work;

**3.** ability to identify several old and new terms.

### *An Interactive Writing Adventure on the Web*

**Grade Level:** Adaptable K–8

**Objective:** Students will identify key elements of plot, construct a Web page, and write a story resolution.

**Time:** 3 hours

**Problem to Be Solved:** Read an interactive story on the WWW. Then, decide the course of the story by clicking on one of two plot scenarios. Using Microsoft Word, write and publish your own version of the next page in the hypertext story.

**Materials:** Computer with Internet access
Microsoft Word
Printer
Pencil or pen

**Procedures:**

**1.** Invite students to travel through the World Wide Web (WWW) to find a collaborative hypertext story.

**2.** Guide the students through a "planned" Net search. (Usually, Net searches are done by the teacher before the lesson begins. This eliminates long searches resulting in hits that are inappropriate for children. In this instance, the search is conducted in a whole group setting under close supervision.) Using your browser's **Find** option, search for "collaborative hypertext stories." Scroll through the hits and locate The Scoop—Interactive Adventure. URL: HYPERLINK <http://www.friend.ly.net/scoop/adventure/index.html>.

**3.** Read the information about the latest interactive adventure story. Be sure to join the mailing list to receive the latest updates on new stories.

**4.** Click on the link to begin reading the interactive adventure.

**5.** Read several pages, and decide the course of the story by clicking on one of two plot scenarios.

## COMPUTER CLASSROOM EXAMPLES (CONTINUED)

### *An Interactive Writing Adventure on the Web (Continued)*

6. Stop the reading of the story at an interesting point.

7. Ask the students to imagine what will happen next in the adventure.

8. Invite the students to write the next webpage for the interactive story.

9. Provide students with discussion time and individual Internet reading time to generate ideas for their continuations.

10. After brainstorming initial ideas, assign students the task of using Microsoft Word to translate their ideas into product form. (It might be a good idea to group students when using this CD-ROM. This will save on time, especially if you only have one copy.)

11. When all the student products are completed, travel back to HYPERLINK <http://www.friend.ly.net/scoop/adventure/index.html> and read the continuation of the adventure. Be sure to print a copy of the hypertext story in case the Website is updated with a new adventure.

**Assessment:** A rubric should include:

1. ability to track story plot;

2. willingness to imagine next phase of story;

3. participation in writing Web page;

4. evaluation of final product.

## TECHNO-TEACHER TIPS

### Creating Homepages

Teachers might be concerned about helping students create homepages because in the past a person needed to know HTML to create a homepage. Fortunately, Web Page Generators are becoming available, so that all a person needs to do is fill in the information required by a template—without using HTML. Web Page Generators are types of software that enable you to create a Web page via a template. Before you take on the task of learning HTML, see whether you can acquire software that will allow you to create a Web page without using HTML.

### Compatibility Issues

Software compatibility is a problem, so you need to think carefully about compatibility issues before you begin a classroom publishing project. If students don't have computers at home or have limited to access to computers outside of school, you should determine how much class time is needed for students to work on their projects.

### Listservs

Consider joining a listserv made up of other teachers involved in classroom publishing projects. Listserv members can provide help when you have questions about classroom publishing projects.

## FREQUENTLY ASKED QUESTIONS

1.  **How can I ensure that all my students get an equal amount of time for publishing their writing on our one classroom computer?**

    Develop a basic schedule allowing each student the same amount of computer time per week. This will depend on grade level, age group, and school activities. In the classroom you will use your computer in many different ways. Structure computer scheduling around these ways. Give students ample time to research using the Internet, word process, and explore new software titles. Consider pairing students and doubling their computer time. In this way they can collaborate, using their computer skills for a longer period of time.

2.  **How can I ensure that all the students in a group do an equal amount of quality work when they produce a class publication?**

    First, provide students with instruction on individual and group responsibilities. For instance, you might explain that when one student in the group misses a deadline, the other group members fall behind. Second, provide a method for students to evaluate themselves and other group members. Explain the system at the beginning of a collaborative project so that students know they will be responsible for evaluating each other. Third, use peer evaluation and self-evaluation to adjust grades for group projects.

## REFERENCES

Angeletti, S. R. (1993). Group writing and publishing: Building community in a second-grade classroom. *Language Arts, 70* (6), 494–499.

Baird, R. N., McDonald, D., Pittman, R. H., & Turnbull, A. T. (1993). *The graphics of communication: Methods, media and technology* (6th ed.). Fort Worth, TX: Harcourt Brace.

Bronzo, W. G., & Simpson, M. L. (1998). *Readers, teachers, learners: Expanding literacy across the content areas* (3rd ed.). Upper Saddle River, NJ: Merrill.

Comstock, M. (1993). Writing together, learning together: Collaboration's two-way street. *Quarterly of the National Writing Project and the Center for the Study of Writing, 15* (4), 29–32.

Doolittle, P. E. (1991). *Vygotsky and the socialization of literacy*. (ERIC Document Reproduction Service No. ED 377 473)

Dragga, S. (1988). The effects of praiseworthy grading on students and teachers. *Journal of Teaching Writing, 7* (1), 41–50.

Kinzer, C., & Leu, D. J., Jr. (1997). The challenge of change: Exploring literacy and learning in electronic environments. *Language Arts, 74,* 126–136.

Leu, D. (1997). Caity's question: Literacy as deixis on the Internet. *The Reading Teacher, 51* (1), 62–67.

Leu, D. J., & El-Hindi, A. E. (1998). Beyond classroom boundaries: Constructivist teaching with the Internet. *The Reading Teacher, 51* (8), 694–700.

Leu, D. J., & Leu, D. (1997). Using the Internet for language arts and literature. In *Teaching with the Internet: Lessons from the classroom.* Norwood, MA: Christopher-Gordon.

Leu, D. J., Jr., & Iannone, P. V. (1998). Just beyond the horizon: Writing-centered literacy activities for traditional and electronic contexts. *The Reading Teacher, 51* (5), 438–443.

Long, R., & Bulgarella, L. (1985). Social interaction and the writing process. *Language Arts, 62* (2), 166–172.

Maring, G. H., Wiseman, B. J., & Myers, K. S. (1997). *Journal of Adolescent & Adult Literacy, 41* (3), 196–207.

Marzano, L. (1990). Connecting literature with cooperative writing. *The Reading Teacher, 43* (6), 429–430.

McEachern, W. R. (1986, November). *Group compositions: A model for report writing.* Paper presented at the annual meeting of the National Council of Teachers of English, San Antonio, TX. (ERIC Document Reproduction Service Report No. ED 283 193).

Music, K. (1988). Conquering trauma with group writing. In Marsha S. Bordner (Ed.), *Strategies in composition: Ideas that work in the classroom.* (ERIC Document Reproduction Service Report No. ED 294 181).

Paeth, B. (1996). Dear Jenny. *Teachers and Writers, 28* (2), 1–6.

Shen, V. T. (1996). The role of hypertext as an interactional medium among fifth-grade students. In D. J. Leu, C. K. Kinzer, & K. A. Hichman (Eds.), *Literacies for the 21st century: Research and practice* (pp. 484–499). Chicago: National Reading Conference.

Tsujimoto, S. E. (1988). Partners in the writing process. In Jeff Golub (Ed.), *Focus on collaborative learning: Classroom practices in teaching English* (pp. 85–92). Urbana, IL: National Council of Teachers of English.

Vincent, G. (1993). Just short of paradise: Collaborative writing in middle school. *English Journal, 82* (7), 58–60.

Yanushefski, J. (1988). Group authorship in the language arts classroom. *Language Arts, 65* (3), 279–287.

Zak, F. (1990). Exclusively positive responses to students' writing. *Journal of Basic Writing, 9* (2), 40–53.

# WORKING WITH SPECIAL EDUCATION AND ESL STUDENTS

Rorie is drawing a replica of a pyramid on a computer screen using a special keyboard that allows him to overcome motor coordination problems due to cerebral palsy. Rorie is able to accomplish quite a bit with the keyboard, but he teams up with Phillipe to write text for the story he and Phillipe are creating about the "Mysterious Pyramid," as they call it. Phillipe helps Rorie type text and Rorie helps Phillipe, who is a nonnative speaker of English, fix verb endings because Phillipe sometimes confuses singulars and plurals.

As their teacher, Mr. James, watches Rorie and Phillipe work together, he recalls the days when Rorie would have been in a class with other " special ed" students and Phillipe would have been sent to the school for immigrant children who spoke very little, if any, English. Yet today Rorie and Phillipe are working together to create a book that they will read to the class. *And the book,* Mr. James says to himself, *will be a professional product because the computer is incredible, simply incredible.*

Mr. James looks around his sixth-grade classroom and sees other students' teams—some with special needs students, some with ESL students, some with students who have great facility with computers, some with students who are eager to use the computer but quite unpracticed in its use. He is again considering the technological magic of computers when he hears Phillipe saying something loud in Spanish. Mr. James turns toward the workstation where Rorie and Phillipe are collaborating and sees Phillipe shaking his fist at the computer screen and speaking rapidly in Spanish. Rorie is laughing.

Mr. James approaches Rorie and asks, "What's the problem?" Rorie blurts out, "Phillipe accidentally pushed the Delete key and our words are gone, so he's angry with the computer." Phillipe, out of words and face flushed, realizes that the class is watching him, so he looks a bit sheepish with embarrassment. Rorie, not at all bothered by the missing texts, explains to Phillipe how to bring back the words by using the mouse and cursor to click Undo Delete on a pull-down menu. Phillipe's eyes are big when the words reappear, and Rorie says, "I guess this really is a mysterious pyramid." Both Rorie and Phillipe laugh and continue working on the story they will present to the class in a couple of days.

Rorie and Phillipe are busy adding text to their book, and Mr. James, smiling, thinks to himself, *Computers are incredible, and I'm glad to be teaching in a school system that provides these kids with such rich technology.*

## TECHNOLOGY IN SPECIAL EDUCATION: THE TIME IS NOW

Teachers in K–8 classrooms face complex challenges when they are called on to provide a rich learning environment for children with unique needs, including ESL and special needs students, while also working with "regular" students. That complex challenge appears to be even more daunting when teachers note that ESL, for example, is a field of study all its own. A person can get a Ph.D. in ESL!

As authors of this book we understand the complex challenge K–8 teachers face when they seek to educate ESL and special needs students in their classrooms, because we found ourselves ill at ease after investigating some of the literature on ESL and special needs students as a prelude to writing this chapter. We had to admit that the task of writing a chapter about using computers with those types of students was out of our reach. So we asked two colleagues to help us. Dr. Janna Siegel Robertson, who is an expert on students with special needs, and Dr. Anita Pandey, who is an expert on ESL, agreed to write sections for this chapter on their respective areas of expertise. But before we present their advice about how to use computers to provide a rich learning environment for ESL and special needs students, Karen Anderson, a long-time teacher of special education, gives an example of how she uses technology in her classroom.

### COMPUTER CLASSROOM SNAPSHOT

#### *Context*

Multimedia software allows the user to create slide presentations. Students can illustrate their stories by selecting the scene, images, and sounds. They can also use text-to-speech that lets them hear their creation read aloud. This activity encourages creativity, cooperation, planning, and research. It allows the teacher the opportunity to meet each student's learning style. It gets the students engaged in the lesson, and the knowledge gained stays with the learners because they have an active role in the end product, they feel pride in their creations, and learning becomes fun!

Some of this software also incorporates animation in the images. One of the first producers of multimedia software was Roger Wagner Publishing with Hyper-Studio. Stanley's Sticker Stories by Edmark, Kids Works by Davidson, Storybookweaver by The Learning Company, and the Amazing Writing Machine by Broderbund illustrate further examples of such software. ClarisWorks also has the capability of creating slide show presentations, as do many other word processing programs.

### *What I Did and Why*

I was a teacher of children with special needs for 22 years. During this time I was fortunate to be part of a state-funded project that put $20,000 worth of computer technology in my classroom. This equipment included a teaching station that was composed of a 32″ television, a Macintosh computer, a laser disc player, and a video recorder. It was from this station that my class created numerous multimedia projects related to various units of study.

I used computer technology, particularly multimedia technology, in my classroom because all the students could get involved. Use of computers in the classroom can improve academic performance, motivate students to learn, enable them to accomplish things that they wouldn't otherwise be able to do, and build self-esteem. I have seen the student with special needs show typical students how to do something on the computer. One way to look at computer technology in relation to the special needs child is that it is an "equalizer."

In one of my favorite activities, I used Kid's Studio by CyberPuppy Software, Inc., to write a language experience story about a field trip to the zoo. From this first slide, students had to re-create the trip in sequential order. Everyone was actively involved in selection of the backgrounds, pictures, sounds, and narration of their creation. I allowed each of them, using text-to-speech, to read a page of the story. If the child had difficulty with reading, I coached him or her prior to the recording. After we were finished, we viewed our slide show. What a great way to get everyone involved and build self-esteem! The faces of the children when they heard their voices on the computer were priceless. This slide show was also used at an open house, where the parents were just as excited to hear their child's voice on the computer. I also printed out the story to include in the class storybook and place on the bookshelf in the reading corner. The children loved reading this compilation of their stories during free reading time. Copies of our story were also sent home to the parents with the assignment of having their child read to them. The children could all read the stories regardless of their reading level.

I used multimedia presentations in various other ways, including book reports, science or social studies projects, and journal writing. We usually kept a class journal, and on Friday mornings we recapped the week.

### *What I Learned*

Multimedia instruction gets the students excited about what they are doing. It teaches much more than content. The students learn proper social skills. Some take leadership roles. They develop necessary planning skills because they have to know what they are doing before they get started. Everyone participates and becomes actively engaged in the project. For the child with special needs, learning can be frustrating and therefore not motivating. But using the computer in school has been proven to be a motivator for *all* children. Multimedia is one way of getting everyone involved.

## TEACHING LITERACY TO STUDENTS WITH SPECIAL NEEDS USING TECHNOLOGY (BY JANNA SIEGEL ROBERTSON)

In the educational climate of integrating students with special needs into the general education classroom, teachers have found it challenging to instruct special needs students who have significantly different reading and writing abilities from other students. In fact, even special education teachers face challenges in broadening the literacy of special needs students. Fortunately, as Karen Anderson's classroom snapshot illustrates, Computer Assisted Instruction (CAI) provides opportunities for students to access computers regardless of the students' physical or sensory disabilities. In addition, the Internet provides information and classroom activities for teachers who work with special needs students.

### *Computer Assisted Instruction (CAI)*

Special needs students can be assisted by CAI because these programs are often self-paced and individualized for each student's needs. For instance, CAI programs allow for assessment, drill and practice, instruction, simulation, or creative productions (Siegel, Good, & Moore, 1996). In fact, research has shown that CAI motivates, teaches, and empowers special needs students as well as helping to improve their communication skills (Bitter, 1993; Cochran & Bull, 1993; Holzberg, 1994). Furthermore, nonverbal or limited verbal individuals have used computers as a major component of communication devices (Bigge, 1991).

Computers create a context for instruction that can provide stimulus (text, audio, and visual) for interaction between instructors and students (Giordano, Leeper, & Siegel, 1996). Indeed, schools are now using videodisks, compact disks, and other software that include interaction with audio and video. In some cases teachers can program questions or directions into the video to create an interactive activity that is customized for their students and their curriculum (Brosnan, 1995). Several different software programs, available in language, reading, and writing development, are designed to accommodate students with cognitive, physical, or sensory disabilities.

Two concerns are related to CAI. One is that it may cause teaching to become more and more automatized, and as a consequence students may socialize less with peers. Considering the current isolation problems of individuals with disabilities, practitioners, in their enthusiasm for embracing exciting instructional opportunities for students with disabilities, should not segregate special needs students in computer labs (Siegel, 1999). Rather, such students should be integrated into computer lab activities with general education students. This can be done with a "buddy" system or with cooperative learning groups.

The second concern is that CAI will be used too much for skill and drill. Woodward and Gersten (1992), for instance, reviewed research studies indicating that special needs students and their nondisabled peers spent comparable amounts of time on CAI, but the special needs students' CAI use was significantly more in the area of drill and practice programs. Technology is available to help special needs students go beyond mere skill and drill, so teachers should consider using that technology.

Students with physical and sensory disabilities sometimes require additional software or hardware modification. Software programs with modifications can be sorted into three categories: Animated Books, Tutorials/Drill and Practice, and Creative/Multimedia Programs. Software in all three categories have accommodations for students of different skill levels and abilities.

## Electronic/Animated Books

The original electronic books were text-based creations that could be read on a computer. The next generation included animated books (hypermedia books) that have been illustrated, animated, and made to interact with their reader. The majority have a read-aloud feature so that nonreaders can participate as well as readers. Lower level readers can read these books at their own pace and have particular words or passages repeated as many times as needed. Because the pictures are animated, there are opportunities for context clues for beginning readers. For example, Broderbund is one publisher of interactive books. In its Living Books series Broderbund selects favorite children's books, such as *Green Eggs and Ham* by Dr. Seuss, and includes a Let Me Play feature, so when a student clicks on the word *ham,* a voice says "ham" and the program reveals a picture of a green ham. Whenever a student clicks on nontext illustrations, a short animation is initiated. For teachers who have trouble showing reluctant readers that words are fun, the Living Books series provides highly motivating and rewarding material.

## Tutorials/Drill and Practice

Some CAI programs teach oral reading, phonics, fluency, comprehension, word attack, grammar, and spelling. Often these programs can be modified to meet a student's specific needs, allowing for improved programmed instruction. One example is the Laureate series for language development for special education and ESL. For instance, in its program on verbs, the animations allow the verbs to come alive. The teacher controls the content and format and can modify the program to either teach verbs or test a student's understanding of verbs. This instructional method allows for continuous repetitions with attractive animations and no negative feedback (only prompts for correct answers until the student's response is correct). The positive feedback cartoons are amusing and motivating to students.

### Creative/Multimedia Programs

The creative "writing to read" programs are some of the most easily adapted to all levels of literacy ability. Programs such as Don Johnson's books enable students to select one of two words per line to make the story their own. The program includes several aspects of drill and practice, because the story is not only read aloud but put to music so that it can be sung. Other creative software leaves much more up to the student. Most software packages include a language experience approach whereby students read their own writing (so it is automatically modified to their level). A favorite set of multimedia software programs is the Imagination Express series from Edmark. It not only enables students to write, illustrate, and publish their own stories but also animates them at a high level of sophistication, making students' books look quite professional. For example, if a student writes a story using the Pyramids program from Edmark, he or she can write about exploring ancient Egyptian ruins and animate and narrate the story, allowing readers to interact with the text by clicking on pictures that use animation or audio. Imagination Express programs are suitable for elementary and secondary students. Other multimedia programs useful for teacher and student creations are Microsoft's PowerPoint and HyperStudio.

## *Assistive Technology*

Even though software programs are essential to provide special needs students with a variety of approaches to literacy education, those students need other technology to have access to the educational technology. That is, they need assistive technology. For instance, augmented keyboards, touch pads, voice commands, and other assistive devices help students with physical and sensory disabilities to master the physical requirements of computers (Siegel, Good, & Moore, 1996). Individuals with disabilities use assistive technology in several ways: communication, environmental control, mobility, education, daily living, employment, and recreation. Teachers, however, have focused on assistive technology that is necessary for literacy (Table 7.1).

The comprehensive list in Table 7.1 includes both "low tech" options, such as a larger pen for a student who has trouble writing, and "high tech" solutions, such as speech synthesizers and hardware and software necessary for individuals with sensory and physical impairments to access computers. In addition, several programs are built into the current operating systems of Macintosh and Windows can be used for students with visual impairments. For instance, the size of the screen view can be enlarged to allow students even with severely limited vision to read text and see graphics. Fewer accommodations are available for individuals with

**Table 7.1**  Examples of Assistive Technology for Literacy

| Literacy Area | Purpose of Assistive Technology | Assistive Technology Equipment |
|---|---|---|
| **Listening** | • Enhances sound and speech reception<br>• Converts speech to text | • Hearing aid, cochlear implant, assistive listening systems<br>• Captioning of videotapes and TV, computer assisted real-time captioning, computer assisted note taking, computer generated speech output |
| **Speech Language** | • Enhances speech production<br>• Supplements/replaces speech with text or graphics that communicate<br>• Supplements/replaces speech production with alternative speech | • Speech amplifier, speech clarifier<br>• Communication board/book, typewriter, portable word processor, computer or communication device<br>• Artificial larynx, tape-recorded speech and computer generated speech output with a variety of input, storage, and retrieval options |
| **Reading** | • Enhances standard text and graphics<br>• Enlarges text and graphics<br>• Converts text and graphics to speech<br>• Converts text and graphics to Braille or other tactile symbols | • Corrective lenses, highlighting, color overlays, manually or electronically changes spacing, screen color/contrast adaptations, pictures/graphics, symbols, sign language cues<br>• Large print books, handheld and screen magnifiers, closed circuit TV, screen enlarging software<br>• Talking dictionary, talking word processor, screen reading system, video description<br>• Braille translation software and Braille printer, refreshable Braille computer output, tactile graphic display systems |
| **Writing** | • Enhances standard writing utensils and supports<br>• Replaces standard writing utensils and supports<br>• Enhances the composition of written expression | • Adaptive grip, larger size, rubber grips or adaptive writing tool; splints or wrist supports; special paper with wider lines, texture; writing guides; slanted, larger or no slip writing surface<br>• Typewriter, electronic note taker, portable word processor, can have Braille input, can have keyboard enhancements, alternative keyboard, alternative input such as switches with scanning, word prediction and macros, computer with voice dictation input<br>• Dictionary or thesaurus (talking), spell checker, grammar checker, abbreviation expansion, word prediction or macros, voice dictation input, multimedia software |

*Note:* From *Assistive Technology in Special Education: Policy and Practice* (pp. 40–41), by D. Golden, 1998, Reston, VA: Council for Exceptional Children. Copyright 1998. Adopted with permission.

hearing impairments because computers are mainly visual, but there are visual cues rather than the "beep" the computer usually makes to get one's attention (Buggey, 1999). For students with motor difficulties, several tools are available to change the sensitivity and speed of the keyboard and mouse. They can be found in the control panel settings or original setup options on most computers.

Occasionally the tools provided in a typical computer are not enough to accommodate a person with very severe disabilities. In these cases, assistive technology provides extra equipment. For example, Braille writers and touch response mouses are available for individuals with little or no sight. Alternative keyboards with touch windows and switches are available for students with limited motor control. Also, infrared " head mouse" options, eye gazing tools, and other innovative technologies enable special needs students to access computers. Several software publishers such as Edmark, Don Johnson, and Laureate incorporate simple controls so that the program will automatically scan, highlighting an object on the screen (often at a speed the student can select), and allow the student to click with the mouse, touch the screen, or push a switch to choose the option. With scanning, students can access simple tutorial or drill and practice programs or even learn to write compositions using on-screen keyboards or word predication software. Often the style of on-screen keyboards or alternative keyboards follows the models used for augmentative alternative communication (AAC) devices.

AAC makes use of two broad methods of inputting information into communication devices or computers. One is random selection of letters, words, symbols, or options; the other gives access to two choices, of which the individual must choose one. To accomplish this input, communication boards offer symbols, pictures, or words to accommodate a student's needs. Often current keyboard layouts are not suitable for input by students with physical or cognitive limitations. Augmented keyboards may have include rearranged keys in more efficient layouts, reduced keys for fewer physical demands, and expanded keys for additional message options. Encoding alternatives also are available with the following options:

- pictures or symbols in which one symbol or picture may have many possible meanings, depending on keys pressed;
- alphabetic encoding, in which one alphabet letter has several meanings;
- enlarged key keyboards;
- abbreviation expansion, in which a few letters allow the whole word to be spoken or written; and
- lexical predication, in which a list of likely options is provided after each letter typed.

The output can be written or spoken. Spoken output is usually provided by computerized voices (speech synthesizers), which are now faster, less mechanistic sounding, and more age and gender appropriate than older versions (Venkatagiri, 1995).

A variety of issues need to be considered when a teacher is deciding which assistive technology device to use. Figure 7.1 is an Assistive Technology Evaluation

To simplify the decision-making process, The Arc has compiled the following checklist to be used by people with mental retardation and their family members when making decisions about assistive technology. While the checklist cannot provide all the questions you need to address, technology-users and their advocates who address all of the questions on this list will have taken the basic steps needed to evaluate and assess an assistive device. The previous narrative can provide more details about the process covered by each question.

Look at the questions below as you evaluate and select devices. Questions are worded so that the optimal response is always "yes." In some circumstances, the question is not applicable (N/A). However, if, after completing the checklist there are too many "no" responses, you might want to reconsider any decisions about the device, at least until you can fill in your information gaps.

**Before you evaluate a device (user questions):**

| | | | |
|---|---|---|---|
| Have you identified your specific need(s) to be addressed by an assistive device? | YES | NO | N/A |
| Are you familiar with environment where you will use the device? | YES | NO | N/A |
| Have you written your goals and objectives down and developed a way of tracking your progress? | YES | NO | N/A |

**Before you evaluate a device (vendor questions):**

| | | | |
|---|---|---|---|
| Does the vendor have a good reputation? | YES | NO | N/A |
| Does the vendor provide demonstration or trial periods? | YES | NO | N/A |
| Is delivery available, and if so, is it prompt and reasonably priced? | YES | NO | N/A |
| Does the vendor provide, or can the vendor direct you to, required training for device use? | YES | NO | N/A |
| Will the vendor assist you in completing paperwork and documentation needed by funding sources? | YES | NO | N/A |
| Can the vendor modify the device if necessary, and will the vendor provide ongoing support? | YES | NO | N/A |

**After you identify a device:**

**Device Performance Evaluation**

| | | | |
|---|---|---|---|
| Have you seen data to back up performance claims? | YES | NO | N/A |
| Was the device testing conducted by an independent evaluator? | YES | NO | N/A |
| Was testing conducted under circumstances similar to those in which you will be using the device? | YES | NO | N/A |

**Figure 7.1** The Arc: Assistive Technology Evaluation Checklist From "How to Evaluate and Select Assistive Technology," by the Arc, 1994. (ERIC Document Reproduction Service No. ED 376 664)

| | | | |
|---|---|---|---|
| Are device space, electronics, and wiring requirements compatible with your use of the device? With other devices? | YES | NO | N/A |

**Device Convenience Evaluation**

| | | | |
|---|---|---|---|
| Have you tried out the device and found it to be comfortable and convenient to use? | YES | NO | N/A |
| Is the device easily or reasonably transported, stored, and secured? | YES | NO | N/A |
| Can you operate all components of the device without training? If not, is training available? | YES | NO | N/A |
| Are installation and assembly requirements reasonable? | YES | NO | N/A |
| Will the device adapt to changes in your disability? | YES | NO | N/A |

**Device Reliability and Safety Evaluation**

| | | | |
|---|---|---|---|
| Did performance testing include reliability and durability assessment? | YES | NO | N/A |
| Are annual and lifetime maintenance and repair costs reasonable? | YES | NO | N/A |
| Is there a warranty available for the device? | YES | NO | N/A |
| If there is regular maintenance, is someone available to do this work? | YES | NO | N/A |
| Does the device meet federal standards for wiring and construction? | YES | NO | N/A |
| Was safety testing performed in situations similar to those in which you will be using the device? | YES | NO | N/A |
| Will the device require extensive modification? If so, have you determined that this will not impact reliability and safety? | YES | NO | N/A |

**Device Practicality Evaluation**

| | | | |
|---|---|---|---|
| Is the device within your price range? | YES | NO | N/A |
| Does the device meet requirements identified by your funding source? | YES | NO | N/A |
| Does the device address the needs you identified earlier? | YES | NO | N/A |
| Is the device available within a reasonable time? | YES | NO | N/A |
| Is the device consistent with your lifestyle, age, personality, and values? | YES | NO | N/A |
| Do you like the way the device looks, and will you feel comfortable using the device around others? | YES | NO | N/A |
| Have you compared this device with others performing similar functions? | YES | NO | N/A |

**Figure 7.1** *continued*

Checklist that was developed to help teachers, families, and individuals in making this important decision (The Arc, 1994). Because assistive technology selection can be confusing, most school districts hire specialists or contract with outside consultants. The checklist in Figure 7.1 can be a guideline for teachers and parents to use when making decisions about purchasing AT.

## Using the Internet

For teachers who would like additional information about teaching literacy to students with special needs, several excellent sites can be found on the Internet. One is the Literacy Technology Project, which focuses on the writing of exceptional students. This project is sponsored by the Center on Disabilities and Human Development. The site has excellent links to a great selection of information on using technology for literacy with individuals with disabilities. The Web address is <http://www.ets.uidaho.edu/cdhd/littech/lithome.htm>.

A wonderful site for teaching examples that make use of many of the technologies mentioned in this chapter is found at A National Perspective on Special Educators' Use of Technology to Promote Literacy. This site is sponsored by the U.S. Department of Education. There is a thorough literature database on the topic as well as a free downloadable photo-essay book entitled *Technology Links to Literacy: A Case Book of Special Educators' Use of Technology to Promote Literacy* (Craver & Burton-Radzely, 1998). The book gives examples of how seven different schools across the country used technology successfully with special needs students. The Web address is <http://www.abledata.com/Literacy/index.htm>.

Although the Internet provides a multitude of free instructional resources to students and teachers, not all pages are accessible to individuals who use assistive technology. A Website that lists accessible sites is called WebABLE! and is funded through the Yuri Rubinsky Foundation. WebABLE! is the authoritative Website for disability-related Internet resources. WebABLE!'s accessibility database lists hundreds of Internet-based resources on accessibility. The mission of WebABLE!, an initiative of WebABLE! Solutions, is to stimulate education, research, and development of technologies to ensure that people with disabilities have access to advanced information systems and emerging technologies. The Web address is <http://www.webable.com/>.

Another resource related to Internet accessibility is a free Web-based tool called Bobby. It will check any Web page to see if it is accessible to individuals with disabilities. All you do is submit the URL (Web address) to Bobby, and you will receive a full analysis of your Web page. Once a site is deemed accessible, the site can display the Bobby logo. The Web address is <http://www.cast.org/bobby/>.

## Literacy Development and Students With Disabilities

The most important aspect of incorporating technology in the teaching of beginning literacy is to support the natural developmental sequence of learning to communicate, including listening, speaking, reading, and writing. All the CAI and AT (Assistive Technology) tools discussed previously can support children with or without special needs, but children with disabilities often miss many of the opportunities that other children enjoy that support successful early literacy.

Table 7.2, which illustrates general developmental needs displayed by all young children to promote initial concept development, values, and skills, lists ways in which teachers can make a difference using technological and non-technological activities. Most important, the majority of these activities provide solutions to children's problems with literacy whether they have disabilities or not. All students benefit from a well-rounded literacy curriculum, and students with disabilities are no exception.

When teachers use technology to teach literacy, all students—including those with special needs—benefit, particularly because technology can be modified to help them read and write. Assistive technology also enables special needs students to access computers. As more and more accommodations are built into computer hardware and software, all students can benefit from easy access to technology. For example, once speech-to-text input is easy to do, wouldn't we all love to dictate our writing rather than type! Think of how technology can enable all types of students to have equal access to computers, making them a truly user-friendly tool that one day will take no more thought to use than a telephone. As computers become increasingly easy to use, educators will be able to employ them to enhance learning for all students.

# Moving With Technology: Teaching ESL K–8 (by Anita Pandey)

> For educators, the rapid and continuing introduction of new technology into education has outpaced the ability of teachers and developers to evaluate it properly. . . . Somehow, we must try and make sense of what is going on, in spite of the rate of change.
>
> (Levy, 1997, p. 2)

The focus of this section is on how best to utilize existing and emerging technology to teach ESL in K–8 classrooms. The discussion begins with an outline of some of the benefits of using technology to teach ESL in the grade levels specified. Then the kinds of language-instructional technologies currently available are examined, and finally, suggestions are given for their use in class and for independent, student-directed language learning.

In a sense, both instructional technology and ESL are booming "industries," so it makes sense for them to overlap. It is estimated that at the dawn of the millennium, the majority of school-age children in 50 or more U.S. cities are minorities, from homes where English is not the native tongue (TESOL Association ESL Standards). The figures for the variety of instructional technologies currently available, and their utility in this information age, are equally astounding. Some 13 years ago it was estimated that around 10,000 instructional software packages were commercially available for microcomputers (Franklin & Strudler, 1989, p. 1). Today

**Table 7.2**   Developmental Needs of Children With Disabilities

| What Children Need | What Children With Disabilities May Experience | What To Do | Activities |
|---|---|---|---|
| Opportunities to explore and play | Fewer opportunities to learn through active exploration and play because of limited ability to see, move, hear, or communicate | Plan space allowing for special needs; provide materials and experiences that provide input through the senses; make appropriate adaptations to environment | Visits to museums, play groups, computer games, playing with adaptive toys, proper positioning to facilitate play |
| Lots of opportunities to interact with print materials | Limited access to print materials | Provide large print materials, assistive technology, computer technology, language experiences; give family information | Kitchen activities, turn on the closed caption on the television, adaptive writing instruments, text-to-speech software |
| Many opportunities to observe the functions of print, especially at home | Fewer opportunities to see the functions of print modeled | Opportunities to engage children with print; functional classroom settings; make sure child understands what activity is | Read the newspaper, e-mail friends on the computer, create multi-media books, journal writing, classroom activities: taking roll, lunch count |
| Belief that learning to read and write is important | Less emphasis placed on learning to read and write compared to concerns about physical needs and learning self-help skills | Plan to provide appropriate literacy experiences and opportunities to address needs related to the disability; educate families | Making the computer accessible, adaptations to pencils, finding some sort of graphic output |
| Expectations that child has the ability to read and write | Lowered expectations that child will learn to read and write | Model high expectations for family; provide videos and stories about individuals with disabilities | Computer accessibility, educational software, notetakers |
| Many opportunities to communicate with peers and adults in interactive situations | Fewer experiences interacting and communicating with others | Provide a means of communication for the child; provide opportunities for interaction | Electronic communication devices, manual communication boards |

**Table 7.2**   Developmental Needs of Children With Disabilities (Continued)

| What Children Need | What Children With Disabilities May Experience | What To Do | Activities |
|---|---|---|---|
| Knowledge of how sounds in language relate to alphabet | Fewer opportunities to hear sounds, see symbols, and say sounds | Plan activities that engage in learning sound-symbol relationships, games; experiment with writing and reading | Computer software; educational, text-to-speech, tape recorders, imitation games |

thousands more are readily available. The problem is that there is still a huge disparity between the availability of instructional technology and its implementation in schools. This problem was noted in the late 1980s (see Franklin & Strudler, 1989) and still persists.

Teaching ESL to children and adults, or simply teaching ESL learners, can be a very culturally rewarding experience. Even as such teaching requires a sound knowledge of second language acquisition principles, of approaches to teaching ESL (Bhatia & Ritchie, 1996; Larsen-Freeman, 1986), and an appreciation for cross-cultural differences (Clayton, 1996), it also requires an innovative instructor (whether human or technological, although the former is preferable) capable of utilizing a variety of instructional tools at any given point, both inside and outside the classroom (Bush & Terry, 1997; Levy, 1997; Nunan, 1996).

We are currently witnessing an unprecedented growth and proliferation of computer technology and of associated instructional technologies of value to practically every field. Not to harness it—not to take advantage of this vast resource bank—would be a terrible mistake. Yet the value of technology is not always immediately apparent (especially when it changes at a mind-boggling pace). In fact, I want to take a moment to tell you a little about my personal journey in learning about computers.

I didn't use a computer until I was 19 years old. Part of this had to do with fear and part of it with the scarcity of computers in my immediate surroundings. Having grown up in the rural areas of "developing" countries (which are super-advanced as far as human relations are concerned), I was lucky if I had access to a photocopy machine. Computers were rarely visible in these parts, even in the late 1980s when I worked on my Bachelor's degree in linguistics. At the university I attended in West Africa, computers were reserved for students studying computer science. So I typed my undergraduate thesis on an electric typewriter and was pretty proud of it, until I saw what laser printers yielded. So, naturally, I had no idea what e-mail meant until I came to the United States to do my graduate work. By then, I was so afraid of being technologically ignorant that I developed a computer-phobia that kept me away from that mysterious screen and from all those who could have helped me get to know it right away. If it hadn't been for a "tough" professor at the University of Illinois who required that all class papers be typed on a computer and turned in along with a diskette, I would probably not have dared to venture near these "ghastly creatures" for quite a while. I owe that professor many thanks.

I often wonder whether part of my fascination with computer technology has something to do with its total absence in the first 18 years of my life. I keep telling myself that I could have been an "expert" in computer technology if I had had easy access to such technology from the very beginning. So I have a lot more to learn about existing and emerging computer technology, and I'm excited about it.

Technology has permeated most, if not all, fields, and TESOL (Teachers of English to Students of Other Languages) is no exception. In fact, technology-enhanced language teaching can greatly benefit students by expanding the learning environment(s) or opportunities for the dissemination of information and by changing the very definition of language, learning, and teaching (Bush & Terry, 1997; Dunkel, 1991; Gardner & Garcia, 1996; Little, 1996; Voller & Pickard 1996). There is a reason why the Internet and related technologies are associated with the *information age,* with the *Information Superhighway,* even with the *information revolution.*

To explore the ways in which K–8 teachers can use computer technology to promote literacy instruction for ESL students, in the following discussion I will attempt to:

- acquaint K-8 teachers with some of the technological resources currently available for teaching ESL;
- illustrate some of the benefits of using technology to teach ESL;
- suggest some means of effectively incorporating technology in the ESL curriculum at the different grade levels; and
- recommend strategies that K-8 instructors who have ESL students in their classes can use to keep up with advances in ESL instructional technology.

## *Whole Language Learning via Computer Assisted Language Learning*

What has research in computer assisted language learning (CALL) shown? Research in computer assisted instruction (CAI) and specifically in CALL has been going on for two decades (Dunkel, 1991; Levy, 1997). At present, interest in CAI and CALL is at an all-time high due to the sudden acceleration in technological innovations, particularly after the creation of the World Wide Web (Li & Hart, 1996). For the most part, the research points in favor of CALL, drawing attention to its positive points. Grosse and Leto (1999) argue that technology can be extremely useful in teaching ESL "if used correctly" (p. 1). They observe, "Electronic learning breaks down traditional time and space constraints on learning" and instructors interact with more students "than they would have through the traditional classroom format" (p. 7). Grosse and Leto illustrate these points by citing several examples of interactions in virtual English classrooms that allowed for meaningful, real-time exchanges. These days, instructors and students in such classrooms can even make use of the "white board" for illustrative purposes including drawings, which all those participating in the chat room can immediately see on their screens—far more visible, in fact, than the traditional chalkboard.

Yet some fundamental questions still occupy the minds of several researchers, necessitating further research through instructors like us. For example: What is known about the process of language learning that suggests that the learning environment provided by current technology *could* and actually *does* make a difference? How much of the available technology is potentially useful? Clearly, answers to these and other questions can only be found if we unhesitatingly employ CALL with our students, both in the classroom and outside—if we require the use of certain kinds of technology for out-of-class assignments. After all, even if it doesn't yield miraculous language learning, how can it possibly hurt? As Garrett (1996) observes, "[T]he sharpest questions raised by our attempts to understand the role of technology in language learning are really not questions about technology but about language learning itself, and the most significant advantage of technology is its potential to catalyze and to focus our attention on these fundamental issues" (p. xv).

Today, unlike in the 1980s (Olsen, 1980), most instructors and administrators are eager and willing to respond to the technological age, and specifically to CALL. More teachers are being provided with computer labs, TVs, VCRs, CD players, and affordable software packages. Students and instructors who do not have PCs can easily surf the Web at a public, school, or university library. Even getting a free e-mail account is no longer a novelty. Given the accessibility of technology in our society, it is in our best interest to utilize it in teaching.

In fact, early introduction to technology, like early introduction to any language, has an added value—it enables pupils to master technology at an early age and to learn language in context. In particular, CALL is learner-centered and therefore provides for whole language learning (Freeman & Freeman, 1992, p. 4). Moreover, CALL—via e-mail penpaling, see-you-see-me videoconferencing, voice chatting, and Internet sites—exposes children to authentic language, a prerequisite for effective second language learning (Brown, 1994; Diaz-Rico & Weed, 1995; Gass & Selinker, 1995). Also, CALL facilitates autonomous language learning, thereby ensuring the kind of continuity in language instruction that is particularly advisable for the ESL student who does not hear much (or any) English at home and who needs continued exposure to comprehensible input. CALL or technology-enhanced language teaching is also more effort-effective for instructors. Most would agree that preparing for class—making lesson plans that utilize traditional resources such as texts and teacher-talk—is far more time-consuming and cumbersome than adopting the role of a facilitator who monitors students' language progress as they interact with the world through a screen. In ascertaining their students' language progress, ESL instructors are advised to periodically consult the ESL standards for K–8 that can be accessed through TESOL's homepage at <www.tesol.edu/assoc/k12standards/>.

In schools where ESL students make up only a small percentage of each grade level, the number of school hours devoted to ESL may be limited. Given that these students generally have to be taken out of their regular classes to meet with their designated ESL teacher (G. Joe, personal communication), the ESL instructor might not get to meet with a student for more than one to two hours per week. Such an instructor would do well to create self-instructors of these learners—in short, to prepare and encourage them to take advantage of the autonomous language learning that computer-based technology now makes possible. By so doing, the instructor empowers both the students and himself or herself (Freeman & Freeman, 1992; Freire, 1970; Higgins, 1991; Pandey, 1999), and can easily reinforce the one-on-one, face-to-face lessons with CALL. ESL students at different grade levels can then learn English as they construct and expand their knowledge base (Freeman & Freeman, 1996).

Research in second language acquisition has shown that interactive and experiential second language learning is far more effective and advisable than an instructional approach in which teachers attempt to "deposit" knowledge in student "banks" (Cummins, 1989). Dunkel (1991) reminds us that "Although they may not be able to express themselves in English, the young ESL children you are meeting are, in fact, experienced language users" (p. 1). This is something every ESL instructor must keep in mind. In effect, it's a good idea to put ESL students in charge of their own language learning, and CALL makes this easy. As Freeman and Freeman (1992, p. 233) observe, "Faith in the learner expands student potential."

## Technology-Enhanced ESL for Each Grade Level

### The Primary Grades

In a sense, the ESL child feels twice removed from his or her "home" (Clayton, 1996; Rodriquez, 1980). Remember that it is important to be extra-sensitive and genuinely attentive to ESL children because they have been displaced from their comfort zones, from their primary cultural milieus. Because language and culture are intertwined (McKay & Hornberger, 1996; Romaine, 1994), the ESL instructor has to be careful not to usurp a child's primary culture. For K–3 ESL students, you need to use technology that is visually and auditorially stimulating—technology that appeals to a child's sense of sight and hearing. After all, "Children learning ESL are, first of all, children" (Ashworth & Wakefield, 1994, p. 33). A variety of phonics (software) programs, such as Rock 'N Learn, are currently available and have been found to effectively teach ESL students the sounds of the English alphabet, in isolation and in the context of simple words. I am not suggesting that board games like Phonics Adventure (1987) are pointless. Certainly not. I just think it's a good idea to try out the computer-based ones and possibly pretest them with your students before deciding which ones to use in class. You might decide to use a combination or to use one specific kind with your ESL students, particularly after you've done a needs analysis.

In using technology to cover content areas of the curriculum, for instance, for the sake of the ESL students in your class, you might decide to emphasize the language as much as the content or to use content-area teaching as a means to an end (namely, vocabulary and grammar comprehension and expansion). I truly believe that "it takes a village to raise a child," and it takes a collaborative effort—that is, interested staff, students, and community—to make the learning of English as a second language enjoyable, meaningful, and effective. So I recommend that you not rely on the designated ESL teacher to assist the ESL students in your classes.

First-grade teacher Ginger Joe of Oak Forest Elementary School in Memphis had the following to say about the utility of computer-based phonics programs:

> Ever since I started using them with not just my ESL students, but with all the students in my class, I've noticed a remarkable improvement. It's amazing how quickly they learn the alphabet and how to correctly pronounce words that I used to have such a hard time teaching them, even when I used the Hooked-on-Phonics kit! I'd highly recommend the use of such technology. I've also had great success with Kids Pix and Kids Works. It makes me sad to see these brand new computers sitting idle in some classrooms; the teachers just don't use them. Imagine all the extra ESL-learning activities I could do in my class if I had those two or three computers. (personal communication)

Kids Works is a fascinating graphic arts–type clipart program that children find very engaging. It can be used solely for drawing and art, for developing motor skills (like basic word processing, which I myself am slow at because I wasn't introduced to it early enough) and artistic skills, or for other learning tasks. For instance, ESL children could be taught umbrella words like animals, flowers, and birds, and asked to sort and classify the members of these larger categories by using the pictures and graphic representations this particular computer program contains. To use Kids Works, schools simply have to get state licensing. Once the program is installed on one of the school computers, instructors and students can access it from any computer terminal on campus. Another beneficial software program that can be downloaded from the Web is Roxie's ABC Fish, which teaches the alphabet by using music and songs. It is an excellent interactive program for K–3 ESL students.

Kids Pix is an exciting, interactive, talking-computer program of great benefit to first and second graders. Students practice their keyboard/keystroke and typing skills by typing in letters and sounds, and the computer responds by reading (backwards) whatever they enter. For nonsense or misspelled words, the computer can be heard responding "This is not a word." Both Kids Pix and Kids Works can also be employed for autonomous out-of-class learning with K–3 ESL students. Parents can be advised to purchase these programs for their children or to use them at local libraries.

As comprehension precedes production in language learning (Brown 1994), the use of colorful and informative CD-ROMs such as the ones from *Discovery* or *National Geographic* are good for developing the listening comprehension skills of ESL children. Second- and third-grade teacher Laura Constance (personal communication) highly recommends these for use with K–4 ESL pupils. In her words,

"I have found that it greatly enhances the learning experience for pretty much every child. Some of the colors on those CD-ROMs are even better than the colors on TV! My kids are absolutely transfixed, even when I pause for comprehension checks and explanations. They just love them." Elementary ESL teacher Christina Mo also recommends the use of stories on CD-ROM, VHS, and DVD, as stories viewed in movie mode help develop a child's imagination and language skills (pronunciation, expression, listening/comprehension) and can also be used to encourage ESL children to share their life stories with classmates. Numerous nursery rhymes and songs—excellent cultural vignettes—are now available on CD-ROM and can also be used to teach vocabulary, cultural elements, and phonics to ESL pupils in grades K–3.

A colleague recently recommended that I purchase one of the "living books" now readily available at Best Buy, Computer World, Circuit City, or any store that sells computer paraphernalia. These relatively inexpensive "books" run the literary gamut in titles and are absolutely delightful, even for adults like me. One of the things I find fascinating is that they're so realistic and interactive. The oral narrative is accompanied by visual displays of the words and sentences. If you click on any of the highlighted words, you're immediately treated to a delightful medley of extras—colorful images, new scenes in the story, songs, music, dance, and dialogue, so this treat serves as an incentive to those who can "read." It is probably easier and quicker for children "reading" or viewing these stories to make the connections between (1) the sounds and words used in American English, and (2) the words themselves and general usage. The viewer can literally see the characters live their lives and, in a sense, can even establish a rapport with them. One can find any of the Dr. Seuss books, like *Cat in the Hat,* as well as a host of others.

A variety of CD-ROMs for ESL students of different ages and proficiency levels are currently available. The following can be ordered through ALTA/ESL:

- Dynamic Classics (e.g., *Robin Hood, Alice in Wonderland*)
- TRACI Talk CD-ROM series, which enables the learner to ask anything of TRACI—the Teacher Ranging Across the Computer Interface—and is bound to entice anyone with its animation, photos, and the latest in speech recognition technology
- Let's Go Interactive CD-ROM, which features songs, graphics, word puzzles, literate cats, and so on
- Let's Talk English Vocabulary and Pronunciation, which is great for after-school practice with English
- Smart Start English CD-ROM, which promises the learner a 1,000-word vocabulary and makes it possible for a learner to "talk" to onscreen characters in a variety of everyday situations
- New Dynamic English, which makes use of QuickTime video for video lessons, dialogues, and narratives, and advanced speech recognition technology that makes it especially interactive

An attention-getting instructional tool for use with lower level ESL students is a large display monitor to which they can hook up a laptop, powerbook, or PC (G. Joe, personal communication). In this way, cooperative learning can take place, because all computer images, including Internet searches of sites intended for or possibly even created through the collaborative effort of an elementary school class, can be projected on a TV monitor for general viewing. Words and images are enlarged and amplified, and each student does not have to have an individual screen. Moreover, students who are not old enough or responsible enough to do a useful Web search are not made to do so, yet they can learn many sight words in this manner (Gibbons, 1991). Web surfing is not recommended for very young children, as their curiosity might lead them to inappropriate adult sites. Instead, if Web searches are to be used for K–4 ESL students, it's probably a good idea to bookmark four or five sites deemed valuable and to have students browse these and select one or two to focus on for a particular language learning task. It is also not advisable to assign out-of-class Web surfing exercises to pupils in grades K–4, as parent involvement and plagiarism could constitute a problem. This does not mean, however, that ESL students and their parents should not be made aware of the plethora of ESL learning opportunities the Internet—even mere Web surfing—provides.

## The Intermediate Grades: Covering Middle and Higher Linguistic Ground

With fourth through eighth graders, there appears to be a lot more one can do with CALL. For one thing, stories on CD-ROM can be used in conjunction with the same or similar movies on VHS or DVD, so that ESL pupils in grades 4–6 can be introduced to new vocabulary items, especially idioms in context, and students in grades 7 and 8 can be introduced to comparison and contrast as useful analytic tools.

Introducing ESL students in grades 4–6 to word processing is a good start (see Daiute, 1985) in the direction of literacy development in English. The word processing can be as simple as merely typing in displayed or dictated words and sentences (an analogy with copying as a learning device) or as challenging as having them describe and narrate, in their own words, aspects of their sociocultural experiences. Granted, there are a variety of word processing programs currently available, but as Franklin and Strudler (1989) observe, "Once a student has mastered the ideas of word processing and the use of one word processor, the student can easily transfer this knowledge and skill to another word processor" (p. 2). CAI also makes a variety of prewriting activities possible. For instance, you could preselect or bookmark certain Websites and have students practice clustering, listing, mapping, and so on, using the content presented in these sites. Freewriting and focused freewriting could be done on a word processor. Eventually, you can introduce students to revising and editing (including the use of the spell checker and grammar checker) on a word processor. In short, you can bank on CAI or CII to make it relatively easy to introduce all your students—not just the ESL students—to the process approach to writing.

A number of studies have illustrated that students who compose and revise on PCs write better papers and generally have a more positive attitude toward writing than those who do not (see, for example, Roblyer, Castine, & King, 1988). Researchers such as Neu and Scarcella (1991) and Phinney (1991) have found this to be true of ESL students as well. Computer-based testing of ESL students' changing English proficiency is also highly efficient today (see Madsen, 1991; Stevenson & Gross, 1991).

In my experience, ESL and/or bilingual children aged 8 to 12 generally enjoy leadership or instructor roles (Pandey, 1999). Putting them in charge of their own learning—inductively, at least—can be very beneficial. In attempting to meet the challenge of content instruction in the classroom (Hayes & O'Loughlin, 1999), as teachers we optimize learning once we make our students computer-literate. Teachers could have ESL students surf the Internet for content areas covered in class (Gibbons, 1991; Sperling, 1999), so that they come to class prepared to talk about sites of interest and explain why they found those sites interesting. They could make a list of 5 to 10 new words or expressions they came across on the Internet. In pairs or groups, they could even rate the sites. Instead of giving them topics to write about, you could give them the freedom to choose their own via a Web search exercise.

To further develop their reading comprehension and paraphrasing skills, you might even have ESL students summarize short articles or stories—suitable for their age and proficiency levels—that appear on different Websites. In this way the ESL students learn by doing (i.e., in accordance with the principles of task-based second language learning). You could have them e-mail their summaries to you, along with an attachment of the article they selected, so you can guard against plagiarism. You could use e-mail and other Internet programs in a variety of ways (Warschauer, 1999). You could have students keep word logs and construct sentences using newly learned words in context. I have found this to be more helpful than simply having students add more and more items to their word logs. Once a Web "page" or site engages an ESL learner, language learning is inevitable. Focused Web browsing is one means of ensuring whole language learning (Healey & Jackson, 1999; Robinett, 1999; Sperling, 1999, for more stimulating ideas). To make the learning experience more fruitful (i.e., linguistically speaking), a web search exercise could be accompanied by a set of questions or information retrieval prompts. All in all, giving students control over technology is one way of empowering them (Higgins, 1995; Pemberton et al., 1996). This is especially true of ESL students, many of whom may be computer-phobic, as they may have little or no knowledge of computers and associated technologies.

For guidelines on selecting and recommending sites suitable for content-based intermediate courses, you might wish to consult Healey and Jackson (1999). Additional criteria for the evaluation of instructional materials of use to ESL pupils can be found in Chapter VII of the *Foreign Language Framework* of California's Department of Education (California State Department of Education, 1989). As Diaz-Rico and Weed (1995, p. 121) observe, "A critical aspect of any lesson is the proper selection and use of materials." Technological resources are much like videos-cum-texts, only more sophisticated and often more interactive. Material selection must be guided by two primary criteria: (1) Are the content objectives for the lesson adequately presented by the material? and (2) Is the material comprehensible? The second is probably a less critical issue for Websites, which are generally multipaginal and multidimensional, catering to different learning styles.

A variety of online ESL textbooks are now available for ESL learners, both children and adults. One that contains samples of authentic dialogues recorded in different contexts and glossaries for functional idioms and context-specific vocabulary items, as well as test-your-knowledge exercises at the end of each "chapter," is the *Online ESL Conversation Textbook,* accessible at <http://deil.lang.uiuc.edu/students/r-li5/book/>. The unit on shopping was written by the author of the present piece [Pandey] and, like the others in this "text," is suitable for ESL students in grades 6–8. The following are some resource sites that K–8 (ESL) instructors could use with their students. Keep in mind that the URLs might change. If that happens, a keyword search should help.

1. <http://www.everythingESL.net/>
2. <http://www.tapr.org/~ird/Sjones/index.html>
3. <http://www.tcom.ohiou.edu/OU_Language/>
4. <http://www.deil.uiuc.edu/resources/TESOL/>
5. <http://humanities.byu.edu/ELC/teacher/> This site contains ESL lessons and accompanying teacher training modules.
6. <http://www.aitech.ac.jp/~ckelly/sub/questionss.html> A collaboration hub, this site features various questions posed by readers, and responses to these. Topics range from ethics, to culture and traditions, to social and political problems, to ESL instructional advice.
7. <http://eslcafe.com/ideas/sefer/cgi?display/> This site presents the ESL Cafe's Cookbook of Ideas for the ESL/EFL Classroom.
8. <http://www.itec.sfsu.edu/students/k12/resources.html/>
9. <http://iac.snow.edu/faculty/dogden/vis/tesollistserve.html/>
10. <http://www.tesol.edu/>
11. <http://www.ling.lancs.ac.uk/staff/visitors> This site contains links to valuable resources and lesson plans.
12. <http://members.xoom.com/> This site features an e-mail mentoring project that instructors can join. The chat room is worth entering, and the "star questions," posed by teachers around the world, are thought-provoking.
13. <http://darkwing.uoregon.edu/~call/reseource.html/> This site contains a variety of resources, including listservs for students, keypals, content-rich sites, synchronous and asynchronous communication, and student-centered sites.
14. <http://www.gsn.org/> The Global Schoolhouse site provides Lightspan Page one and other cutting-edge software packages for free to K–12 teachers.
15. <http://eslworldwide.com/>

These are just a few of the Websites that invite ESL instructors to share their questions, concerns, and instructional ideas with other professionals—all of great value to any ESL instructor. Most provide links to other pages of instructional interest and the e-mail addresses of professionals in the field. The use of different search engines (e.g., Lycos, Excite, Yahoo) is likely to yield other sites devoted to, or at least applicable to, CALL.

Some Websites that are targeted specifically at ESL students, and that could be recommended for independent, out-of-class language learning and practice, include the following:

1. Marty Levine's site, which, as the site creator himself observes, "is easily adaptable for use in grades 7–12." </http://www.csun.edu/~hcedu013/>

2. *The Internet TESOL Journal* <www.uoregon.edu/~call/student.html>

3. Grammar Page <www.gallaudet.edu/~engwweb/grammar>

4. <http://lc.byuh.edu/CNN_N/CNN-N_page.html> Entitled "CNN Newsroom & Worldview for ESL," this site contains interesting vocabulary and grammar exercises for ESL students.

5. Dave's ESL Cafe <www.eslcafe.com>

6. Ex*Change <http://www.deil.lang.uiuc.edu/exchange/projects/>

7. Tower of English which contains an e-mail penpal page, a chat room, and links to other sites of interest. <www.clocktower-elc.freeserv.co.uk>

8. ESL on the Web <deil.lang.uiuc.edu/web.pages/esl.html>

9. Karin's ESL Party Land <www.eslpartyland.com/teach3.htm>

10. Randall's ESL Cyber Listening Lab <www.esl.lab.com>

Ex*Change, recipient of the Megallan 4-star award for creativity and language teaching, was one of the first of these sites (see Li & Hart, 1996). When it was first created in 1996, its readership grew to over 100 readers per day from over 45 countries. It currently consists of five sections: learning resources, culture cafe, interaction point (with chat room and penpaling options), current news and events, and stories. It was even rated as the best Internet site for ESL students in the publication entitled *The Internet for English Learners* targeted at Korean students in 1996 and published by ALC Press, Seoul.

E-mail penpaling is highly recommended for seventh and eighth graders, as it gets students in the habit of writing in English and also encourages them to establish new friendships. If your ESL students have American pen pals, they are likely to learn American cultural artifacts much more quickly and in the context of friendly exchanges. What better way to acquaint them with cultural issues of great import, such as the culture of the American classroom, the culture of dating, the relatively ungendered culture of interaction, and so on. Teichmann (1994, p. 64) discusses how German and American children were effectively linked via e-mail and videoconferencing. The resultant cross-cultural exchange, conducted in English, was insightful and interesting to both sides.

As most of these sites have bulletin boards and chat rooms, instructors could employ them for synchronous and asynchronous language learning/teaching. Even ESL sites such as Paolo Rossetti's Online English, intended for adult ESL students, can easily be adapted for use with fourth through eighth graders.

Existing Websites geared toward CALL are not the only resources an ESL instructor need depend on. For instructors who prefer to design their own Web-based language learning and assessment exercises, a variety of Internet-based resources and design tools are available (Figure 7.2).

The e-Lective Language Learning System (Cummins, 1998) is another valuable technological resource. Well suited to older ESL students, it provides all kinds of texts (poems, stories, plays) in electronic form accompanied by visuals and sound effects, so that it is more "authentic" than the text provided in traditional formats like books and audiotapes. ESL instructors could also employ interactive software programs like Daedalus Interchange or First Class, both readily available and used in many writing centers around the world, particularly in writing-across-the-curriculum programs.

## How to Keep Up With ESL Instructional Technology

There are many ways for keeping up with instructional technology of direct value to K–8 ESL students. One is to subscribe to *The TESOL Journal,* which features articles on the utility of new software or technology programs (see Cummins, 1998, for example); book notices; ads for CALL-type resources; and Christine Maloni's helpful tips for Net surfing, appropriately dubbed "Wandering the Web." TESOL's homepage also contains useful links to resource sites of interest to K–12 ESL instructors.

For those who have not done so, it's a good idea to subscribe to both the *TESL-List* and the *Linguist List,* as you can read about instructional tools and/or materials that other professionals in the field have employed, and you can pose questions about virtually anything related to the field. Moreover, subscribing to these listserves enables you to observe and participate in a variety of discussions on topics ranging from materials to instructional tools and approaches to teaching ESL. You can learn about new resources, ongoing research projects, regional conferences in the field, and electronic journals that put out calls for abstracts and contributions. Perhaps the main advantage of subscribing is that doing so makes it possible to connect with thousands of professionals from all around the world in a matter of minutes—far less time, in some ways, than that spent in face-to-face interactions with just one or two individuals. Levy (1997, pp. 254–256) provides valuable information on how to subscribe to a variety of CALL-related listservs.

Many school boards provide teachers with incentives to take graduate courses to improve their teaching and, if they want to work with ESL students, to get an add-on endorsement. ESL teachers should take advantage of these opportunities by enrolling in courses in instructional design or instructional technology. Either individually or with the assistance of your colleagues, apply for one of the many technology grants the Board of Education annually makes available, so that your

---

**Learning About the Internet**

---

**Understanding the Internet**
http://www.screen.com/start

**Internet Assistant On-Line Companion**
http://www.vmedia.com/hpia.html

**Dummy's guide:**
ftp://ftp.eenet.ee/pub/guides/bdg/bdg_3.html

**The Internet Bookshop:**
http://www.bookshop.co.uk

---

**General Software and Hardware**

---

**Apple Computers Inc.:**
http://www.apple.com/

**IBM:** http://www.ibm.com

**Sun** (including interactive Java language and Hot Java browser): http://www.sun.com/

**Microsoft:**
http://www.microsoft.com/

**Adobe:**
http://www.adobe.com

---

**Web Page Design**

---

**HTML Tutorial: introduction**
http://www.cwru.edu/help/introHTML/intro.html

**HTML:**
http://www.w3.org/hypertext/www/MarkUp/MarkUp.html

**Web construction (Internet Australia):**
http://byerley.cs.waikato.ac.nz/~tonym/html-intro/

**Java:** programming for the Internet: http://java.dnx.com/

**Java tools:**
http://www.construct.net/tools/java

**Writing java programs:**
http://java.sun.com/tutorial/java/index.html

**Netscape services:**
http://home.netscape.com/home/how-to-create-web-services.html

---

**Figure 7.2**    The Internet Assistant

**Macromedia:**
http://www.macromedia.com

**Virtual reality forum:**
http://vrml.wired.com/

**State of the Art in Human Language Technology Survey:**
http://www.cse.ogi.edu/CSLU/HLTsurvey

## Language Teaching or CALL Sites

**TESL-EJ: North America:**
http://www.well.com/www/sokolik/tesl-ej.html

**TESL-EJ: Asia:**
http://www.kyoto-su.ac.jp/information/tesl-ej/

**EUROCALL:**
http://www.cti.hull.ac.uk/eurocall.htm

**TELL Consortium:**
http://www.cti.hull.ac.uk/tell.htm

**EFL ODL Project (Ruth Vilmi):**
http://www.hut.fi/~rvilmi/email-project.html

**Foreign language resources on the Web:**
http://www.itp.berkeley.edu/~thorne/HumanResources.html

**The Language Center (Sussex University):**
http://www.sussex.ac.uk/langc/intro

**The Language Center (Warwick University):**
http://www.warwick.ac.uk/WWW/faculties/arts/LangC/

**The Language Center (Oxford University):**
http://info.ox.ac.uk:80/departments/langcentre/

**On-CALL:**
http://www.cltr.uq.oz.au:8000/oncall

**Foreign language teaching forum:**
http://www.corland.edu/www_root/flteach.html

**Language lists:**
http://www.info.ox.ac.uk/departments/langcentre/langlists.html

**The CALL Cookbook:**
http://www.owlnet.rice.edu/~ling417/

**SL-Lists: ESL/EFL students' e-mail discussion lists:**
http://www.latrobe.edu.au/www/education/sl/sl.html

**Figure 7.2**    *continued*

school can invest more in instructional technology. And be an avid user of the technology yourself, so that apart from being able to anticipate your students' reactions to it, you get a good feel for how best to utilize it. Try to create an environment that is conducive for learning. We all know that learning takes time, effort, and encouragement, especially when the urgency to communicate is not strong. We have to constantly remind ourselves that linguistic miracles, like most miracles, are rare and that second language learning does not occur in a linear series of well-defined stages. For this reason, I try to pay more attention to the message, rather than the form, in what my ESL students say or write. In my view, our students should be our first priority, and if CALL or technologically enhanced language learning can make a difference in their learning, what are we waiting for?

## COMPUTER CLASSROOM EXAMPLES

### *Writing About the Pyramids*

**Grade Level:** 5–8

**Objective:** TLW create and print a 5–10 page book using Imagination Express.

**Time:** One hour introduction, one hour to create a rubric with students, and then 30 minutes a day for five days to complete. After completion three more hours for critique, revision, and presentation will be needed.

**Problem to Be Solved:** The students are to create childrens' books for younger students showing what they have learned in the unit on Ancient Egypt.

**Materials:** computers
Imagination Express Pyramids by Edmark

**Steps:**
1. The teacher can introduce the assignment by showing the sample e-book to the class.
2. For students who have never made a book using Imagination Express, one hour of instruction may be required on how to add text, backgrounds, and pictures to the story. All students should be encouraged to add animation and sound to their stories as well.
3. Criteria will be set in a rubric co-constructed with students. These criteria may include the number of sentences, correct grammar and spelling, a title to the story, characters given names and interacting with each other, and points for including material from the unit on Ancient Egypt. Usually in rubrics, more points are given for students who develop their story more fully than those who follow the minimum criteria.
4. Students will create their stories with assistance and reminders about items in the rubric. If any students do not have an idea for a story, they should listen to the ideas in the story idea section.
5. After completion, students should evaluate their stories in small groups using the rubric.
6. After being given feedback, they will get one more hour to improve their stories.
7. The stories will then be presented orally to the class to demonstrate sounds and animations. These will be presented to younger children as deemed appropriate by the teacher.

**Assessment:** In the writing rubric, usually no more than five criteria are identified. Students are assigned one to three points for minimal, average, and excellent achievement of the criteria. The grades are determined by the teacher only on the final product, not on the intermediate feedback given by other students.

**Modifications for Students:** The best aspect of writing stories is that they are easily adapted for students. A student with writing difficulties may write simpler sentences but can improve his or her story with more animation. Another student may need modifications

## COMPUTER CLASSROOM EXAMPLES (CONTINUED)

### *Writing About the Pyramids (Continued)*

**Modifications for Students (Continued):** to the rubric but can still participate with the class. Assistive technology (AT) can be used with Touch Windows or switches for students with motor problems. If AT is not available, a student with motor difficulties can also instruct another student on what to put in the book. Even a student with significant delays can enjoy having the stories read to him or her and clicking on the animations.

### *The Tortoise and the Hare: Bilingual Vocabulary*

**Grade Level:** 2–4

**Objective:** TLW identify 5–10 words in a language that is different from their native one.

**Time:** One school week. One hour to read the story; 30 minutes a day for four days to practice for assessment.

**Materials:** One computer
*Living Books: The Tortoise and the Hare* by Broderbund

**Steps:**
1. The teacher can introduce the assignment by having the story read aloud to the students in Spanish and in English.
2. Students who have never seen a Living Book will need to be shown how to click on a word with the cursor to have it read aloud.
3. Students will be placed in groups with both Spanish and English native speakers. The students will select five words they do not know (from a list provided by the teacher) and will have to identify and pronounce the words in both Spanish and English. The native speaking students will assist the non-native speaking students with pronunciation.
4. Daily activities can be used to reinforce the new words. Some activities can involve reading the story on computer or the book. The Play with Me feature allows for student interaction. The teachers guide has several worksheet activities that can be modified to include words from both English and Spanish. Students can develop their own study aids such flash cards and quizzing themselves. For cooperative groups, a teacher can design four activities that the students rotate to on different days to practice the words.
5. The students are assessed in groups on the final day. The number of correct words in the native and non-native language is assessed.
6. Groups that learned different words should share them with the class.

**Assessment:** Students should receive credit for the words they learned in the other language and also for the success of their group members. Each student receives points for the words his or her group members learned as well as his or her own. This promotes the cooperative aspect of the lesson.

## TECHNO-TEACHER TIPS

### Licking the Keyboarding Problem

A number of special needs students have disabilities that keep them from success at the keyboard. The answer to their problem is the voice-activated computer or voice-activated software available for existing computers. Explore the possibilities by typing "voice-activated computers" into a reliable search engine.

### Computer Supervision

Getting enough hardware seems to be the easy part for the majority of programs these days. For most teachers the hard part is organizing, supervising, and helping special education students succeed with information technology. Points to consider:

1. You, the teacher, must keep up to date with your software knowledge. The choices for good software (we have mentioned Laureate) are multiplying as this book goes to press. Keeping students interested and challenged at the same time requires you be in a continual upgrade mode.

2. Have backup projects waiting in the wings for two reasons: the unpredictable nature of computers to crash, and the waning interest of some students as they get tired with tasks or finish early.

3. Remember that as lucky as you are to have an aide, it is your job to keep the aide up to skill level with computer use. This could take extra time, but it is well worth the effort.

### Helpful Websites

Are you in the market for yet another helpful Website? Try <www.cast.org/>. This is the homepage for the Center for Applied Special Technology. Featured are Teaching Strategies and Teaching Tools. The former offers a section on using software to customize special learning situations.

## FREQUENTLY ASKED QUESTIONS

1. **What would be your recommendations for software with doable tasks for my early education special needs kids?**

    Laureate Special Needs Software is one of the best. It not only has tasks for mixed abilities but offers a built-in database that keeps a record of student performance. This is an excellent feature for measuring progress. Another package worth checking out is Wiggleworks, a reading program also designed for mixed abilities.

2. **I've just been issued a beautiful, big-screen electronic chalkboard that should help me present in my special ed lab. Is there some good software for projecting on this size screen?**

   Try Boardmaker. For ease at building visuals for your snazzy new screen, it works very well. You simply type in the name of something simple and it will produce a picture. For example, type in *bathroom* and it will provide an image of a toilet. It's great for the basics and fun to use.

3. **The concept of sharing isn't working too well with the few computers I have, especially during the little free time I give to my special needs students. What happens generally is that the boys are a little pushy and tend to dominate. Any suggestions?**

   Yes. The problem is not only with special needs students. Research suggests that boys gravitate toward computers more readily than girls and that girls need more encouragement to jump in. You might want to ride herd on an equal time policy, however you handle it. And don't let the girls get discouraged.

4. **I've been an ESL teacher for many years and am thinking of taking advantage of an opportunity to teach overseas. I use technology, but I'm not sure what to expect to find in the way of computers in a number of non-mainstream countries I'd like to go to. Any suggestions?**

   You've no doubt gotten a list of schools that are advertising for ESL teachers. These schools will have e-mail addresses, and you can go online and ask the right questions about software, PC/Mac status, and the like. With any luck, the school will have a Website. If the school doesn't have an e-mail address, you don't want to go there. Pack up all your own software. Regardless of what a school says about its technology, count on it being worse. Good luck on your new adventure.

## REFERENCES

ALC (1996). *The Internet for English learners.* Seoul: ALC Press.

The Arc. (1994). *How to evaluate and select assistive technology.* Arlington, TX: Arc. (ERIC Document Reproduction Service No. ED 376 664)

Ashworth, M., Wakefield, P. (1994). *Teaching the world's children: ESL for ages three to seven.* Markham, Ontario: Pippin.

Bhatia, T., & Ritchie, W. (Eds.). (1996). *Handbook of second language acquisition.* New York: Pergamon Press.

Bigge, J. L. (1991). *Teaching individuals with physical and multiple disabilities* (3rd ed.). New York: Macmillan.

Bitter, G. G. (1993). *Using a microcomputer in the classroom* (3rd ed.). Needham Heights, MA: Allyn & Bacon.

Brosnan, P. A. (1995). *Learning about tasks computers can perform.* Columbus, OH: ERIC Clearinghouse for Science, Mathematics, and Environmental Education. (ERIC Document Reproduction Service No. ED 380 280)

Brown, H. (1994). *Teaching by principles: An interactive approach to language pedagogy* (3rd ed.). Englewood Cliffs, NJ: Prentice Hall.

Buggey, T. (1999). Assistive technology for learners with special needs. In G. R. Morrison, D. Lowther, & L. Demeulle, *Integrating computer technology in the classroom.* Upper Saddle River, NJ: Prentice Hall.

Bush, M., & Terry, R. M. (1997). *Technology-enhanced language learning.* Lincolnwood, IL: National Textbook.

California State Department of Education. (1989). *Foreign language framework.* Sacramento: Author.

Clayton, J. B. (1996). *Your land, my land: Children in the process of acculturation.* Portsmouth, NH: Heinemann.

Cochran, P. S., & Bull, G. L. (1993). Computers and individuals with speech and language disorders. In J. D. Lindsey (Ed.), *Computers and exceptional individuals* (2nd ed., pp. 143–158). Austin, TX: PRO:ED.

Craver, J. M., & Burton-Radzely, L. (Eds.). (1998). *Technology links to literacy: A casebook of special educators' use of technology to promote literacy.* Calverton, MD: Macro International.

Cummins, J. (1989). *Empowering minority students.* Sacramento: CABE.

Cummins, J. (1998, Spring). e-lective language learning: Design of a computer-assisted text-based ESL/EFL learning system. *TESOL Journal,* 18–21.

Daiute, C. (1985). *Writing and computers.* Reading, MA: Addison-Wesley.

Diaz-Rico, L. Weed, K. Z. (1995). *The Crosscultural, language, and academic development handbook: A complete K–12 reference guide.* Boston: Allyn & Bacon.

Dunkel, P. (Ed.). (1991). *Computer-assisted language learning and testing: research issues and practice.* New York: Newbury House.

Franklin, S., & Strudler, S. (1989). *Computer-integrated instruction inservice notebook: Elementary School.* Eugene, OR: International Society for Technology in Education.

Freeman, Y. S., & Freeman, D. E. (1992). *Whole language for second language learners.* Portsmouth, NH: Heinemann.

Freire, P. (1970). *Pedagogy of the oppressed.* New York: Continuum.

Gardner, D., & Garcia, R. B. (1996). (Ed.), *Interactive video as self-access support for language learning beginners.* In R. Pemberton et al. (Eds.), *Taking control: Autonomy in language learning* (pp. 219–232). Hong Kong: Hong Kong University Press.

Garret, M. (1996) Foreword. In G. Giordano (Ed.), *Literacy: Programs for adults with developmental disabilities,* (pp. vi–xv). San Diego: Singular Publishing.

Gass, S., & Selinker, L. (1995). *SLA: An introduction.* Mahwah, NJ: Lawrence Erlbaum.

Gibbons, P. (1991). *Learning to learn in a second language.* Portsmouth, NH: Heinemann.

Giordano, G., Leeper, L., & Siegel, J. (1996). Computer assisted literacy programs. In G. Giordano (Ed.), *Literacy: Programs for adults with developmental disabilities.* San Diego: Singular.

Golden, D. (1998). *Assistive technology in special education: Policy and practice.* Reston, VA: Council for Exceptional Children.

Grosse, C. U., & Leto, L. J. (1999). Virtual communications and networking in distance learning. *TESOL Matters, 9* (1), 1–7.

Hayes, J., & O'Loughlin, J. (1999, Summer). Meeting the challenge of content instruction in the K–8 classroom. *TESOL Journal,* 18–21.

Healey, D., & Jackson, N. (Eds). (1999). *1999 CALL interest section software list.* Burlingame, CA: Alta.

Higgins, J. (1991). *Fuel for learning: The neglected element in textbooks and call.* Paper presented at the meeting of TESOL, New York, NY.

Higgins, J. (1995). *Computers and English language learning.* Oxford: Intellect.

Holzberg, C. S. (1994). Technology in special education. *Technology and Learning, 14* (7), 18–21.

Larsen-Freeman, D. (1986). *Techniques and principles in language teaching.* New York: Oxford University Press.

Larson-Freeman, D., & Long, M. (1991). *An introduction to second language acquisition research.* New York: Addison-Wesley.

Levy, M. (1997). *Computer-assisted language learning.* Oxford: Clarendon Press.

Li, R-C., & Hart, R. S. (1996, Winter). What can the World Wide Web offer ESL teachers? *TESOL Journal,* 5–9.

Little, P. (1996). Freedom to learn and compulsion to interact: Promoting learner autonomy through the use of information systems and information technologies. In R. Pemberton et al. (Eds.), *Taking control: Autonomy in language learning* (pp. 203–218). Hong Kong: Hong Kong University Press.

Madsen, H. (1991). Computer-adaptive testing of listening and reading comprehension: The Brigham Young University approach. In P. Dunkel (Ed.), *Computer-assisted language learning and testing: Research issues and practice.* (pp. 237–258). New York: Newbury House.

McKay, S., & Hornberger, N. H. (Eds.). (1996). *Sociolinguistics and language and language teaching.* Oxford: Oxford University Press.

Neu, J., & Scarcella, R. (1991). Word processing in the ESL writing classroom: A survey of student attitudes. In P. Dunkel (Ed.), *Computer-assisted language learning and testing: Research issues and practice* (pp. 169–188). New York: Newbury House.

Nunan, D. (1996). Towards autonomous learning: some theoretical, empirical, and practical issues. In R. Pemberton et al. (Eds.), *Taking control: Autonomy in language learning* (pp. 13–27). Hong Kong: Hong Kong University Press.

Olsen, S. (1980). Foreign language departments and computer-assisted instruction: A survey. *Modern Language Journal, 64* (3), 341–349.

Pandey, A. (1999). *Children as effective language teachers.* Manuscript based on a talk presented at the annual TESOL convention, Seattle, March 19, 1998.

Pemberton, R., et al. (Ed.). (1996). *Taking control: autonomy in language learning.* Hong Kong: Hong Kong University Press.

Phinney, M. (1991). Computer-assisted writing and writing apprehension in ESL students. In P. Dunkel (Ed.), *Computer-assisted language learning and testing: Research issues and practice* (pp. 189–204). New York: Newbury House.

Robinett, T. (1999). *Frameworks for teachers: a self-paced internet training program and resource guide specifically designed for teachers.* Burlingame, CA: Alta.

Roblyer, M. D., Castine, W. H., & King, F. J. (1988). Computer applications have "undeniable value," research shows. *Electronic Learning, 8,* 38–47.

Rodriquez, R. (1981). Aria: Memoir of a bilingual childhood. In *Hunger of Memory: An autobiography, the education of Richard Rodriquez,* Boston: D. R. Godine.

Romaine, S. (1994). *Language in society: An introduction.* Oxford: Oxford University Press.

Siegel, J. (1999). Utilizing technology for the inclusion of individuals with mental retardation. In P. Retish & S. Reiter (Eds.), *Adults with disabilities: International perspectives in the community.* Mahwah, NJ: Lawrence Erlbaum.

Siegel, J., Good, K., & Moore, J. (1996). Integrating technology into educating pre-service education teachers. *Action in Teacher Education, 17* (4), 53–63.

Sperling, D. (1999). *Dave Sperling's Internet guide: for English language teachers.* Burlingame, CA: Alta.

Stevenson, J., & Gross, S. (1991). Use of a computerized adaptive testing model for ESOL/bilingual entry/exit decision making. In P. Dunkel (Ed.), *Computer-assisted language learning and testing: Research issues and practice* (pp. 223–236). New York: Newbury House.

Teichmann, D. (1994). Connecting through e-mail and videoconferencing. *Technology and Learning, 14* (8), 49–66.

Venkatagiri, H. S. (1995). Techniques for enhancing communication productivity in AAC: A review of research. *American Journal of Speech Language Pathology, 4* (4), 36–45.

Voller, P., & Pickard, V. (1996). Conversation exchange. A way towards autonomous language learning. In R. Pemberton et al. (Eds.), *Taking control: Autonomy in language learning* (pp. 115–132). Hong Kong: Hong Kong University Press.

Warschauer, M. (1999). *E-mail for English teaching: Bringing the Internet and computer learning networks into the language classroom.* Burlingame, CA: Alta.

Woodward, J., & Gersten, R. (1992). Innovative technology for secondary students with learning disabilities. *Exceptional Children, 59,* 407–421.

# INDEX

**192**